The Death of Scripture and the Rise of Biblical Studies

OXFORD STUDIES IN HISTORICAL THEOLOGY

Series Editor
David C. Steinmetz, Duke University

Editorial Board
Irena Backus, Université de Genève
Robert C. Gregg, Stanford University
George M. Marsden, University of Notre Dame
Wayne A. Meeks, Yale University
Gerhard Sauter, Rheinische Friedrich-Wilhelms-Universität Bonn
Susan E. Schreiner, University of Chicago
John Van Engen, University of Notre Dame
Geoffrey Wainwright, Duke University
Robert L. Wilken, University of Virginia

WHAT PURE EYES COULD SEE
Calvin's Doctrine of Faith in Its Exegetical Context
Barbara Pitkin

THE UNACCOMMODATED CALVIN
Studies in the Foundation of a Theological Tradition
Richard A. Muller

THE CONFESSIONALIZATION OF HUMANISM IN REFORMATION GERMANY
Erika Rummell

THE PLEASURE OF DISCERNMENT
Marguerite de Navarre as Theologian
Carol Thysell

REFORMATION READINGS OF THE APOCALYPSE
Geneva, Zurich, and Wittenberg
Irena Backus

WRITING THE WRONGS
Women of the Old Testament among Biblical Commentators from Philo through the Reformation
John L. Thompson

THE HUNGRY ARE DYING
Beggars and Bishops in Roman Cappadocia
Susan R. Holman

RESCUE FOR THE DEAD
The Posthumous Salvation of Non-Christians in Early Christianity
Jeffrey A. Trumbower

AFTER CALVIN
Studies in the Development of a Theological Tradition
Richard A. Muller

THE POVERTY OF RICHES
St. Francis of Assisi Reconsidered
Kenneth Baxter Wolf

REFORMING MARY
Changing Images of the Virgin Mary in Lutheran Sermons of the Sixteenth Century
Beth Kreitzer

TEACHING THE REFORMATION
Ministers and Their Message in Basel, 1529–1629
Amy Nelson Burnett

THE PASSIONS OF CHRIST IN HIGH-MEDIEVAL THOUGHT
An Essay on Christological Development
Kevin Madigan

GOD'S IRISHMEN
Theological Debates in Cromwellian Ireland
Crawford Gribben

REFORMING SAINTS
Saints' Lives and Their Authors in Germany, 1470–1530
David J. Collins

GREGORY OF NAZIANZUS ON THE TRINITY AND THE KNOWLEDGE OF GOD
In Your Light We Shall See Light
Christopher A. Beeley

THE JUDAIZING CALVIN
Sixteenth-Century Debates over the Messianic Psalms
G. Sujin Pak

THE DEATH OF SCRIPTURE AND THE RISE OF BIBLICAL STUDIES
Michael C. Legaspi

The Death of Scripture and the Rise of Biblical Studies

MICHAEL C. LEGASPI

UNIVERSITY PRESS

OXFORD
UNIVERSITY PRESS

Oxford University Press, Inc., publishes works that further
Oxford University's objective of excellence
in research, scholarship, and education.

Oxford   New York
Auckland   Cape Town   Dar es Salaam   Hong Kong   Karachi
Kuala Lumpur   Madrid   Melbourne   Mexico City   Nairobi
New Delhi   Shanghai   Taipei   Toronto

With offices in
Argentina   Austria   Brazil   Chile   Czech Republic   France   Greece
Guatemala   Hungary   Italy   Japan   Poland   Portugal   Singapore
South Korea   Switzerland   Thailand   Turkey   Ukraine   Vietnam

Copyright © 2010 by Oxford University Press, Inc.

Published by Oxford University Press, Inc.
198 Madison Avenue, New York, NY 10016
www.oup.com

First issued as an Oxford University Press paperback, 2011

Oxford is a registered trademark of Oxford University Press

All rights reserved. No part of this publication may be reproduced,
stored in a retrieval system, or transmitted, in any form or by any means,
electronic, mechanical, photocopying, recording, or otherwise,
without the prior permission of Oxford University Press.

Library of Congress Cataloging-in-Publication Data
Legaspi, Michael C.
The death of scripture and the rise of biblical studies / by Michael C. Legaspi.
    p. cm.
Includes bibliographical references and index.
ISBN 978-0-19-539435-1 (hardcover); 978-0-19-984588-0 (paperback)
1. Bible. O.T.—Criticism, interpretation, etc.—History. 2. Michaelis, Johann David, 1717–1791.
I. Michaelis, Johann David, 1717–1791. II. Title.
BS1160.L385 2010
221.609'033—dc22   2009027400

Printed in the United States of America
on acid-free paper

You are right to despise the paltry imitators who derive their religion wholly from someone else or cling to a dead document by which they swear and from which they draw proof. Every holy writing is merely a mausoleum of religion, a monument that a great spirit was there that no longer exists; for if it still lived and were active, why would it attach such great importance to the dead letter that can only be a weak reproduction of it? It is not the person who believes in a holy writing who has religion, but only the one who needs none and probably could make one for himself.
—Friedrich Schleiermacher, "On the Essence of Religion" (1799)

The two main principles of the so-called historical criticism are the Postulate of Vulgarity and the Axiom of the Average. The Postulate of Vulgarity: everything great, good and beautiful is improbable because it is extraordinary and, at the very least, suspicious. The Axiom of the Average: as we and our surroundings are, so must it have been always and everywhere, because that, after all, is so very natural.
—Friedrich Schlegel, *Critical Fragment* no. 25 (1797)

Why do you seek the living among the dead?
—Luke 24:5

Preface

Consider two scenes. The first takes place in an Eastern Orthodox church. The liturgy of St. John Chrysostom is under way. From behind the icon screen, the priest comes into view, carrying overhead, in solemn procession, an ornately bound, gold-plated volume: the Book of the Gospels. All stand. There is incense in the air. Acolytes, candles in hand, stand by to illuminate the reading of the Gospel. In that moment, the people are told not to look, to follow texts with their eyes, but rather to listen. The priest proclaims, "Wisdom! Let us attend!" and the people go silent. In the liturgy, the faithful see the Bible in procession, hear it in song, and venerate its holiness and authority with signs of loyalty and submission. The one thing the faithful do not actually do during this service, however, is *read* the Bible. It is always read *to* the people by someone else. Written words voiced by readers and expounded by preaching are transmuted into oral and immediate ones. The second scene is a biblical studies seminar in a university classroom. It too is filled with people. They sit, not stand. At the center is a long table. On it are many Bibles, various copies in assorted languages: Hebrew, Greek, Syriac, Latin. Some lie open, others are pushed aside into impromptu stacks. They share the table with other writings: teacher's notes, photocopies, reference works, dictionaries, grammars, commentaries. The atmosphere is sociable but cerebral, quiet but static. Heads are bowed, but over books. There are readers here too, but the oral performances are tracked closely by others whose eyes are attuned carefully to common texts. There is speech, but no song or prayer.

Spoken words belong only to individuals. The texts focus readerly vision. Commentary is controlled.

In both scenes, the Bible is at the center. In the first, its words are invisible, fleetingly oral, melodic. In the second, they are visible, unmoving, inscribed and fixed on pages. The two scenes represent very different enterprises. Yet they are not different because they embody different assumptions, discourses, and communal identities, though this is certainly the case. They are different, ultimately, because they have come into being by virtue of independent realities and by way of separate histories. They are different because the two groups, as a result of these histories and realities, are actually engaged with different Bibles: a *scriptural* Bible and an *academic* Bible.

This book tells the story of the academic Bible, how and why it came into being. It begins at a moment when the scriptural Bible evoked by the liturgical scene above had already receded to the margins of modern Western cultural and public life. The Reformation engendered a crisis of authority in which authority itself—its location, its nature, its sources—was contested. As a result of this crisis, the ecclesial underpinnings of the scriptural Bible became too weak, too fragmented to sustain its place at the center of Western Christendom. It was moved to the boundaries, where, throughout the sixteenth and seventeenth centuries, it fueled confessional and anticonfessional theological programs, some critical and others traditional. Many of the tools and much of the material that would later be used to create the academic Bible were developed in the two centuries following the Reformation. Yet the academic Bible did not come into being until the eighteenth century, when biblical criticism took shape at the modern university as a *post-*confessional enterprise. The academic Bible was created by scholars who saw that the scriptural Bible, embedded as it was in confessional particularities, was inimical to the sociopolitical project from which Enlightenment universities drew their purpose and support. Given the choice between the scriptural Bible and something else, university men, the fathers of modern criticism, chose something else.

This book is not a tale of divorce, confrontation, or apostasy. It assumes that the scriptural Bible, in its many Jewish and Christian forms, has its own complex, conflicted history, but it adds nothing to that history. It also assumes, as eighteenth-century critics assumed, that by the time of the German Enlightenment the era of scriptural Bibles and their confessional sponsors had already passed in Europe and that a new vision of a society ordered by postconfessional governments was taking hold. In German universities, then, the academic Bible was a successor, not a competitor, to the scriptural Bible. The image of the two Bibles may seem too totalizing, too dichotomous to some. One might object, for example, that there are churchly and academic communities (the latter certainly heirs to the German university tradition) that believe the two are complementary—indeed, *must be* so.

They hold that genuinely faithful, intellectually satisfying, and morally responsible biblical interpretation depends on the vigorous influence of critical biblical scholarship on religious belief. The two Bibles, on this view, not only coexist, they also support one another. I do not deny that theologians, biblical scholars, and churchmen of various sorts have worked out constructive relations between the two Bibles and the interpretive modes they represent. Intellectually earnest interpreters often see the two Bibles as representing real and profound antitheses between history and revelation, faith and reason, and the like. And they believe that they must be held in a kind of creative tension. However, in actual practice, the relation has not, in my opinion, yielded decisive solutions to perennial theological, moral, and philosophical questions in the history of interpretation. It tends rather to employ modern criticism as a prophylactic against fundamentalism and to treat traditional belief in biblical authority as a distant source of social and cultural capital for the academic enterprise. In other words, the intellectual stakes turn out to be low, and the social ones quite high. From a historical point of view, then, grand antitheses (or antinomies) between History and Revelation, the Secular and the Sacred, Science and Religion, and so on seem rather like mythologies retrojected onto the history of modern scholarship—all the more so because the antinomies themselves predate modern critical consciousness, and the modern project itself, as will be clear, was distinctly social in orientation. Intellectual antinomies were not discovered by modern scholars; they were redeployed by them. Ultimately, though, this book is not a work of theology but rather of history, and others are surely in a better position to argue questions concerning the relation of the Bible to truth, history, faith, reason, etc., on systematic grounds. Yet a long and clear historical perspective, one stretching back to the origins of modern criticism at the university, shows that dualism is, in fact, warranted.

At the center of this story is one figure in particular who had a large share in the creation of the academic Bible: Johann David Michaelis (1717–1791). A few introductory remarks about him are in order. Michaelis was one of the most important biblical scholars of the eighteenth century. His life coincided with the flourishing, in the German lands, of the "conservative" or "mainstream" Enlightenment. Michaelis and his contemporaries, figures like Christian Gottlob Heyne, Johann Gottfried Herder, and, seminally, Immanuel Kant, opened new paths for integrating religion and culture into modern, progressive political and social frameworks. Their work did not manifest the kind of aggressive heterodoxy associated with the radical or early Enlightenment. Instead, German academics preserved many traditional moral and religious forms (for example, the authority of the Bible) by retaining them critically and self-consciously, as historical contingencies amenable to new intellectual projects. Michaelis belongs to this milieu. As we will see, his contributions exemplified a conservative progressivism that took the cultural obsolescence of confessional Christianity for granted and aimed at the creation of an irenic social order based on reason, morality, and the growing power of the state. Also important for this study is the fact that Michaelis was a university man. He was born and educated at one (Halle), and he lived, worked, and died at another (Göttingen). The German Enlightenment (*Aufklärung*) saw the founding of new universities and the reform of existing ones. It gave rise to a new "idea of the University," one oriented toward the social and political goals of the conservative Enlightenment. Because the academic Bible was a creation of the German university in this period, the university has a prominent role in this book. Finally, though Michaelis was a scholar of both Old and New Testaments, this study focuses on the Hebrew Bible and the ancient Near East. His work on the Old Testament, ancient languages, and Hebrew antiquities shows dramatically what was involved in the creation of a new discourse, a new approach to the authority of the Bible. It offers greater scope for examining the kinds of scholarly maneuvers, philological and historical, that were used to remake the Christian scriptural inheritance. References to the "Bible" and things "biblical" in this book, then, more often than not refer particularly to the Old Testament.

This book contains six main chapters, which can be divided into two parts. The first three chapters describe the broader conditions for the rise of the academic Bible. The latter three offer a focused examination of specific ways that Michaelis accommodated the study of the Bible to these conditions. Chapter 1 argues that the Bible in the West ceased to function as catholic scripture in the period following the Reformation and that, as a result, biblical scholars turned increasingly toward the Bible as *text* to rehabilitate it. Schisms, religious wars, and the manifold effects of confessionalization created a fragmented religious environment that yielded modes of scholarship aimed at exploiting, reinforcing, or repairing this fragmentation. Yet these efforts all assumed an inert textual Bible that needed to be reactivated and reintegrated into specific cultural and religious programs. In the sixteenth and seventeenth centuries, biblical scholarship operated on a Bible that was moving from "scripture" to "text." Chapter 2 takes up this story at Göttingen, Germany's premier Enlightenment university in the eighteenth century. Because the Bible had become a weak and contested textual inheritance, it needed to be rehabilitated if it was to endure in public life. It was not at all clear that the study of the Bible in any form would have a place at a new university, especially one created by the government to educate civil servants and noblemen in the rational, tolerant spirit of the age. Yet, at Göttingen, academics succeeded in folding the humanities, though tied strongly to ancient texts and traditions, into a modern, statist enterprise. Chapter 3 shifts briefly away from the study of the Bible and focuses on two classical philologists at Göttingen, Johann Matthias Gesner and Christian Gottlob Heyne. The study of the Bible and that of the ancient Greek and Roman world were closely intertwined in early modern Europe and deserve to be studied in concert more than they are. In the case of Göttingen, the study of Greece and Rome offers a very close parallel to the study of the Bible. Gesner and Heyne were contemporaries of Michaelis who, like Michaelis, found themselves in a precarious but promising situation: they had to adapt the study of ancient, authoritative literature to the realities of the new university, or simply fade into the background. Gesner and Heyne adapted. Their vision of a critically reconstructed antiquity fully intelligible to modern ideals resembles the picture of ancient Israel that Michaelis, through nearly five decades of tireless research and publication, labored to produce.

Because of the close parallels between the work of Michaelis and that of his colleagues in classical studies, Michaelis's reconstructed Israel may be understood as a "classical Israel." The second half of the book offers an examination of how Michaelis replenished the cultural value of the Bible by turning the ancient Israelites into a kind of classical civilization. Chapter 4 begins with Michaelis's program for the study of the Hebrew language. His ideas on Hebrew are important because they show that, for him, the Bible had to be embedded in a deep and dead past before it could be operated on and, ultimately, revivified. Michaelis believed that a scientific understanding of Hebrew, for example, was only available by separating it from its afterlife in a living, rabbinic Judaism and by shedding the theological exceptionalism that had made Hebrew a divine or primeval language to many. Not only did Michaelis succeed in relativizing religious interpretive frameworks, he argued that they were actually a hindrance to a true understanding of the Bible. Chapter 5, in a similar vein, marks the importance of aesthetics in Michaelis's recovery of a classical Israel. Building on the work of English critic Robert Lowth, Michaelis argued that the psalms and prophecies of the Old Testament could be fruitfully analyzed as "biblical poetry" or "ancient Israelite poetry," apart from their theological or religious value. Lowth and Michaelis were important figures in the eighteenth-century turn toward a primitive yet sublime poetics of feeling—a poetics in which Israelite literature, of all literatures, had a central place. As this chapter shows, though, "biblical poetry" was not a discovery but an invention. This new concept allowed scholars to operate independently of scriptural frameworks for understanding the Bible, namely, the canons by which religious communities organize their Bibles. Those grouped as "prophets," for example, could just as well be classed with the "poets" found in all parts of the Bible, thus transforming them from foretellers of Christ into poets of personal passion. Chapter 6 describes Michaelis's efforts to remake the figure of Moses. As we will see, Michaelis was not alone in wanting to reinterpret the significance of the great prophet. Yet his Moses, an enlightened, poetic genius and the paragon of classical Israel, rested on unusually erudite foundations. Michaelis denied that the Old Testament, as scripture, had any kind of direct relevance or authority in modern life. His work on Moses showed how a scholar could apply the tools of history and philology to remake the biblical tradition, to see the value of biblical figures by new, nonconfessional lights. The Conclusion discusses the fate of Michaelis's classical project, its reception among contemporaries and successors. It also offers a larger perspective on Michaelis's legacy.

A clear understanding of the history of modern criticism has important implications for the study of the Bible today: its aims, contexts, and, indeed, its future. It turns, I believe, on the way that the problematic relation between the scriptural and academic Bibles is ultimately negotiated. The two are opposed to one another, but I believe it is necessary to reconceive the nature of this opposition. Too often it has been seen, unhelpfully, as an expression of stale antitheses between reason and faith, history and revelation, the secular and the sacred. The history of modern biblical criticism shows that the fundamental antitheses were not intellectual or theological, but rather social, moral, and political. Academic critics did not dispense with the authority of a Bible resonant with religion; they redeployed it. Yet they did so in a distinctive form that has run both parallel and perpendicular to churchly appropriations of the Bible. Why biblical critics at the university first developed this form, how they succeeded, and what is to be done with it are questions at the heart of this book.

One of my mentors once told me of a cagey academic veteran who was accosted by a curious researcher somewhere deep in an archive. Not wanting to offer a direct response to the inevitable question, "What are you working on?" he paused and said sagely, "We only ever work on ourselves." Writing this book, I have found that there is more than a little wisdom in this. These days, one does not come by the energy and interest for the study of eighteenth-century philologists very easily. Yet, I have consistently been drawn forward by a desire to address deep-seated questions about the nature and purpose of my own academic involvement with the Bible. These questions took root in graduate school, when, at the beginning of my studies, I had the privilege of taking Peter Machinist's course on the history of biblical scholarship. He encouraged my interest in this subject, eventually agreeing to supervise the research on which this book is based. I thank him for his teaching, his support, and his scholarly integrity. When, at a late stage of graduate study, my interests began to carry me beyond biblical studies, Ann Blair (source of the anecdote above) was willing to take a remedial student under her wing. She has taught me much about the workings of historical scholarship and the strange world of the intellectual historian. The defects in my historical scholarship, though, are my own. I thank her for supervising my research, helping me through various academic stages with wisdom and good will, and, finally, for continued friendship and advice.

I must also thank three other former teachers who have shaped this work. Gary Anderson has been a source of valuable encouragement and a fine example of excellent scholarship that reaches beyond the university. Readers of this book will recognize the influence of James Kugel's work on the history of biblical interpretation. In charting a new path for this field, he has managed that rarest of scholarly feats: erudition that culminates in clarity of vision. Jon Levenson's work on historical criticism has been enormously helpful to me. I thank him for humor, insight, and, above all, for asking important and uncomfortable questions about the modern study of the Bible.

I also thank Jonathan Sheehan for incisive comments on an earlier draft of this work. I was told by another scholar that I had the "misfortune" of publishing a work on eighteenth-century biblical criticism after Jonathan's own excellent book on the same topic had already appeared. Misfortune indeed. By providing invaluable help to me, though, Jonathan generously turned my misfortune into an opportunity for me to make a distinctive contribution. I have learned a great deal from him. Suzanne Marchand and Anthony Grafton also helped me to think through many themes, topics, and issues associated with this period. Though my debts to these scholars and many others will be evident, responsibility for this book's numerous shortcomings rests solely with me.

It has been a pleasure to work alongside colleagues in the Department of Theology at Creighton University, who have provided help, support, and advice. I thank members of the Theology Department Writers' Group who read and commented on parts of this work: John O'Keefe, Rich Miller, Eileen Burke-Sullivan, and Brian Sholl. Fr. William Harmless, SJ, has taught me a great deal about research and scholarly writing, and his advice on specific matters was reliably sound and incisive. Ron Simkins, Nicolae Roddy, and Leonard Greenspoon have stimulated my thinking on a number of issues related to biblical criticism. The acerbic Rusty Reno has been an invaluable friend, interlocutor, and mentor. He has sharpened my understanding of my own research, helping me to see the theological background of modern biblical criticism with greater conceptual clarity. I thank him and all my Creighton colleagues.

I would also like to thank Ulrich Schindel, professor emeritus in the Seminar für Klassische Philologie at the Georg-August-Universität in Göttingen, for wise and generous guidance during my year in Göttingen. I could not have completed this work without a background in the history of classical scholarship. Prof. Schindel not only understands this history; as successor to Gesner and Heyne, he also embodies it. Prof. Rudolf Smend, professor emeritus in the Theologische Fakultät at Georg-August, has also been a source of valuable knowledge and assistance. I hope one day to know as much about Michaelis and the history of biblical scholarship as he does.

In the last several years friends have thought through many of these issues with me: Alexander Burgess, J. Randall Short, Aaron Rubin, and colleagues associated with the Orthodox Center for the Advancement of Biblical Studies (OCABS). In this latter group, I thank Nicolae Roddy, Fr. Vahan Hovhanessian, Deacon Michael Azar, Timothy Clark, and Richard Benton. Along with these men, I gratefully acknowledge the leadership and guidance of the founder of OCABS, Fr. Paul Nadim Tarazi of St. Vladimir's Orthodox Theological Seminary.

I wish to thank Keith Faivre, Mariana Templin, and the excellent editorial staff at Oxford University Press for invaluable assistance. Special thanks go to Cynthia Read for her expert help and guidance in bringing this project to fruition. Support for this project was provided by the German Academic Exchange Service (DAAD), which made it possible to conduct research at Göttingen in 2004–2005. I also received support from Harvard University's Graduate School of Arts and Sciences, Creighton University's Graduate School, and the Kripke Center for the Study of Religion and Society at Creighton University. I gratefully acknowledge the support of the Templeton Foundation, the Arete Initiative at the University of Chicago, and the Defining Wisdom Project for funding and support. Additional thanks are due to staff at the Niedersächsische Staats- und Universitätsbibliothek and the Forschungsbibliothek at the University of Göttingen; the Andover-Harvard, Houghton, and Widener Libraries at Harvard University; the Regenstein Library at the University of Chicago; and Creighton University's Reinert-Alumni Memorial Library, especially interlibrary loan specialist Lynn Schneiderman. Thanks also to Oxford University Press for permission to use a previously published article of mine ("Recovering the Third Culture: Johann David Michaelis and the Study of Hebrew Language and Civilization," *History of Universities* XXI/2 (2006): 159–201), which forms the basis of chapter 4. Translations of German and Latin words and passages used in this book, unless otherwise indicated, are my own.

Finally, thanks go to my family, especially to Lois Crist, Bryan and Becci Crist, and Luciano and Candelaria Legaspi, for unfailing love and support. I thank my sons Josiah and Cato, who illuminate the reading of the Gospel, and my daughters Olivia and Ana, who lend their voices to the liturgy. And thanks most of all to Abby, without whose strength, encouragement, and patience my work would be impossible. She has taught me, simply, to love the truth. This work is dedicated, with affection, to her.

Contents

1. From Scripture to Text, 3
2. Bible and Theology at an Enlightenment University, 27
3. The Study of Classical Antiquity at Göttingen, 53
4. Michaelis and the Dead Hebrew Language, 79
5. Lowth, Michaelis, and the Invention of Biblical Poetry, 105
6. Michaelis, Moses, and the Recovery of the Bible, 129

   Conclusion, 155

   Notes, 171

   Bibliography, 199

   Index, 215

   Index of Biblical References, 221

The Death of Scripture and the Rise of Biblical Studies

1

From Scripture to Text

> Texts, like dead men and women, have no rights, no aims, no interests. They can be used in whatever way readers or interpreters choose.
> —Robert Morgan and John Barton, *Biblical Interpretation*[1]

Scripture died a quiet death in Western Christendom some time in the sixteenth century. The death of scripture was attended by two ironies. First, those who brought the scriptural Bible to its death counted themselves among its defenders. Second, the power to revivify a moribund scriptural inheritance arose not from the churches but from the state. The first development was the Reformation, and the second was the rise, two hundred years later, of modern biblical scholarship.

For over a millennium, Western Christians read and revered the Christian Bible as Scripture, as an authoritative anthology of unified, authoritative writings belonging to the Church. The scriptural Bible was neither reducible to a written "text" nor intelligible outside a divine economy of meaning.[2] It was not simply the foundation of the Church's academic theology; it also furnished its moral universe, framed its philosophic inquiries, and fitted out its liturgies. It provided the materials for thought, expression, and action, becoming what Northrop Frye famously called the "great code" of Western civilization.[3] As the book at the center of Western Christendom, the Bible functioned scripturally. However, in the wake of the traumatic religious divisions of the sixteenth century, the fractured Church ceased to be a unified body capable of maintaining a coherent claim on the Bible as *its* Bible. Because both Roman Catholics and Protestants claimed the Bible, in different ways, as their own, the Bible could no longer function unproblematically as Scripture. Its nature and authority had to be explicated and legitimated with reference to extrascriptural concepts, whether juridically, as among Catholics, or doctrinally, as among Protestants. Over the course of the post-Reformational controversies, the Bible showed itself to be a contested legacy for Western Christians, ultimately devolving into a multiplicity of bibles with distinct canons, separate ecclesial contexts, and prolific theological superstructures. What had functioned centrally in the life of the Church became, in the early modern period, a kind of textual proving ground for the legitimacy of extrascriptural theoretical understandings: at first theological and polemical and then, over time, literary, philosophical, and cultural. As a text, an object of critical analysis, the Bible came into clearer focus; however, as Scripture, the Bible became increasingly opaque.

It took time and a set of conducive circumstances for the full import of this transformation to become evident. A central argument in this book is that the development of biblical studies as an academic discipline in Germany more than two hundred years after the Reformation was an outworking of what might be called the "death of Scripture." The works of Spinoza, Hobbes, Simon, Peyrère, and others bear witness to the fact that the kinds of philological, critical, and historical analyses of the Bible associated with modern biblical studies were already well attested by the latter part of the seventeenth century. What is not well understood is why these did not give rise to an organized, institutional, and methodologically self-conscious critical program until the late eighteenth century. Nor is it widely understood why this took place in the German lands when few or none of the most notable critical precursors were German. Confusion on these questions belies a wider and more pervasive uncertainty about the origin and nature of the modern discipline of biblical studies itself. The rise of the discipline depended on two developments. The first was the opacity of the Bible, which was a result of the division of the Church. This is clear, for instance, in long-standing controversies between scholastics and humanists—and later between Catholics and Protestants—over the use and authority of the Vulgate. According to its defenders, the Vulgate was not merely a version of the Bible. Rather, in light of its position at the center of Latin Christianity, the Vulgate *was*, functionally, the Bible itself. When removed from the center and dissipated among irreconcilable textual traditions, the Latin Bible, the scripture of the Western Church, died a kind of death. Second, the loss of the Bible's scriptural character created the need for a new understanding of the Bible's relation to modern culture.

It was not simply deep curiosity about the language, form, and content of the Bible that spawned the ambitious research programs of eighteenth-century biblical scholars. In the decades surrounding the turn of the eighteenth century, the prestige of the Bible in the Western world was at an all-time low. Skeptics, rationalist critics, and proponents of the new science published widely and influentially on the state of its textual corruption, the unreliability of its historical narratives, the crudeness of its style, and, in some cases, the fanciful, even childish quality of its stories. It was, to many elites, a book no longer worth believing. Richard Popkin has argued persuasively that skepticism toward the Bible had its roots in an intellectual crisis provoked by prolonged, unresolved theological disputes about how to guarantee the truth of Catholic and Protestant hermeneutics.[4] The harsh and violent realities of religious division in the centuries following the Reformation featured sharp criticisms of traditional belief, on the one hand, and intensification of confessional interpretation and polemical theology on the other. What developed in the mid-eighteenth century was not a new awareness of the "human" or "historical" character of the Bible. Rather, it was the realization that the Bible was no longer intelligible as scripture, that is, as a self-authorizing, unifying authority in European culture. Its only meanings were confessional meanings: Catholic, Lutheran, Reformed. If the Bible was to find a place in a new political order committed to the unifying power of the state, it would have to do so as a common cultural inheritance. This was the great insight of German academics working at new and renewed institutions during the age of Enlightenment university reform. They mastered and activated the older scholarship—by then two centuries' worth of philological, text-critical, and antiquarian learning—in an effort to embed the Bible in a foreign, historical culture. In this way, they introduced a historical disjunction that allowed them to operate on the Bible as an inert and separated body of tradition. They used historical research to write the Bible's death certificate while opening, simultaneously, a new avenue for recovering the biblical writings as ancient cultural products capable of reinforcing the values and aims of a new sociopolitical order. The Bible, once decomposed, could be used to fertilize modern culture.

No biblical critic of the eighteenth century did more to exploit and articulate the significance of these developments than Johann David Michaelis. Michaelis was the leading biblical scholar of his generation and the most accomplished Orientalist of the eighteenth century. From his position at the Georg-August-Universität in Göttingen (hereafter Georgia Augusta), Michaelis wrote important works, trained scores of influential scholars, commanded large international audiences, and built his reputation as the world's expert on the ancient context of the Bible. Founded in 1737, Georgia Augusta quickly became a center of the German Enlightenment. In its early, heady days, Michaelis formalized methods of biblical study and research programs there that accorded with the social and political realities of the Enlightenment university. These shaped the academic study of the Bible at Göttingen and other centers of the new science of the Bible (*Bibelwissenschaft*), notably Jena, the reconfigured university at Halle, and Humboldt's new university at Berlin (founded 1810). It is not without justice that historians of scholarship have often called Michaelis one of the fathers of modern biblical criticism. Michaelis provided the conceptual framework that would allow contemporary scholars to activate older modes of erudition in the creation of a new disciplinary study of the Bible. In groundbreaking work on Hebrew language, law, poetry, and antiquities, Michaelis argued that an explicit recognition of the Old Testament's deadness, its status as an ancient literary corpus discontinuous both with Christianity and with Judaism, was the first step in retaining its relevance. Modeling his work on neohumanistic attempts to reinforce the social and cultural ideals of the *Aufklärung* through the study of (dead) Greek and Latin literature, Michaelis approached the Old Testament as the literary remainder of an ancient Israelite society. As Rome and especially Greece furnished ideals for the eighteenth-century Germans, Israel, too, could be made a relevant resource for the new cultural, social, and political order. This was part of an effort to disengage biblical interpretation from confessional paradigms and make a new, cultural Bible shorn of scriptural properties the centerpiece of an irenic political theology. In pursuing this, Michaelis initiated and formalized a number of projects that would stand at the center of modern criticism for generations to come: for example, the scientific study of Hebrew as an ancient Semitic language (rather than a divine or primeval language), literary criticism of biblical poetry, and the historical criticism of legal materials in the Bible. In these ways, Michaelis was a foundational figure for the discipline and an important figure within a wider transformation of biblical interpretation in academic culture.

This book, however, is not simply an intellectual biography of Michaelis. It is also a revisionist account of the early history of biblical scholarship. A correct understanding of this history is essential to contemporary discussions about the role of biblical criticism in academic theology. One of the more important trends in the academy within the last few decades has been the renewal of interest in the theological interpretation of Scripture. This interest has coincided with a growing sense among many that the discipline of biblical studies, once dominated by historical criticism and lately fragmented by multiplied methodologies, has become increasingly incoherent. In his justly famous work on hermeneutics, *The Eclipse of Biblical Narrative*, Hans Frei showed that biblical criticism of the eighteenth and nineteenth centuries lost contact with the Bible's most prominent feature: its narrative shape. Frei's work influentially questioned whether a hermeneutics preoccupied with historicity and predicated upon a referential theory of meaning could yield a theology that did justice to the actual shape, content, and thought-forms of the Bible. In the decades since Frei, many theologians have continued to look for ways to disengage theology from historical criticism and reconnect it more closely to the language of the Bible itself.

The notion that biblical studies have entered a period of crisis has become a commonplace among biblical critics. According to one prominent scholar, Brevard Childs, the discipline has been marked by "methodological impasse, conflicting private interpretations, loss of clear direction, extreme fragmentation, unbridgeable diversity, and even a deep sense of resignation."[5] Childs's comments refer to developments within the discipline, such as the decline of classic documentary criticism in the twentieth century, profound reevaluations of historical conclusions based on newer archaeological approaches, and the profusion of new methods, some programmatically "postmodern," which refuse to give priority to historical and philological inquiry as traditionally practiced. Yet the disorientation of the discipline also has to do with its ambiguous relation to theology and the Bible's large religious readership. On the one hand, biblical scholarship has operated independently of and, at times, antagonistically toward professional theologians and church leaders. Here the names of Peyrère, Spinoza, Reimarus, and D. F. Strauss come to mind. On the other hand, biblical studies have benefited from religious patronage and furnished indispensable support to ambitious programs of various sorts: for example, the rationalist programs of German theologians in the eighteenth century, *Kulturprotestantismus* in the nineteenth, and the North American "biblical theology" movement in the twentieth. This mixed history has allowed historians of scholarship to characterize the relationship in disparate ways: either as beholden to religious categories or as fundamentally inimical to religious reading.[6]

What a close look at the origins of modern criticism shows is that the discipline is best understood as a cultural-political project shaped by the realities of the university. As an academic discipline, it shared in the fundamental paradox at the heart of *Religionswissenschaft*. In order to maintain the critical distance necessary for objective understanding, scholars of religion created ways of studying their subjects that insulated them from the thing that gives religion power: its claim on the loyalties of the individual.[7] In this way, biblical scholarship bore a necessary relation to religious communities, promoting understanding of their bibles. Yet critical scholars also reserved the right to modify or reject the beliefs and interpretive disciplines that gave religious communities their distinctive confessional shapes. Biblical scholarship, as a discipline, had no *programmatic* interest in theological heterodoxy (or orthodoxy). Its overriding concern was the creation of a new postconfessional mode of biblical discourse, one that remained open to religion while opposed to interpretation consciously shaped by particular religious identities. Jon Levenson describes the contemporary state of affairs, which has its roots in these developments: "The academy must refuse everything to scholars as faithful members of religious communities, but it must give them everything as individuals; they must become critics."[8] The goal was and is irenicism. Before modern biblical criticism can be properly evaluated, this essential point must be understood.

This perspective on origins, though, must not be identified with a theory of secularization that explains the rise of biblical scholarship as an instance of the decline of religion in the face of antireligious opposition. Such theories have played large and small roles in attempts to describe the career of the Bible in the modern world. Paul Hazard, for example, in his famous work on the fateful "crisis of European conscience," portrayed biblical criticism as a key instance of secularization, dividing Europe between Christian traditionalists and their radical, freethinking opponents.[9] Early modern biblical criticism may be understood, on this view, in terms of a larger historical trajectory marked by a decline in the prestige and significance of Christianity. A secularization theory of this type, though, is not useful in describing what most biblical scholars in this period were actually trying to accomplish. One finds very few invectives against religion among the treatises, monographs, and dissertations of philologists and theologians actively engaged in the study of the Bible in the early modern period. Something like the distinction between "secularization" (a process) and "secularism" (an ideology) is useful here. Though critical efforts may have contributed to secularization, few critics were secularists: "secularization" does not speak to motive. The total disappearance of Christianity would have seemed, to all but a handful of radicals in the eighteenth century, undesirable if not inconceivable.

Similarly, modern biblical criticism has been explained as one instance in the rise of a pervasive historicism that overspread the human sciences in Germany at the turn of the nineteenth century. Thus Robert Leventhal points to the "emergence of hermeneutics" in this period, a generalized theory of interpretation that was "a specifically German reaction to transcendental philosophy and its ahistorical, even anti-historical predisposition."[10] German thinkers, on this view, stressed the untranslatability of historical cultures and understood interpretation of literary, philosophical, and religious texts as an attempt to provoke what Leventhal has nicely termed a "clash of discursive worlds." Similarly, Peter Hanns Reill argues that the pragmatic historicism of the *Aufklärer* set them apart from their French and British counterparts. They created a new form of historical inquiry attentive not to the "purified facts" of the antiquarians or attuned to the stale moralism of the polyhistorians but rather oriented toward a total system of causes and driving forces in the human past, which, in turn, could be used to solve long-standing problems in law, theology, and other disciplines.[11] There can be little doubt that historicism, as a kind of governing belief, was crucially important to many forms of intellectual inquiry in the period: philosophy, theology, law, and aesthetics. It is thus useful to speak of the centrality of historical understanding to eighteenth-century biblical critics. Indeed, modern biblical criticism is often referred to simply as "historical criticism" or "historical-critical method." Nevertheless, historical understanding was never an end in itself. If Herder, Lessing, and Schlegel sought a "clash of discursive worlds," professional biblical scholars in the same period, while doing their share to bring it about, could not allow the Bible to remain consigned to an alien discursive world. Historical research was expected to throw up new bridges of understanding even as it destroyed old ones. Without slipping into exemplar history, historical research had to become, in Reill's term, "pragmatic." It had to be useful to life.

A much more promising way to understand the relation of theological readers to modern biblical scholarship, especially that of the Enlightenment, is to see it as a cultural enterprise aimed at overcoming confessional loyalties while preserving Christian intellectual and religious forms. Jonathan Sheehan has argued along these lines that translators and biblical scholars in the eighteenth century set the stage for the "forging of a cultural Bible."[12] Sheehan characterizes the efforts of translators, critics, and exegetes in a fresh and compelling way, not simply as antecedents to later developments like secularism or historicism but rather as examples of a constructive program in their own right. In doing so, he reckons seriously with the self-understanding of eighteenth-century figures. The efforts of biblical scholars in this period must be understood as part of a larger attempt to shore up the authority of the Bible by rearticulating its cultural relevance and, as Sheehan has shown, by creatively demonstrating its value as a philological, moral, aesthetic, and historical resource. The perspective taken in this book reflects a view of the eighteenth century that is in substantial agreement with the transformation thesis at the heart of Sheehan's important work. Yet it extends and refines that thesis in two ways. First, in order for the Bible to become an Enlightenment Bible or a cultural Bible, it had first to be divested of its scriptural character. This amounted not simply to transformation but rather to revivification. Because the Bible could no longer be invoked as catholic scripture, the paths to understanding it lay within specific confessional hermeneutics. Scriptural bibles had to be left aside before the Bible, as a cornerstone of European culture, could be received again. The "death of scripture" and the rise of a nonconfessional Bible described here bring the religious legacy of modern criticism as a constructive response to the fracturing of Christendom into clearer view. Second, it attaches this legacy in a specific way to the institutional environment at Enlightenment universities like Michaelis's Georgia Augusta. For it was there that university reformers made the hallmark of the modern critical project, political irenicism, a first-order intellectual virtue and an explicit goal of academic culture. Earlier German scholars guided by Protestant scholasticism, Pietism, and neohumanism in the seventeenth and eighteenth centuries preserved and cultivated the critical tools and erudition that would ultimately be necessary to decompose the Bible. It fell to their successors at the university to revivify it. The Enlightenment not only led to the forging of cultural Bibles; it also produced the modern academic Bible.

In order to set the stage for this account, I offer, in this chapter, a brief account of the fate of the Bible as scripture in the sixteenth and seventeenth centuries. I use the example of Erasmus to illuminate the effects of humanism and the role of the church on biblical interpretation, arguing that religious schism and the eclipse of the Vulgate engendered new, nonscriptural interpretive modes. Finally, I connect the "textualization" of the Bible in the seventeenth century to conditions created by the religious divisions of the preceding century, suggesting that textualization emerged as a strategy for managing appropriations of the Bible in the religiously conflicted world of early modern Europe.

The Death of Scripture

In claiming that biblical scholarship operated on the Bible as text and not as scripture, I wish to signal a historical shift, to mark out distinct but adjacent hermeneutical territories. The point is not to hold up a scriptural Bible as kind of Platonic form compared to which the modern academic Bible is only a derivative, distorted, and secondary reality. It is rather to invoke the "death of scripture" as a theological and historiographic characterization of the preconditions of the eighteenth-century scholarly enterprise. Modern scholars inherited a moribund Bible, which, after the Reformation, had ceased to function as catholic scripture in a divided Europe. In place of confessional modes of reading which only seemed to perpetuate war, obscurantism, and senseless religious division, they created a new program for retaining the cultural authority of the Bible, one that would secure for it a place in what Carl Becker famously called the "heavenly city of the eighteenth-century philosophers."[13] Before this took place, though, the Bible had first to become a text.

The late fifteenth and early sixteenth centuries spanned a tumultuous and consequential period. Political and ecclesial developments, which were decades and centuries in the making, contributed to a rapid, violent sundering of Western Christendom. The erosion of papal authority and the rise of powerful monarchies, the influence of late medieval reform movements, the invention of the printing press, and the growth of populations and urban economies in Western Europe all played important roles. Among contributing factors to the Reformation, the one most decisive for the new approaches to biblical interpretation that grew out of the Reformation, however, was the constellation of attitudes and activities identified with Renaissance humanism. Jacob Burckhardt famously characterized the Italian humanists of the Quattrocento as progenitors of modern secularism responsible for breaking free of the medieval Christian past by turning to pagan antiquity. According to Burckhardt, they created an alternative culture that was a "competitor with the whole culture of the Middle Ages, which was essentially clerical and was fostered by the Church." The humanists spawned "a new civilization, founding itself on that which lay on the other side of the Middle Ages."[14] Since Burckhardt's time, though, historians have refined Burckhardt's thesis in important ways, challenging the decisiveness of the break between medieval and Renaissance cultures on the one hand and the programmatic secularism of Renaissance classicism on the other.[15] In light of these challenges, Renaissance humanism is better described as a broad, religiously flexible, and civic-minded educational program encompassing the humanities (*studia humanitatis*) and a movement, furthermore, rooted in medieval appropriation of classical sources. One of its distinctive features was the study of classical texts in their original languages—preeminently Latin but also Greek and, later, Hebrew. This gave rise to the Renaissance ideal of the *vir trilinguus* and the close association of political and religious renewal with fresh appropriations of ancient learning. Humanism was a reformatory enterprise energized at all points by philology.

There was a clear affinity between the humanist program, captured in the slogan *ad fontes* ("to the sources"), and the *sola scriptura* principle of the Reformers. Humanists and reformers placed the study of ancient texts in their original languages at the center of programs that allowed them to access the touchstones of Western culture. In this, both groups were opposed to scholasticism. Though humanists and scholastics shared a good deal, such as a concern to adapt pagan learning to Christian purposes, the debate between them formed an important background to the textualization of the Bible. The scholastics insisted on the primacy of systematic theology in the theological curriculum, upholding her traditional place as "queen of the sciences." Philology, on this view, was merely the "handmaiden" of theology. To scholastic theologians, the Bible was the source of theology. It contained timeless truths that needed to be clarified and organized by reason. These truths transcended historical and cultural boundaries. In subordinating the literal sense of the Bible, where philology was helpful, to the spiritual senses of the Bible, scholastic theologians integrated the Latin Bible into a long and variegated theological and philosophical discourse stretching back to Augustine. They emphasized the role of rigorous logic, careful distinctions, and manifest demonstrations in maintaining and extending this discourse. To many scholastics, humanist insistence on philology seemed impertinent and wrongheaded.

Humanists cultivated rhetoric and eloquence in direct opposition to what they regarded as the tortuous barbarisms of scholastic thought. Scholastics, for their part, believed that rhetoric was out of place in theology. Of what value, for example, was Ciceronian eloquence in explaining clearly how the host remains bread while becoming the body of Christ? To humanists a philological examination of the Bible showed that it bore witness to a living historical reality. It was not simply a Latin sourcebook for scholastic disputation. As Alister McGrath points out, in turning to the text of the New Testament humanists sought "moral and doctrinal insights" through "literary and historical analysis." They sought to encounter Christ and recapture the "vitality of the experience of the early church." *Ad fontes*, as a reform program, extended to the Bible. Yet even as humanists learned Hebrew and Greek, they recognized the biblical text as "an intellectually modest source incapable of bearing the dialectical weight imposed upon it through the theological speculation of the schoolmen."[16]

Focus on the text of the Bible allowed the humanists to create invidious comparisons between the liveliness of the New Testament and the sclerotic systems of the scholastics. It allowed the reformers, though, to create an even sharper opposition between the text of the Bible and the traditional theology of the Church. For all of their similarities, humanists and reformers differed significantly in their aims. Where humanists sought to reform the Church by restoring the humanities and adopting a simpler, more ethically robust form of Christian piety, the reformers attacked the central doctrines of the Church and its very right to pronounce authoritatively on scriptural matters. There had been reform movements and criticisms of the Church before Luther. But Luther's challenge, according to Euan Cameron, was a frontal assault on the "principal strength and justification" of the Church, for Luther believed that souls were "saved by the direct intervention of a sovereign God considering only his own inclination to mercy, rather than the sinner's disposition." Luther succeeded in impressing on his followers "the remorselessly coherent logic" of this message, which "entailed and demanded that one abandon the search for qualitative 'grace' through acts of ritual, ceremonial piety done in the face of Mother Church."[17] Cameron also points out that if a new doctrine of justification was the first pillar of the reformation, then *sola scriptura* was the second. For the reformers borrowed from humanists by using the text of the Bible as a basis for criticizing the present state of the church. *Sola scriptura* stood for an effort to "*oppose* parts of a 'tradition' which was seen as pernicious" by comparing it to a particular version of the Gospel message.[18] A textual recovery of the Bible was essential to changes sought by reformers, just as it was important—though to a different degree—to humanists in the fifteenth and sixteenth centuries. Humanists aided and abetted the textualization of the Bible. Protestants turned textualization into a theological principle.

Erasmus attempted to embrace humanist reforms without abandoning a scriptural hermeneutic. Despite fundamental differences, Erasmus and Luther shared a common interest in restoring the text of the Bible.[19] Over the course of three decades, from 1505–1535, Erasmus published works on the biblical text. The first in this vein was the *Adnotationes* of Lorenzo Valla. Valla is often credited with stimulating Erasmus's interest in biblical philology. After encountering Valla's critical notes on the Vulgate New Testament, Erasmus eagerly produced a new edition of them in

1505. In subsequent years, he devoted himself to a study of the Greek text, and in 1516 his *Novum instrumentum* appeared. This included an explanation and defense of the project, an edition of the Greek text of the New Testament alongside Erasmus's Latin translation in parallel columns, and, finally, notes on the translation itself. The work was retitled *Novum testamentum* in the second edition of 1519, and it appeared under that name in the editions of 1522, 1527, and 1535. Within this time period, Erasmus also published editions of the church fathers as well as popular expositions of New Testament books. The latter, intended for a lay audience, were called *Paraphrases* and were issued for every book of the New Testament except the book of Revelation.

Erasmus applied himself diligently to the text of the Bible. A quote from the preface of the 1516 *Novum instrumentum* offers the theological rationale for his textual labors:

> ... our chief hope for the restoration and rebuilding of the Christian religion ... is that all those who profess the Christian philosophy the whole world over should above all absorb the principles laid down by their Founder from the writings of the evangelists and apostles, in which that heavenly Word which once came down to us from the heart of the Father still lives and breathes for us and acts and speaks with more immediate efficacy, in my opinion, than in any other way. Besides which I perceived that that teaching which is our salvation was to be had in a much purer and more lively form if sought at the fountain-head and drawn from the actual sources than from pools and runnels. And so I have revised the whole New Testament (as they call it) against the standard of the Greek original, not unadvisedly or with little effort, but calling in the assistance of a number of manuscripts in both languages.[20]

Erasmus's theological vision is clear in this quotation: the restoration and revitalization of the Christian Church depends upon an active engagement with the scriptures, a learned reappropriation of the Christian faith, a return *ad fontes*. He draws a contrast between a fountain gushing with clear water, issuing from the Bible and the teachings of the fathers, and stagnant pools and tiny runnels, the pedantry and vanity of scholastic theology.

In his editorial work on the Greek New Testament, Erasmus prepared the way for a revision of the text and authority of the Vulgate. Not only did Erasmus use available manuscripts to present the reader with the Greek text, he also included his own Latin translation based on the Greek. The significance of a new Latin translation was not lost on Erasmus's scholastic opponents, who came to the defense of the Vulgate. In a carefully documented study of the debate between Erasmus and his opponents, Allan Jenkins and Patrick Preston outline various ways in which

Erasmus's biblical philology posed a challenge to scholasticism.[21] Scholastic theology was based on a Latin theological tradition that grew out of the Vulgate, used Aristotelian philosophical categories to express timeless biblical truths, identified salvation with intellectual assent to these truths, and, finally, derived its authority precisely from its own traditional character. By dislodging the Vulgate from the center of theological inquiry, Erasmus questioned the reliability of theologians who could not read the Bible in its original languages. Erasmus rejected the philosophical frameworks of the scholastics and commended scripture not as source material for elaborate theologies but rather as edification for the Christian believer and as an essential venue for encountering Christ. Erasmus bypassed the scholastic tradition and forced the interpreter to confront the Bible anew, making text-critical judgments and translational decisions as necessary, as an essential discipline in the cultivation of *philosophia Christi*.[22]

Erasmus was an outspoken critic of scholastic theologians, and his New Testament project challenged their authority in the ways that Jenkins and Preston have identified. Yet the controversy over the Vulgate also shows that the very concept of scripture, and not merely the authority of the scholastics, was at stake in the debate. To critics of Erasmus, the "philological principle" (the claim that correct knowledge of the Bible depends on knowledge of the text in its original languages) compromised the authority of scripture. Of these critics, few were more concerned to safeguard the authority of the Vulgate than Paris-trained theologian Pierre Cousturier (Petrus Sutor; 1475–1537). In a 1525 work directed against the scholarship of Erasmus and Lefèvre, entitled *De tralatione Bibliae et novarum reprobatione interpretationum*, Cousturier took Erasmus to task. In dislodging the Vulgate, Cousturier argued, Erasmus was not simply questioning the authority of a translation, he was undermining scripture itself. The Vulgate formed the basis for theological judgments rendered by theologians, councils, and fathers throughout the history of the Church. To question the authority of the Vulgate while acknowledging its historic centrality was simply to contradict oneself, for what made the Vulgate *scripture* was precisely this history. Cousturier argued that it was "not reasonable that the whole church, which has always used this edition and still both approves and uses it, should for all these centuries have been wrong. Nor is it probable that that all those holy Fathers should have been deceived and all those saintly men who relied on this version when deciding the most difficult questions in general councils."[23] Scripture functions in an authoritative and obligatory way within the context of a community shaped by a coherent economy of meaning. The Vulgate functioned in precisely this way in the Western Church prior to the application of the philological principle by the reformers in their vernacular translations and commentaries. Theologians like Cousturier saw that the humanists could not displace the Vulgate without sacrificing the scriptural character of the Bible and turning it into a foreign textual body.

Though Erasmus did not agree with Cousturier on this point, he clearly appreciated the role of the Church in interpreting the Bible as scripture. This is clear, for example, in Erasmus's debate with Luther. There was much for Luther to like in Erasmus's program. Both men criticized clerical abuses, endorsed the study of biblical languages, and opposed scholastic theology with its heavy reliance on Aristotelian frameworks. Luther also believed, as Erasmus said in the 1516 preface, that Christian teaching should be acquired *e fontibus*, in lively encounter with the Bible itself. Yet when Luther applied for Erasmus's support in 1518, Erasmus politely demurred. He did not want to enter the fray by throwing support behind the controversial Luther, thus giving his scholastic opponents an opportunity to criticize his humanistic reforms by linking them with schism. He wrote a warm but careful letter to Luther in 1519, indicating that he would not intervene in ongoing disputes: "I keep myself uncommitted, so far as I can, in hopes of being able to do more for the revival of good literature."[24] As the Luther affair escalated, though, Erasmus became increasingly critical of Luther's blunt, aggressive, and divisive actions. He complained to colleagues like Justus Jonas that Luther's actions were entirely out of keeping with Christian humility and a desire for the peace of the Church. Though he disapproved of Luther, Erasmus was often connected by his opponents to Luther and accused of being a secret sympathizer. Eventually, Erasmus felt it necessary to oppose Luther publicly. In 1524, Erasmus published his *Discourse on Free Will* as a challenge to Luther on a topic of great importance to him: the role of man in salvation. Erasmus ultimately argued in this work for the validity of "Christian skepticism." Because the biblical evidence for the freedom or bondage of the will was not, in Erasmus's view, decisive, prudence requires the interpreter to suspend individual judgment. And because this is an issue on which the Church has pronounced itself, Erasmus claimed that one ought to accept the teaching of the Church that the will is free. Luther, in his reply, disagreed with the substance of Erasmus's position, but he also attacked the notion that skepticism is a genuinely Christian posture, arguing that Christians are distinguished by what they believe and not by what they doubt. The Holy Spirit, Luther wrote famously, is no skeptic. Erasmus explained that his skepticism was not dogmatic but prudential, a safeguard against rashness and not a refusal to affirm the truth. The ultimate value of a skeptical approach was to prevent the individual interpreter from losing contact with the larger interpretive community. Richard Popkin explains Erasmian skepticism as a concession to the weakness of human intellect: "the superstructure of the essential belief is too complex for a man to judge. Hence it is easier to rest in a sceptical attitude and accept the age-old wisdom of the Church on these matters than to try to understand and judge for oneself."[25]

Erasmus certainly believed that the Church possessed age-old wisdom and that individual intellects could be dangerously fallible. The deeper issue underlying

Erasmus's skepticism, though, was his ecclesiology, specifically his view of how the Bible functions within the framework of tradition and ecclesial authority. For someone who gained fame as a critic of the Church, Erasmus nevertheless retained a high view of the Church throughout his life. Consider this striking declaration from 1527:

> How much the authority of the Church means to others I do not know: to me it means so much that I could have the same opinions as the Arians and Pelagians if the Church had accepted what they taught. The words of Christ are enough for me, but people should not be surprised if I follow the Church as their interpreter; convinced of its authority, I believe the canonical Scriptures.[26]

For Erasmus, the authority of the Church was the basis for receiving the Bible as Scripture. The Bible is a "canonical" reality and not simply a textual one. Erasmus understood the appeal of Arianism and Pelagianism. He appreciated, then, that orthodoxy was not simply a matter of rejecting false doctrines like these by individual recourse to the biblical evidence. It was a matter of loyalty to the Church. For Erasmus, the Scriptures were revelatory witnesses to divine speech and action, which bear close and careful study in their own right: few in Erasmus's day were as devoted to the text of the Bible as he. Yet Erasmus also insisted that interpreters measure their own work against the tradition. Erasmus wrote that "we do not depend upon any dreams of our own, but seek it out of the writings of Origen, Basil, Chrysostom, Cyril, Jerome, Cyprian, Ambrose, or Augustine." Luther, by contrast, claimed that "through the Holy Spirit or the particular gift of God, each man is enlightened so that he can judge in complete certainty in what concerns himself and his own personal salvation, and decide between the doctrines and opinions of all men."[27] In insisting that one consult the Fathers, Erasmus advocated an interpretive mode oriented above all toward the consensus of the Church on doctrinal matters. Luther, it is fair to say, did not. The difference between Erasmus and Luther surely had to do with differences in their temperaments and political situations. Yet it also had to do with differing conceptions of scripture. As Erika Rummel has pointed out, for Erasmus, "concord marked and defined the true Church, which was the recipient of God's word and the guardian of spiritual truth."[28] The Bible was the possession of the Church, and the Church, by definition, was a peaceable and coherent body united by Christ. To read the Bible *against* the Church, or in a way that divided the Church, was to misunderstand fundamentally what the Bible is and is for. When pressed, Erasmus showed that for him it was the reality of the Church as an old, wise, and united body that was decisive for biblical interpretation. His life and work show what was involved in one attempt to retain an ecclesial framework for a scriptural Bible in an age of criticism and religious division.

Toward the end of his life, Erasmus published a meditation on Psalm 84, *On Mending the Peace of the Church* (1533). However, the peace of the Church, already in ruins in Erasmus's day, would not be mended. The division of the Western Church created a new environment for biblical interpretation, one in which the textuality of the Bible became a primary and deeply problematic concern in a way that it had not been before. The great question among seventeenth-century interpreters was whether the Bible, in light of its textual characteristics, was perspicuous, whether its wording and meaning were self-evident or not.[29] This is not surprising. Anabaptist conventicles, spiritualist sects, and antitrinitarian groups grew precipitately out of reform movements of the 1520s and 1530s. By the middle of the sixteenth century, the Reformation had remade societies and governments: churches and territories across Europe lay in a patchwork of state-sponsored confessions, with the division between Lutheran and Reformed often as rigid as the one between Catholics and Protestants. Theologian Ephraim Radner, in an insightful and important book on the theological consequences of Christian division, describes the situation faced by Catholic and Protestant biblical interpreters: "That two portions of a divided Church could never, in the face of their critics or antagonists, persuasively extricate themselves from the circularity of their criteriology was a realization quickly made by both controversialists and religious scoffers."[30] For each group, the presence of the *other* Christian confession, which also claimed fidelity to the Bible, made it necessary for each group to defend its distinctive mode of biblical interpretation. As Radner points out, though, there was no noncircular way to ground biblical interpretation in distinctive criteria. For example, apologists might defend Protestant individualism or Catholic institutionalism as suitable interpretive modes on the basis of biblical teachings; yet these teachings were gleaned from the text by way of the very modes they were supposed to vindicate. Building on Radner's analysis, R. R. Reno has argued that theology after the Reformation included two trends: a Roman Catholic tendency toward "juridical supersessionism" and a Protestant tendency toward "doctrinal supersessionism."[31] In each case, the need to create separation from and establish superiority over the other led Catholics and Protestant interpreters to emphasize beliefs and practices that they did not share with one another. Theology and biblical interpretation, then, were conducted at the margins of the respective traditions, where differences were to be found, and not at the centers, where common ground existed. Reno sums up: the Bible proved "an insufficient basis for distinguishing between Protestant and Catholic"; as a result, "the shared language of Scripture" could not be the "primary source of theological precision and judgment."[32] To the wide community of interpreters throughout Europe, the Bible was no longer intelligible or usable simply as scripture belonging to the faithful; it became a repository of textual material for parallel theological superstructures. This is clear, for example, in the institutional shape taken by Protestant churches in the second half of the sixteenth century. This period saw the rise of catechisms and the reappearance of scholastic method. Protestants created or remade laws, schools, churches, and universities. Cameron describes it as the reflex of an "intellectual imperialism of colossal proportions" by which the "rarified scruples of literate intellectuals" became a "complete pattern of new belief, worship, and Church polity" for whole societies.[33] The Bible and the right of the individual to interpret it were qualified in this arrangement. Biblical teachings were organized into catechisms and standardized in confessions; serious interpretation was reserved for scholars proficient in biblical languages. Protestants and Catholics formalized and established theological identities, staking out positions on an ecclesial divide. Because the Bible belonged to all churches, and each was divided from the others, it belonged to none. Reading or hearing the Bible was not sufficient for understanding it. One first had to choose where to stand.

The Textualization of the Bible

Theological conflict engendered other types of conflict in the sixteenth and seventeenth centuries, from skirmishes to full-blown wars. In this time, the textuality of the Bible, or rather its textual disorder, became the focus of intense research programs for biblical scholars in England, France, Spain, the Dutch Republic, and the German territories. On the one hand, textualization, with its roots in Renaissance humanism, preceded the Reformation and supplied the reformers with the tools and learning to challenge the Church. On the other hand, textualization intensified as a *result* of religious division. In disputing with one another, Catholics and Protestants paid close attention to the textual character of the Bible. If, for example, a Roman Catholic appealed to Matthew 16:18 ("You are Peter and upon this rock I will build my church") to demonstrate the primacy of Peter and the establishment of the papacy, then a Protestant, with recourse to the Greek text, may well have raised a grammatical point weakening the connection between "Peter" and the "rock." Peter (Gk. *petros*) is a proper, masculine noun, only ever functioning as a personal name in the New Testament, while "rock" (Gk. *petra*) is a common noun of feminine gender. When Christ juxtaposes the two, an argument might run, he does so disjunctively. Thus *petra* refers to something other than Peter: either Peter's faith, as Luther thought, or to Christ himself, as Origen proposed. In response, though, a Catholic apologist might have replied as Mathias Bredenbach did in 1560, arguing that Jesus spoke Aramaic and, in the Syriac Peshitta version that most closely approximates Jesus' tongue, the two words are identical: *kêpa* ("rock").[34] Theological identities were at stake even in "small" disputes over the meaning of the text of the Bible.

Crises provoked by the Reformation, however, did not only intensify interest and investment in biblical interpretation. They also created the conditions for a stringent textualism that functioned to objectify the Bible, remove it from its larger ecclesial contexts, and turn it into a kind of hermeneutical battleground. A stringent approach to the textuality of the Bible, or rather to its state of textual corruption, became, within only a few generations, a fundamental premise for Catholics and Protestants in their respective theologies of scripture. The nature and extent of this textualization of the Bible in the seventeenth century is illustrated by the remarkable collaboration of Reformed scholar Louis Cappel (1585–1658) and French Oratorian Jean Morin (1591–1659).

Both were involved in the heated controversy over the age and origin of the Masoretic vowel points in the Hebrew Bible. The traditional Jewish view in the sixteenth century was that the consonants and vowel points of the Hebrew text were both part of the original Sinaitic revelation. The reformers and their Roman Catholic opponents, by contrast, asserted that the vowel points were comparatively recent and of human origin. In 1538, Elias Levita (1469–1549), a leading Jewish scholar in his generation, provided a definitive refutation of the antiquity of the vowel points in his *Masoret ha-Masoret*. In the wake of Levita's challenge, the earlier Christian consensus evaporated. Roman Catholic theologians, relying on Levita's scholarship, argued that the vowel points, which were only added later, were necessary to understand the consonantal text. Thus, they reasoned, Protestants committed to *sola scriptura* and *veritas hebraica* did not have direct access to the Old Testament. Not only were they reliant upon tradition for their understanding of the Bible, they were reliant upon *Jewish* tradition. To escape this predicament, many Protestants took sides with Jewish traditionalists and affirmed the antiquity and divine origin of the vowel points. Their great champions in this effort were the Buxtorfs of Basel, Johannes the elder (1564–1629) and Johannes the younger (1599–1664), the most influential and respected Christian Hebraists of their time.

The Buxtorfs' most famous opponent, though, was not a Catholic polemicist. It was philologist and fellow Protestant Louis Cappel. In 1624, Cappel published anonymously a work entitled *Arcanum punctuationis revelatum*, or *Mystery of the Points Revealed*. In it he provided a devastating refutation of the elder Buxtorf. Cappel argued that debates in the Talmud refer not to the pointing activities of the Masoretes but to interpretive problems that arise from working with an unpointed text. Cappel also adduced various historical and philological arguments for the antiquity of the points; for example, that Jerome and the translators of the Septuagint knew nothing of pointed texts, that the names of vowels and accents have Aramaic and not Hebrew names, and that the marginal *qere*, which show how to pronounce the *kethib*, are, oddly, never pointed. Cappel argued further that unvocalized Hebrew consonants, contrary to Buxtorf's opinion, do not permit arbitrary readings. Like Arabic,

Hebrew, he argued, is perfectly readable without vowels; its syllabic structure and the occasional use of consonants to stand for vowels (*matres lectionis*) prevent the consonantal text from being fatally indeterminate. Finally, Cappel showed that the Masoretes developed the system of points in order to fix the tradition of vocalization no earlier than the second half of the first millennium of the Common Era.

Cappel was roundly denounced by his Reformed colleagues. Yet this did not deter him. In subsequent decades, he undertook a larger and more extensive work on textual problems in the Bible. In 1650, he published his *Critica sacra*, the work for which he is best known. In the *Arcanum*, Cappel demonstrated the fallible and historical nature of the vowel points. In the *Critica sacra*, he demonstrated that the consonantal text of the Hebrew Bible is likewise susceptible to change, corruption, and human interference. The work consists of six books in which Cappel provides, in orderly fashion, a detailed presentation of variant readings attested in the versions (Targumim, Vulgate, Septuagint, and Samaritan Pentateuch) and in the ancient witnesses (the New Testament, Josephus, and the Talmud). Cappel argued, in light of the numerous discrepancies presented there, that each source potentially bears witness to the authentic biblical text but that no single version may be equated with it. Cappel thus distinguished between the perfect, divinely inspired autographs (now lost) and the imperfect copies that later scribes and translators produced. Exegetes must consult the versions and arrive at independent and informed judgments as to the precise wording of the text. They must determine the phonetic or orthographic sources of textual corruptions and, on the basis of evidence and transparent reasoning, provide the *sensus planior et commodior* (clearer and more suitable sense). They must also be free to offer, when appropriate, conjectural emendations. Responsible interpretation, according to Cappel, begins with an intelligible, critically established text.

When Cappel had difficulty finding a publisher for the *Critica sacra*, it was the French priest Jean Morin who came to his aid. Morin, who was enthusiastic about the work, helped Cappel find a publisher in Paris, where the book first appeared. Morin had converted to Catholicism as a young adult and joined the Oratorians. He quickly found a place among polemicists seeking to expose the incoherence of Protestant hermeneutics. Before collaborating with Cappel, Morin in 1628 produced a three-volume edition of the Septuagint. Morin is also known for his work on the Samaritan Pentateuch, which was first brought to Europe in 1616 and which Morin edited for the Paris Polyglot Bible in 1632. Morin argued that readings found in the Samaritan Pentateuch, on the whole, supported those of the Septuagint. Thus, Catholics were correct in preferring the Septuagint to the Masoretic Text, which the Protestants took as the basis for their Old Testament. Not surprisingly, Morin also joined forces with Cappel against those who maintained the antiquity of the vowel points. Morin maintained that the Jews had willfully corrupted the

Hebrew text such that no Christian could rely on it in good conscience. The net result for Morin was a ringing reaffirmation of the Church's historic preference for the Septuagint and Vulgate over the Masoretic Text. Morin thus rejected the notion of a pristine Hebrew text to which the reformers might return, arguing instead that the textual history of the Bible itself manifests the importance of tradition in transmitting and safeguarding the Church's great textual inheritance. If the text needed the Church for its survival, then *a fortiori* it needed the Church to explain its meaning. Morin reflected and reinforced the Tridentine strategy for preserving and articulating the coherence of Catholic identity: to shore up Rome's claims to juridical priority and order in the realm of biblical interpretation. As Morin put it succinctly: "It is [God's] will that men depend upon priests."[35] As a Protestant, Cappel did not accept the theological conclusion that Morin drew from Cappel's own work on the vowel points and textual disorder of the Hebrew text. Cappel, for his part, believed that the disorder of the text did not ultimately compromise its perspicuity. He held that nothing pertaining to faith and morals was textually disputable, and a conscientious interpreter with philological training could employ sound text-critical method to recover the proper readings of disputed passages. Cappel turned to a scientific methodology aimed at rehabilitating the text. In this way he safeguarded *sola scriptura*. Philologists, in this scheme, might be necessary, but not priests. What unites Morin and Cappel, though, is more significant than what divides them. Both regarded the historically conditioned character of the biblical text as a first-order problem. To Protestants and their Catholic opponents, the Bible was not a self-evident scriptural inheritance guiding the faithful but rather an indeterminate object whose meaning and authority had to be established from outside the Bible itself, either by appeal to authority or the exercise of critical judgment. But the Bible qua Bible was a disputed book in a confessional no-man's-land.

As we have seen, textualization was one of the *causes* or contributing factors in the reformers' attitude toward the Bible. As the example of Cappel and Morin shows, it was also a *result* of divisions and theological disputes wrought by the Reformation. As the seventeenth century wore on, however, textualization was also advanced as a *remedy* to these same divisions. The new focus on textualization lay at the heart of attempts to unify and overcome religious division, to use critical science to regularize interpretation and save the text from confessional abuse. Humanists began to assume critical postures toward traditional learning and church doctrine as early as the fifteenth century. Anthony Grafton, for example, has shown how the Italian humanist Poliziano (1454–1494), in bringing unprecedented rigor and historical precision to philology, used the solvents of criticism to purify contemporary culture by clearing away dubious learning and exposing its corrupt sources. Poliziano adduced the well-known dictum of a church father, Cyprian, in support of his own program: "Custom unsupported by the truth is long-lived error."

This appeal to the example of Cyprian, Grafton writes, set up a "starkly dramatic comparison" between "the need for pure classical texts and the need for an incorrupt Christianity," which gave Poliziano's method "a moral as well as a philological edge."[36] The "edge" arose from the possibility that eagle-eyed philologists, training their gazes on ancient texts, might prove familiar customs and cherished religious and philosophical ideas to be the products of ignorance, degradation, or, even worse, deception. Lorenzo Valla (1407–1457) proved on philological grounds that the *Donation of Constantine*, which purported to grant the western half of the Roman Empire to the pope, was composed centuries after Constantine. His *Adnotationes* on the Latin New Testament, which remained unpublished during Valla's life, proved a menace to the authority of the Vulgate, posed by a man with no ecclesial or spiritual authority. The philologist, then, developed a new kind of authority in religious and cultural questions simply by dint of expertise—an authority, moreover, that functioned, as a matter of principle, independently of ecclesial loyalties.

It was a small step from a philology that functioned outside the boundaries of religious identity to one that could actively *arbitrate* religious disputes and end confessional discord. Humanists like Valla succeeded in identifying the "truth" of a text, to a great degree, with its historical authenticity. And because they had the skills and knowledge to interrogate its historical situation effectively, they believed that they could offer interpretations and evaluations of texts that transcended the circular, self-serving readings offered by confessional interpreters. Thus the optimism of noted classical philologist Joseph Scaliger (1540–1609): "I wish to be a good grammarian. Religious discord depends on nothing except ignorance of grammar."[37] Peter Miller has shown, in his valuable survey of the "theology of Polyglot Bibles," that this same sentiment guided the textual endeavors of a wide range of scholars in the sixteenth and early seventeenth centuries.[38] This period saw the production of massive Bible projects completed throughout Europe, which featured not only the collation of manuscripts in the original biblical languages but also of ancient versions and, through annotations, apparatuses, and prefaces, compendia of current scholarship as well. The four major polyglots were published at Alcalá de Henares (Complutensian Polyglot), Antwerp, Paris, and London. They were overwhelming in their size and erudition, confronting the user with a mass of raw material from which an understanding of the biblical text was to be won. The first three enjoyed the support and patronage of the Roman Catholic Church; the London project, under the leadership of Brian Walton, was funded by prepaid subscriptions and carried out by a team of English scholars. Miller offers a general characterization of the seventeenth-century philological enterprise as a response to wars of religion "fueled by ignorance" and "actively abetted by obscurantism." Miller explains: "It was precisely because the interpretation of Scripture had become the cause of such laceration in the body of Christendom that it was imperative to create an instrument that, by eliminating the possibility of casual misinterpretation, could deprive the contentiousness of the oxygen it needed to thrive."[39] The visual representation of (sometimes) conflicting textual traditions side by side might seem a strange way to quell interpretive disagreements. Yet it was precisely the "outing" of textual difference, the gathering in and frank acknowledgement of "errors," that scholars like Walton found hopeful. To bring the imperfect, heterogeneous text of the Bible out into the open was to prepare the way for an ecumenical, methodologically transparent mode of interpretation. Scribal errors and the kind of textual corruption manifest in a polyglot—things regarded by theological liberals as *adiaphora*—did not ultimately disturb Walton and his collaborators. Rather, the polyglot would allow for the "repair" of the text and the discernment of a divinely orchestrated consensus among the versions.[40] The polyglots were impressive monuments to the early modern textualized Bible, showcasing the knowledge, skills, and technologies of an emerging biblical science. They also bore witness to the irenic, ecumenical aspirations of scholars like Walton, and indeed Erasmus before him, who turned to the text of the Bible to advance the peace of the church.

Among seventeenth-century biblical interpreters, the most famous irenicist was Baruch Spinoza. In chapter fourteen of his *Tractatus theologico-politicus*, Spinoza acknowledged the divisive aspects of textualization, recalling a Dutch proverb: *Geen ketter sonder letter* ("No heretic without a text").[41] The public, accessible character of texts facilitates their use and interpretation by sects and individuals. The reformational controversies are nothing if not a testimony to the plastic character of the Bible and the vital connection between sects and texts. Though individual Protestant sects (ironically) affirmed the perspicuity of scripture as an article of faith, the wars of religion and political turmoil in Spinoza's own Amsterdam convinced him that even if the Bible were perspicuous, it was still dangerously susceptible to misinterpretation. Like Walton, Spinoza believed that it was possible and, indeed, necessary to set forth a way of interpreting the Bible that would stem sectarian violence. Spinoza set out to accomplish this, first by setting aside theological judgments and confessional frameworks for understanding the Bible, which he regarded as the "prejudices of theologians" and mere "human fabrications" passed off as "divine teachings." Having disposed of these, the reader must turn to the text itself:

> In this way—that is, by allowing no other principles or data for the interpretation of Scripture and study of its contents except those that can be gathered only from Scripture itself and from a historical study of Scripture—steady progress can be made without any danger of error, and one can deal with matters that surpass our understanding with no less confidence than those matters which are known to us by the natural light of reason.[42]

What the interpreter stands to learn from the Bible is identical with what makes it divine: in Spinoza's words, "true moral doctrine." Spinoza's rationalistic, narrowly textual hermeneutic allows him to limit the sphere of the Bible's influence to ethics, which he subsequently identifies with a minimal monotheism and the duty to live justly and charitably. Careful philological study of the Bible shows that concerns with modern philosophical, political, legal, or scientific questions are alien to the Bible. The Bible contains the ancient historical record of a specific civilization, which is firmly embedded in the language and thought patterns of its time. Historical and textual investigation shows that it is neither timeless nor universal. Attempts to use the Bible to address modern questions, especially political ones, are unwarranted. The freedom to philosophize, according to Spinoza, is actually preserved *on biblical grounds*, on the basis of what reason shows the Bible to be.

The discovery of what is "true" is a crucial element of Spinoza's biblical criticism. The quest to discover what is true in and of the Bible is not, for Spinoza, a metaphysical one. He does not seek, by his philological inquiries, to discover the sense in which the Bible itself contains Truth or offers metaphysical precepts that are ratified by reason and experience. Rather, the effort to ascertain what is true, as Jonathan Israel has pointed out, is "a historical-critical and linguistic exercise anchored in a wider naturalistic philosophical standpoint."[43] That is, it is an attempt to uncover the original aims of the biblical writers, to learn how the Bible corresponds—is true to—the intent of its writers. Spinoza regarded this quest as something fully accomplished in his own work. For him, the quest *must* culminate in the candid admission that the Bible, when read in light of its intended meaning, has an important but severely restricted purpose: to teach charity. According to Spinoza, the rule of charity can be honestly gleaned from the Bible, but that is all. The Bible is of no help to philosophy, and it becomes dangerous when invoked in political discussions. These points are borne out by the truths of criticism. To examine the text of the Bible rationally and independently is to perceive its limitations. Spinoza's program was not constructive. What little of value that could be gained from the Bible could be ascertained from reason itself. Philology and historical understanding allowed the critic to play defense, to prevent religious and political leaders from manipulating the Bible and curtailing intellectual freedom by using the authority of the Bible to sanction superstitious or self-serving behaviors. But the Bible, apart from its use in the teaching of charity, had no role to play in modern life. Spinoza's mode of textualization, then, was irenic because it embedded the Bible in ancient history, where it would no longer be able to trouble modern life. Spinoza's program provoked opposition in part because it cut across traditional understandings of the Bible and, indeed, early modern sensibilities about the continued relevance of the Bible. Yet his *Tractatus* was not the logical and inevitable conclusion to the textualizing trajectory that I have sketched for the sixteenth and seventeenth centuries. It was simply one (radical) possibility.

Conclusion

Given this background, it is not surprising that modern biblical scholarship has been inarticulate with respect to the scriptural character of the Bible. James Kugel has made this point in his magisterial survey of ancient and modern biblical interpretation, concluding ultimately that modern criticism is "completely irreconcilable" with religious reading.[44] Kugel argues persuasively that the very notion of a Bible depends upon a mode of reading and interpretation that is, in turn, based on a particular understanding of what the Bible is. According to Kugel, it was only because ancient communities of faith received disparate texts as a unified body of divine writings, often cryptic in meaning but always relevant in application, that these texts became a "Bible" at all. Modern biblical scholars, though, ruled out these ancient, religious readerly assumptions, seeking rather to uncover the Bible's true meaning in history, that is, the meaning its separate texts would have had before they *became* a Bible at all. On this view, modern biblical scholarship is not really about the Bible, which is the creation and possession of religious communities, but about the history of the materials that later constituted the Bible.

In chronicling the transition from scripture to text, I wish to offer a compatible but slightly different perspective on the relation of modern scholarship to the Bible. Like Kugel, I believe that the relation of modern biblical scholarship to the Bible and the religious readership for whom the Bible remains vitally important is problematical. The chief characteristics of modern biblical scholarship as it emerged in the eighteenth century were preoccupation with the textuality of the Bible, qualification of its authority, a turn to referential theories of meaning, and a focus on the world *of* the Bible (rather than the world as seen *through* the Bible). Humanists, of course, had been interested in the textual traditions and original languages of the Bible since the time of Valla, long before the Reformation controversies and the rise of biblical studies. But textual research after the Reformation intensified dramatically, yielding, for example, the era of the great Polyglot Bibles. The objectivity of the Bible, its status as a thing, a text, to be managed, reinterpreted, and recontextualized, formed the basis for a whole spectrum of postreformational interpretive projects. Schism, wars of religion, and the hermeneutical aporia arising from the intellectual crisis of the Reformation created a problematic environment for biblical interpretation. They contributed to what I have called scriptural opacity, with the authority, meaning, and location of the Bible all becoming contested questions. In the main, biblical scholarship did not adopt a Spinozan posture toward an opaque and problematic Bible. Scholars more often resembled Morin and Cappel, who assimilated the results of an emerging textual science to their own confessional programs. Whether a person sided with Morin and the magisterium or with Cappel and the redemptive powers of sacred criticism, he or she had first to reckon with a contested and disordered text. Still others worked in the vein of Erasmus and Walton, who believed that philology could repair the textual disorder of the Bible and heal the wounds of religious division, prompting the renewal and restoration of the Christian church.

By the middle of the eighteenth century, masters of text—philologists, classicists, and orientalists—emerged as leaders in the new academic biblical science. As scholars focused on textual disorder, the authority of the Bible as an obligatory touchstone for contemporary life also weakened. The Bible became, instead, an exotic "resource" for political philosophy, ancient history, and poetics. Instead of looking *through* the Bible in order to understand *the truth about the world*, eighteenth-century scholars looked directly at the text, endeavoring to find new, ever more satisfactory frames of cultural and historical reference by which to understand *the meaning of the text*. In the eighteenth century, scholars working in new settings set their sights high. It would not be enough for them simply to rehabilitate and unify the Christian church. It would be necessary to bring the Bible itself back to life for the sake of society, Western culture, and modern man. The goal was not reform but revivification. And the setting was not the church: it was the Enlightenment university.

2

Bible and Theology at an Enlightenment University

> The academic lecture and the sermon are so different that, if done well, they will in time only corrupt one another.
> —Johann David Michaelis, *Raisonnement über die protestantischen Universitäten*[1]

In his life, Michaelis claimed many titles, but "theologian" was not one of them. The son of a Halle professor, he had come to Göttingen to teach Bible and Near Eastern languages in the philosophical faculty. He made overtures to the theology faculty, offering to teach in dogmatics and ethics. His reputation as a learned man with a skeptical and lukewarm religious personality, though, caused trouble. It was said of him that he did not care for the "spirit" of religion but only for its "skin."[2] Another opponent complained that Michaelis did not come to church on a regular basis.[3] Michaelis was rebuffed. Not one to doubt himself, he dismissed the rejection itself as an example of small-minded territorialism and envy of his brilliance. He shook the dust from his feet. To Michaelis, the study of the Bible no more needed a theological framework than a proper understanding of the Augsburg confession required knowledge of Syriac. Michaelis, for his part, would show that the Bible, quite apart from dogmatics, was directly relevant to modern life. Just how it was possible for a Bible separated from theology to have contemporary value was not clear to many churchmen and scholars in his day. Here Michaelis saw his opportunity. He not only saw that the Bible could stand at the center of a new, socially relevant scholarly enterprise, he believed that he was the man for this particular job and the philosophical faculty of the Enlightenment university was the right place to do it.

In this chapter, I will explore the social and intellectual contexts of the Enlightenment university, paying particular attention to their effects on the study of theology and the Bible. I will also examine the early history of the University of Göttingen, known as Georgia Augusta (named after its founder King George II), and discuss some of the characteristic features of scholarly work at Göttingen. It is important to understand how new notions of the university in general and developments at Göttingen in particular shaped Michaelis's enterprise. Because Michaelis began his professional career at Georgia Augusta within a decade of its founding, the earliest history of the University is especially illuminating. In his thirty-six years there, Michaelis served in several key positions and helped Georgia Augusta secure its preeminent position. In time, Michaelis became known (unofficially) as *der Regent von Göttingen*.[4] How and why a biblical scholar should have attained such prominence at a "postconfessional" university, in a period associated with the declining influence of theology, is an interesting and important question.

The Eighteenth and Nineteenth Centuries: A Brief Sketch

In the nineteenth century, there were two kinds of universities: German universities and those that wanted to be German. Or so it seemed. In this period, German universities established themselves as leaders in the natural and human sciences and, unlike their seventeenth-century forebears, as centers of genuine intellectual innovation. Not only did the universities create giants like Hegel in philosophy, Niebuhr, Mommsen, and Wilamowitz in classics, Böckh and de Lagarde in philology, Ranke in history, Gauss and Riemann in mathematics, and von Harnack in theology; the German university, as a new kind of institution, also became the symbol of the *modern* university. It was the envy of the world, exporting the doctoral *Seminar* and the powerful *Wissenschaftsideologie* for which it stood to universities across Europe and North America. On American soil, for example, Cornell, Johns Hopkins, and the University of Chicago were new institutions in the mold of the German research university. These posed challenges in the late nineteenth century to the dominance of their older counterparts, most of which were built on the British model. In time, though, they would all become, in scholarly ethos if not form, venues for the Teutonic mind.[5]

How, then, to understand the extraordinary success of the German university? Historian Thomas Howard, in a definitive treatment of the German university in the nineteenth century, points somewhat surprisingly to academic theology. Howard seeks to understand "the evolution of the modern German university from the vantage point of theology and the evolution of modern theology from the vantage point of the university."[6] As Howard successfully argues, the pairing makes good sense. To begin, Schleiermacher, the architect of the quintessential German university, the University of Berlin, was himself a theologian. Over the course of the nineteenth century, academic theologians succeeded in assimilating theology to the realities of the modern state in order to ensure the continued survival of their discipline. The fate of theology at the university contains a paradox: by innovating, the Germans conserved. Striking a Faustian bargain with the growing power of the state, they maintained their religious and cultural inheritance by folding the authority of the Bible and of the Protestant theological tradition into the larger programs of *Verwissenschaftlichung* (scientization), *Entkonfessionalisierung* (deconfessionalization), *Professionalisierung* (professionalization), and *Verstaatlichung* (nationalization)—all programs centered at the university.[7] The end result of these programs, as the success of Harnack's defense of academic theology in the early twentieth century shows, was the firm establishment of theology among the scientific disciplines at the modern university. What exactly Harnack defended, though, was neither historic Reformational theology nor even traditional Christian belief. Rather it was "a critical, academic, scientific and, indeed, profoundly statist" enterprise, not the "apologetic, practical, confessional, or ecclesial" one more familiar within the history of the Christian churches. Howard astutely and cautiously questions what sort of religious value the theological *Wissenschaft* of Harnack, which Howard compares somewhat unfavorably to patristic theology, might ultimately have. Howard is too principled a historian to condemn Harnack, but it is difficult to escape the impression that Karl Barth, who comes on the scene to challenge the rigid academism and Erastian ecclesiology of his former mentor, is a heroic, though perhaps overwrought, figure in Howard's narrative. What Howard blandly calls a "redefinition of Protestant theology" and a "new departure in Christian intellectual and institutional history" he lets Barth condemn as a disastrous forsaking of the eternal Word for the multiplication of scholarly words.[8] Howard's story, then, begins with the improbable rise of the university in disparate German lands after the Napoleonic wars and ends (ominously) with the maturation and emplacement of theology as a scientific discipline in the service of an ambitious, powerful, sophisticated, and statist German regime.

It is helpful to keep the nineteenth and early twentieth centuries in view. The *Verwissenschaftlichung, Verstaatlichung, Entkonfessionalisierung,* and *Professionalisierung* of academic theology documented so fully and skillfully by Howard all mark out trajectories, as we will see, that have their roots in the second half of the eighteenth century. Yet the eighteenth-century figures with whom we are chiefly concerned, Michaelis above all, operated in a different milieu, one that knew nothing of the ultimate consequences of Kant's *decennium mirabilis*, the battle of Waterloo, the

Unionskirche of 1817, Hegel's *Phenomenology of Spirit*, the 1848 revolutions, or the "blood and iron" of Bismarck. By the same token, the study of the Bible in the eighteenth century should not be understood merely in terms of the remarkable transformations of the nineteenth century, lest its characteristic features be unduly obscured. For example, German biblical scholarship of the nineteenth century, exemplified by the likes of De Wette, Ewald, and Wellhausen, revolved to a great degree around source criticism and the reconstruction of biblical history. It was, on the whole, technical and specialized, oriented heavily toward textual science, comparative Semitic philology, and biblical antiquities. In the fashion of classical *Alterthumswissenschaft*, biblical scholars merged the Lower and Higher Criticisms to produce definitive accounts of the historical development of biblical texts, from their putative oral prehistories to their appearance as heavily redacted, late-stage editions. They seemed to delight in creating scientifically reconstructed alternatives to the familiar salvation history (*Heilsgeschichte*) of the Christian tradition; these allowed them and their students to perceive more clearly the political dynamics, historical forces, and human contours of the ancient societies that produced the Bible. Theirs was a sophisticated effort to lay bare the historical messiness of the Bible. This apparently deconstructive enterprise, though, often coincided with elaborate philosophical reconstructions of the ethical and religious meaning of biblical texts. For instance, De Wette, preeminent Higher Critic, understood Christianity, purified by Kantian analysis, in transcendental terms, as the cultivation of religious perception and sensibility. Berlin biblical scholar Wilhelm Vatke married stringent historical criticism to evolutionary schemes inspired by Hegel. Gerhard Ebeling sees in this dual commitment to historical disorder on the one hand and transcendent meaning on the other a reflection of Protestant hermeneutics. As Luther heard the divine Word in the human words of the Bible and clung to personal faith in the midst of existential uncertainties and against the forces of history, so too Protestant interpreters intensified the historical murkiness of the Bible in order to make a hard-won understanding of its divine element appear all the brighter.[9] Moreover, this supposedly liberative Protestant disposition, according to Ebeling, always stood in contrast to the faith of Roman Catholics, a faith which was compelled by ancient, institutional power. Catholic faith did not soar above history; it was mired in it.[10] It is not surprising, then, that German scholars developed a reputation for being rigorous, methodical, and scientific in historical work, on the one hand, and metaphysically adventurous in their religious thinking on the other.

Both Protestant hermeneutics and the institutional trajectories identified by Howard played roles in the eighteenth century. Yet, in this period, the Reformation and the statist orientation of the university were refracted differently than they were in the nineteenth century. In the eighteenth century, biblical scholarship was not narrow, text-obsessed, and focused exclusively upon history. As we will see, it took place against the backdrop of a much wider horizon. Once biblical scholarship was definitively "disciplined" at places like Bonn and Berlin in the nineteenth century, philologists strove to become scientific saints and ascetics. They began to resemble the *Wissenschaftler* sketched so memorably by Max Weber in 1919. Weber described the scholar as a socially alienated, science-intoxicated figure whose "personality" is derived from intense devotion to his subject; his "vocation" is internal because the old social, moral, and metaphysical dimensions of scholarly work have largely lost their significance.[11] Not so the university men of the eighteenth century. The *Aufklärer* were worldly, sociable, pragmatic, and polymathic. In the age of Enlightenment university reform, German scholars like Michaelis did not follow many English Deists, French *philosophes*, or Enlightenment radicals in scorning or minimizing the Bible. Their strategy, by contrast, was to maximize the Bible, to renegotiate its relation to modern life on as large a scale as possible. Unlike their professionalized successors, they did not justify their enterprise merely on the basis of its *wissenschaftlich* bona fides, its abstract status as a rigorous science that does its part, alongside the other disciplines, to push back the frontiers of ignorance. Rather, biblical critics in the eighteenth century activated older modes of erudition in order to make the Bible useful to life, as, indeed, their institutional setting required them to do. The Bible's residual authority predisposed them toward the belief that it could be profitably related to all areas of life. Their scholarly mode, then, consisted principally in their acting on this belief. Thus, they read the Bible in order to understand its aesthetic power and to harvest political insights. They turned to it as a resource for understanding ancient law and developing long, historically rich views of human society. In their hands, the Bible became a resource for moral philosophy and the study of language. *Aufklärer* did not employ forcefully the nineteenth-century Protestant rationale for biblical scholarship, according to which the Bible was a filth-encrusted gem waiting to be restored. On this view the "solvents of modern criticism" were said to clear away religious interpretations, the unfortunate "accretions of ages," which long obscured the beauty and power of the Bible.[12] In the main, the guiding light of our eighteenth-century figures was not a beautiful vision of what criticism as a theological enterprise might look like. It was rather, for them, a matter of what biblical criticism, as a university subject, might *do*, what it might contribute to the education of men who would one day run the governments under which they themselves would have to live.

Therefore, I believe it is correct to identify the "Enlightenment Bible" with pragmatic efforts to forge a new "cultural Bible," as Jonathan Sheehan has persuasively done. "Culture" evokes the expansiveness and worldliness of eighteenth-century engagement with the Bible. Focusing especially on the production of new editions of the Bible, Sheehan charts the efforts of "a host of scholars and literati who together forged a model of biblical authority that could endure in a post-theological era."[13]

By translating and annotating the Bible, theologians, critics, poets, and churchmen created new religious and intellectual forms. In England, the aim for scholars like Richard Bentley was largely a defensive one, a "holding action, an attempt to prevent harm" to the Bible from Deists like John Toland. In Germany, though, Sheehan demonstrates that the remaking of the Bible with scholarly tools, first of all, fueled intraconfessional religious rivalries between Pietists and orthodox Lutherans.[14] Pietist efforts, exemplified most powerfully by the Berleburger Bible (1726–1740), merged contemporary scholarship with the vernacular Bible, marking an important step in the long divorce of the Bible from confessional (in this case Lutheran orthodox) theology. Once learned Pietists opened a nonconfessional path for academic biblical scholarship, the stage was set for disciplinary projects that ultimately yielded a panoply of new "Bibles" at even greater removes from traditional Christian theology; thus, as Sheehan illustrates, the "documentary Bible" of the philologists, the "moral Bible" of Enlightenment pedagogues, the "literary Bible" created by poets and men of taste, and the "archival Bible" of historians, antiquarians, and ethnographers. Sheehan's survey of the Bible as it was represented and remade in the various media of the Enlightenment is not simply a tour: it is a tour de force. It bears powerful testimony not principally to the diminishment of religion so often associated with the Enlightenment but, indeed, to its "transformation and reconstruction."[15]

These "new Bibles" assumed the opacity and irrelevance of the "old Bible." Sheehan points appropriately to the role of sectarian conflicts and wars in German lands in the seventeenth century. These created the religious instability that led, ultimately, to the rise of reform movements and heterodox groups, which, in turn, weakened confessional churches.[16] Though this no doubt created a "market" for new Enlightenment bibles and a sense that the Bible ought to be rehabilitated, the deeper causes of scriptural opacity lie, as I argue in chapter 1, with the Reformation itself. The realities of religious division, dramatized but not created by conflict and war, effectively prevented Western interpreters from reading the Bible above all as scripture, from hearing it as divine revelation impervious to private interpretation and clearly audible as the voice of men carried along by the Holy Spirit (1 Peter 3:20–21). Distinctive interpretations of the Bible, in the absence of Christian unity, became necessary signposts and markers on the Western religious landscape. For Western Christendom as a whole to recover a catholic mode of interpretation focused on the theological core of the Bible, the churches would have had to lay down arms and recover their lost unity. Instead, religious divisions persisted. In the seventeenth and early eighteenth centuries, the Western churches only multiplied confessional Bibles and reinforced existing barriers.

The point here is that it was in the eighteenth century that biblical scholars turned decisively to the *university* to recover not just an Enlightenment Bible or a cultural Bible but a *universal* or catholic Bible, one capable of fostering the unity once associated with the scriptural Bible. The civic, aesthetic, and philological bibles created by Enlightenment scholars were, to an important extent, initiatives of the university. To focus on the university is to see why—if religious strife had long exhausted the early modern, Western church—the moribund scriptural Bible was remade so influentially in the eighteenth century. For it was in this period that universities were created or remade expressly to serve the interests of the state. To be sure, German universities still retained confessional identities and vestiges of their ecclesial origins. Yet, as will be clear, these confessional identities and the theological faculties traditionally associated with reinforcing them were deliberately suppressed in this period. This yielded an interesting irony. The clearest and most notable example of a "secular" university in the period was the University of Göttingen, founded in 1737. Its founders stripped the theological faculty of its traditional powers and preeminence and thrust theology into the lowest position that the discipline, to that point, had ever occupied at a European university. Yet, it was precisely here, as we will see, that Michaelis first put in place a program for interpreting and appropriating the Bible, one that proved decisive for modern biblical scholarship. The mode of academic university criticism that was created in the Enlightenment context, in turn, became central to the larger, enormously influential modern theological project that radiated outward from German universities in the nineteenth and twentieth centuries. To focus on the university is also to understand other elements of the modern critical project. The primary rationale for academic engagement with the Bible, as intimated above, was irenic. Eighteenth-century German universities were state initiatives tasked with managing the confessional aspects of higher education in pragmatic and irenic ways. It was in the interest of many institutions to create modes of biblical scholarship that were maximally inclusive, or, in the case of Lutheran Göttingen, sufficiently acceptable to nobles from Anglican, Catholic, and Reformed backgrounds. It is not surprising that this approach to the Bible, which relied heavily upon empirical models of linguistic and historical study borrowed from classical philology,[17] lent shape and support to the larger project of recovering a scholarly, nonconfessional Bible. The ideal of an academic ecumenism, by which scholars of various religious persuasions could work cooperatively to produce interpretations of the Bible in accord with the canons of modern rationality, became modern criticism's leading light.[18] Marooned by confessional interpreters, the Bible entered the university through the back door, where it would find new life.

Michaelis on the Enlightenment University

Enlightenment university professors were expected to stand in the very center of public life, at home as much in the assembly and ministerial cabinet as in the library and lecture hall. Few biblical scholars in the eighteenth century embraced their civic duties more cheerfully or cultivated their public personae more enthusiastically than Michaelis. Operating in this public capacity, Michaelis published anonymously, in 1768, the first of four volumes on German universities, *Raisonnement über die protestantischen Universitäten in Deutschland*; the final volume, in which he identified himself as the author, appeared in 1776. Michaelis's widely read *Raisonnement* stands at the beginning of a tradition of professorial critiques of the university by scholars in the period.[19] Michaelis's analysis is especially useful here, not only as a clear and influential expression of how universities were understood in the German Enlightenment but also as a source of insight into Michaelis's perspective on the relation between biblical scholarship and society.

Michaelis's overall point in the *Raisonnement* is that the university must redound to the glory and benefit of the state. Whatever else it does, it must do this. Michaelis admired the English, who, in their wisdom, supported only two universities.[20] Students and resources were concentrated at Oxford and Cambridge, which were able, as a result, to bear the burdens of being national universities. Political realities in the German lands made similar centralization impossible, so the numerous universities scattered across Germany had to learn how to succeed with fewer resources under the aegis of small, confessional governments. Michaelis began by waving off the university's old religious raison d'être. Michaelis declared that it was no longer reasonable to assume that a university's primary value consisted in its ability to advance the Christian faith: the era in which one might have founded a university for the "preservation and spread of the Protestant religion" had long since passed; even the founding of Pietist Halle actually reflected a mixture of religious and political motivations.[21] After dismissing religion, Michaelis denied that universities exist to create knowledge. Though universities could play a positive role in the development of innovative scholarship, Michaelis did not believe that the primary function of universities was intellectual: "It is not actually the duty of a school, whether high or low, to improve the sciences or make new discoveries: rather, it is the business of a few geniuses, or, if one wants a public institution, a learned society." In fact, Michaelis opined, many universities actually hinder scientific progress.[22] The only clear rationales for the existence of the university, then, were social and economic. German states stood to gain quite a lot from their universities in this regard. Michaelis echoed Hanoverian cameralist J. D. Gruber in emphasizing that excellent universities not only kept native sons home, thus ensuring that the educational "thaler" of *Landeskinder* (territorial subjects) remained in the local economy; they also attracted students and money from rival territories. Thus, wise cameralists should also see to it that living conditions at universities were optimal, with local industries like clothiers, paper mills, breweries, and wineries allowing wealthy students to maintain high standards of living. After all, it was too much to ask that professors, even famous ones, attract and retain such students if the university at the same time expected these wealthy students "to forego familiar comforts" during their studies.[23] Thus, one scholar has aptly characterized the educational theory of Michaelis as a "narrow, *Kleinstaat*-centred" one, amounting to an "admonition to watch the balance sheet."[24]

Michaelis's academic mercantilism, however, was not insensitive to the social value of the university. Michaelis believed that universities did not exist primarily to produce scholars. Rather, their proper roles were to introduce the academically inclined to authentic scholarship and, beyond this, to educate students broadly so that they would possess a modest understanding of scholarship and enough theoretical knowledge to succeed in a professional career (*Amt*). "Who can expect more than this," Michaelis asked, "in three or four years' time?"[25] So much for the individual. On a larger level, though, Michaelis believed that universities played a crucial role in society. He took for granted that the flourishing of the arts and sciences would be desirable by the lights of any theory of statecraft (*Staatskunst*). Michaelis's hierarchical vision of society placed universities toward the top. He assumed that their direct sphere of influence would be fairly small. But because the university trains the clergy and the nobility, it would be able to effect social change from the top down. In this consists Michaelis's optimistic vision of a social order reinforced and stabilized by an educated ruling class. Though oriented toward the wealthy and aristocratic, Michaelis also saw a social benefit in having poor and middle-class students at the university. Poor students, though less stable, might learn to emulate their betters.[26] Middle-class students would be inclined to bring with them proper upbringing, reliable work habits, and the desire—not always shared by their aristocratic counterparts—"to really learn something, and to acquire merit."[27]

To strengthen the claim that the cultivation of scholarly disciplines had social value, Michaelis examined the discipline that appeared to have the *least* social utility, theology, and argued that it could not be safely neglected by cameralists:

> If theology is beset by barbarism and ignorance, then one can only expect religious frauds to deceive the citizens and even the leaders: they will not spread reasonable and useful morality but, instead of these, traffic in many useless, incomprehensible, or erroneous propositions; and if several zealous teachers of such a religion rise up and others oppose them enthusiastically, then useless quarrels would arise over nothing, which would nevertheless be capable of unsettling the state. But the state avoids this danger if theology is drawn from the Bible with sufficient linguistic competence and if it is enlightened by philosophy: and even if, owing to the greatness of human corruption, it produces only a few Christians, the reasonable morality of the pulpit will

> nevertheless attract many good citizens. It will train still more effectively the obedient citizen who, because of his duties, treats it as a law. Because of its ongoing connection to philosophy, ancient languages, and history—in short, to many sciences related to biblical research—theology will cultivate scholarship and therefore help improve and promote the taste and knowledge of the people ... I am actually of the opinion that whoever wants to cultivate a people has much to gain from a learned theology with a partly philosophical and partly philological flavor. Such a theology would have all forms of knowledge as its by-product and ultimately spread among the masses that serve the church and, as they fan out in all cities and villages throughout the entire land, give rise to new research and knowledge.[28]

Theology for Michaelis, then, had several functions. One purpose was to tamp down and head off religious extremism. Religion, on this view, was a garden, and critical theology a weed-killer. The vision of theology as a tool to be wielded not against particular religions but against religious strife itself, as we will see, remained central to Michaelis's own work and the modern critical project as a whole. In this quotation Michaelis expressed the hope that theology would bring about a new renaissance. More precisely, he believed that a new approach to the Bible would show how pleasant and useful scholarship in general could be: if it could clarify the Bible so effectively, then it might also enrich one's understanding of politics, literature, and society. This renaissance, however, did not materialize in the way that Michaelis hoped.[29]

On the whole, Michaelis's perspective on the university was unremarkable. By the time Michaelis published the first volume of the *Raisonnement*, cameralist Johann Justi (1717?–1771) had already written definitive treatments of "police science" (*Policey-Wissenschaft*), or the aspect of governance taken up with the supervision, enforcement, and quality control of state institutions.[30] For Justi and other Prussian cameralists, the university was a state institution (*Staatsanstalt*) subject to state oversight. Scholars, as state employees and vendors, had to be managed appropriately: hired, fired, disciplined, praised, or cajoled until they fell into line with the educational ministry. In this period, the "original ecclesial and corporate character of the universities was being lost."[31] Professors' roles reflected the dominance of the state in the affairs of the university. As Notker Hammerstein has pointed out, professors were supposed to turn subjects into "educated servants of the state," "tolerant churchmen," and men "able to meet the high demands of rationality."[32] Teaching and scholarship, above all, supported these aims. It is, admittedly, a little arresting to read that a scholar like Michaelis, and not simply a functionary somewhere within the Prussian or Hanoverian bureaucracy, understood the scholarly vocation of the university professor in such statist terms. Yet it should not be a surprise. According to William Clark, "academia first lost its theological, transcendental mission in the Enlightenment." It is well to remember, then, that the cameralists and, indeed, a good share of university men were "thinkers of the Enlightenment," or, as he puts it, "cold-blooded pragmatists."[33]

Envisioning Georgia Augusta

In the fall of 1737, a young woman from Erfurt, Sidonia Hedwig Zäunemann, came to Göttingen to offer her poetic talents. She was one of several poets to participate in the inaugural celebration marking the opening of the new university. With the establishment of Georgia Augusta, she suggested, the Germans finally had their Athens: "Athens, that was once verdant in bloom, has lain for ages under ash and stone ... Where is its glory? Where is its fame?" She then addressed the Muses who once lived there: "Take heart! (*Getrost!*) George, the head of the Britons ... builds and grants you another sanctuary. You need only go to the Leine [River] and see for yourselves a new thing arise ..." Finally, she announced that "this newly built Leine-Athens has now, with great splendor, become your dwelling ... how powerful is Reason here transfigured, illuminated, and cheered!" For this, the poet received from the *Prorektor* of the university, three months later, a "well-deserved poetic crown."[34] Zäunemann was neither the first nor the last to refer to Göttingen as a "new Athens" or an "Athens on the Leine."[35] In 1807, for example, Göttingen student Friedrich Thiersch also described his university as an earthly "colony" for the Muses.[36] In conjuring images of homeless Muses taking residence among the "bright little lanes" of Göttingen (in Thiersch's words), admirers like Thiersch and Zäunemann signalled the dawn of a new yet old era. They pointed to the novelty of Georgia Augusta, on the one hand, and to the classical ideals of reason, inquiry, and personal cultivation on the other. Zäunemann's forceful "Gestrost!" captures the adventure, scope, and self-consciousness of the enterprise. The founders of the university saw themselves as overcoming the deadness of the past in order to restore vitality and relevance to the scholarly enterprise. By portraying Georgia Augusta as home to the Muses, inaugural poets conjured the artistic, literary, and cultural achievements of Athens. And like Athens, the new university would stand at the center of a new civilization—one of reason, utility, and taste (if not of beauty, goodness, and truth). The "Athenian" dimension of the "new Athens," or the revival of actual Hellenic ideals, would stand at the center of the Göttingen enterprise somewhat later, in the second half of the century;[37] however, it was "newness" that defined Georgia Augusta in its first decades.

How, then, to understand this newness? In his magisterial treatment of the modern research university, William Clark argues that the evolution of the modern university entailed a change in how authority was exercised and conceived. Where traditional authority, vested in Church and State, gave the medieval university its religious and juridical cast, Clark argues, the modern university was created largely by statesmen-reformers. These cameralists, in endeavoring to bring the university in line with newer political and economic conditions, emplaced bureaucracies and bureaucratic rationality while minimizing traditional authorities. The most interesting aspect of Clark's analysis, however, is the suggestion that the triumph of rational over traditional authority at the university was incomplete: charisma, which had inhered in traditional forms of authority, remained essential even to so-called rational forms of authority, so that one may discern a "charismatic transfiguration of reason" within the modern university.[38] Clark turns to Prussian minister Friedrich Gedike (1754–1803), "the secret (anti)hero" of his massive book, to lay bare the cameralistic machinery of the University of Göttingen and the persistence of charisma as a kind of powerful academic currency there.[39] While conducting an extensive scouting tour of universities across Germany, Gedike wrote a travelogue in which he recorded his observations. What impressed Gedike most on his visit to Georgia Augusta was the strong esprit de corps among Göttingen academics, an immense pride born from a comically high level of institutional self-regard. As Gedike noted, "One can often, to be sure, hardly keep back a smile when one hears many Göttingen academics speaking in such enthusiastic tones, as though outside the city wall of Göttingen neither light nor erudition is to be found."[40] To its critics, the University of Göttingen was a *wissenschaftlicher Fabrik*, an academic factory specializing not so much in scholarship as the business of scholarship. Göttingen scholars, on this view, were academic *Geschäftsmänner* trading in a "scholarly racket."[41] Yet what counted was the scholarly image that it cultivated; what made Georgia Augusta the epicenter of the academic German Enlightenment was the charisma it developed in and around its celebrity professors, scholarly journal, massive library, and learned societies. At Göttingen, that academic charisma mill, the history of universities seems finally to have reached modernity. Abandoning the traditional curriculum, stepping outside the church's sphere of influence, and trading shamelessly on its own *Ruhm* (fame), Georgia Augusta, it is perhaps not too much to say, became the first modern university.[42]

Nevertheless, it remains true that, for all of its innovativeness, Georgia Augusta was patterned explicitly after an older school: the University of Halle (founded 1694). The first curator at Göttingen and the leading figure in the university's founding was Hanoverian Privy Councilor Gerlach Adolph Freiherr von Münchhausen (1688–1770). Münchhausen studied at Halle in its first few decades, when Halle would have been the site not of one Enlightenment but of three. Ian Hunter has identified, in Halle's founding period, "three rival Enlightenment movements" centered on the civil philosophy of jurist Christian Thomasius (1655–1728), the antischolastic Pietism of August Hermann Francke (1663–1727), and the metaphysical rationalism of Christian Wolff (1679–1754).[43] Thomasius, a follower of Pufendorf and a founding member of the law faculty, was a progressive with new ideas for the study of law; he argued, for example, that a government oriented toward "natural law" was better positioned to overcome religious strife and division. Francke, the man responsible for institutionalizing the earlier Pietism of Spener and Arnold, fostered a religious outlook oriented toward pragmatic social renewal and an inward spirituality. Wolff was perhaps Halle's most famous and influential scholar early on, a leading light in the republic of letters. Like Leibniz, his mentor, Wolff was a brilliant polymath. Wolff became controversial at Halle when his insistence on rational transparency and his advocacy of autonomous reason in the formation of moral and religious opinions engendered stiff theological opposition. Thomasius, Francke, and Wolff, though clearly very different from one another, were able to play important roles at the same institution in part because they found common cause in opposing orthodox Lutheran confessionalism. Wolff the philosopher had no use for it. Thomasius resented its narrowness (*Enge*) and Francke its emptiness (*Leere*).[44]

The relation of the new university to Lutheran orthodoxy was one of the most crucial issues in the founding of Halle. The founding father of the Hohenzollern dynasty, John Sigismund, adopted Calvinism in 1613, and his successors, including Friedrich III, the founder of Halle, maintained a strong Reformed identity. Though the Hohenzollern rulers were personally Reformed, the territory as a whole was Lutheran. Despite prodigious efforts throughout his reign (1640–1688), the Great Elector, Friedrich Wilhelm, failed to convert the Lutheran estates or the territory as a whole to the Reformed confession. Friedrich III continued his father's efforts to raise the profile of Calvinism in the territory and mitigate "grassroots Lutheran antipathy" toward the Reformed.[45] Friedrich III, then, had compelling reasons to make the new university Lutheran, but not *very* Lutheran. Since orthodox Lutheran universities elsewhere in Brandenburg-Prussia (Frankfurt an der Oder, Königsberg, Duisburg) had caused problems for the Hohenzollerns before, Friedrich III did not want the new university to become a tool for the orthodox to trouble the crown and the Reformed churches.[46] The Elector also had a clear interest in creating a university that would outstrip the renowned university of his hated rival in Lutheran Saxony, the University of Leipzig. Thus Friedrich III turned largely to Pietists to build the new school, for the Pietists had been successful in creating an intellectually vibrant and socially potent form of nonorthodox Lutheranism.

In their zeal to create a new institutional home for the Pietist movement, the Pietists displayed a willingness to wed their religious program to sweeping educational reforms. At Halle there was an emphasis on praxis in scientific work and vocational training as well as a freer theological atmosphere. The law faculty took precedence over all others, including theology, and professors prided themselves on innovative pedagogy and curriculum and the use of the German language in instruction.[47] More significantly, Halle successfully dispensed with that foundation of medieval learning, the *Autoritätsprinzip*. In the view of Münchhausen and his advisors, professors in too many places still accepted the outmoded notion that education consisted of the faithful transmission of authorized knowledge. Halle had been among the first and most notable German universities to reject the *Autoritätsprinzip* in an open and self-conscious way. As the first of the German Enlightenment universities, Halle exemplified the way higher education in the period served the aims of "a monarchical court bent on using [the university] to provide the state with a deconfessionalized ruling elite."[48]

Georgia Augusta, no less than Halle, reflected the aims of a strong central government to create a new institution in direct service of a "deconfessionalized" state. When George II, Elector of Hanover and ruler of Great Britain, visited his Hanoverian territories in 1729, the poor condition of the schools was brought to his attention. The lone university in the area, Helmstedt in Brunswick-Lüneburg, seemed small and déclassé to forward-thinking educational ministers and, in any event, less suitable for the training of noble youth than the fashionable *Ritterakademien* (knightly academies) that already existed.[49] In 1732, Hofrath J. D. Gruber formalized the rationale for a new Hanoverian university.[50] In it Gruber explained why a new university would serve the king's interests. After praising the king for expanding the territory, Gruber pointed out that this created a need for a university of adequate size to serve the territory. Without such a university, the king risked the loss of 100,000 thaler a year that his own *Landeskinder* would spend attending universities in other lands.[51] By this time, Halle had already succeeded in drawing away many of his subjects. Implicit in Gruber's reference to other lands was a call for George to challenge its patron, his hated Prussian rival and cousin Friedrich Wilhelm I.[52] Gruber also appealed to royal vanity: a "Georgia Augusta Academy" would redound to the monarch's glory, serving as a lasting monument to the king's patriotism and love of science.[53] Finally, Gruber included a detailed breakdown of expenses and income associated with the new initiative, arguing, on the basis of this, that a new university promised maximum profit with minimal financial risk.

The king was persuaded. That same year, he granted oversight of the entire project to Münchhausen, whose first step was to solicit opinions (*Gutachten*) and recommendations from scholars and government officials. Gruber advised him to focus on faculty: "the highest and most important thing is to have skilled, learned, and well-known professors in all faculties."[54] J. L. Mosheim, then professor of church history at Helmstedt and a favorite of Münchhausen, echoed the point and offered specific ways to make a university attractive to professors. To lessen their teaching burdens, he proposed the creation of a college of adjunct professors that could be managed by the "triple enticement of money, honor, and hope," which, practically speaking, meant modest pay, the right to wear a modified version of the professorial robe, and the possibility of promotion. These teachers, holders of the master's degree, would be permitted to hold public lectures of their own (but only for free), prepare the *acta eruditorum* (a current listing of academic publications) for the university, and meet formally twice a week. To keep professors' research programs moving, Mosheim proposed the creation of a learned society (*eine Sozietät der Wissenschaften*) and a society for the study of German language and history alongside the university.[55] These opinions express the perception that skilled and renowned professors, the very embodiments of academic charisma, were a sine qua non, even as they illustrate that this priority would have far-reaching consequences for the university.

Another question raised by this emphasis on excellent professors was, naturally, the standard by which to measure their excellence. Münchhausen himself understood this in terms of the ability to attract students and build the reputation of the school. This, first of all, was defined negatively: there are things the professor, if he is to "draw a large number of students to himself and bring the vocations to Göttingen," must neither be nor believe. Münchhausen might well have said "radicals and schismatics need not apply." He ruled out any who might be suspected of atheism or philosophical naturalism, citing the positive example of Mosheim, who held forth honorably against "freethinkers" (*Freydencker*) and studiously avoided controversy over "obscure passages of holy Scripture."[56] Münchhausen's advisors were more explicit in forbidding certain points of view. G L. Böhmer of Celle, later law professor at Göttingen, called for the rejection of "men with sharp intellectual profiles," who, at a given time, might be suspected of any of the following:

> naturalism, indifference (*indifferentismus*), Socinianism, enthusiasm, chiliasm, the doctrine of apocatastasis, mystical theology, Macchiavellianism, Hobbesianism, alchemy, Ramism, Cartesianism, or pure Aristotelianism.[57]

This neat summary evinces a clear desire to avoid controversial ideologies, outmoded systems of thought, dogmatism, and extreme positions on either end of the theological spectrum.

Thus Böhmer indirectly attests what became a crucial element of the founder's vision: theological and philosophical irenicism. The interest here was pragmatic. Münchhausen the cameralist knew how to encourage institutional cohesiveness; thus, he "brook[ed] no destructive element," no controversy, faction, or rancor inspired by religious polemics.[58] Destructive disputes were avoided by insisting on fidelity to clearly defined standards and by forbidding excessive disagreement over anything beyond those standards. Section 15 of the original 1737 Statutes of the Theological Faculty described the balance this way:

> Professors should not depart one finger's breadth from basic doctrines taken from Holy Scripture, from the three ecumenical confessions, from the unchanged Augsburg Confession, or from the rest of the symbolic writings that have been accepted by the Lutheran Church, and thus should hold very closely to that which has been agreed upon by all teachers. In controversial questions, modest disagreement is permitted; but the one who holds the rejected opinion should not be named, insofar as it concerns a colleague. Individuals, though, should think twice, if they are inclined to find something new.[59]

Though bound by Lutheran confessional standards, they were not permitted to question or enforce the adherence of others to these standards (their *puritas doctrinae*) as their Halle counterparts could.[60] By withholding the right of censure (*Zensurrecht*) from the theology faculty, Münchhausen took an important instrument of academic power out of their hands.

Philosophical dogmatism was also out of style at Göttingen. Münchhausen's model professor, he once indicated, was Christian Thomasius.[61] A founder of the university at Halle, as we have noted, Thomasius was known for his work on logic and his advocacy of Pufendorfian natural law. A highly regarded jurist, Thomasius maintained a high public profile as the editor of a controversial academic journal in Leipzig.[62] He embodied the scientific, progressive spirit of Halle, without exhibiting any of the world-denying tendencies of the more earnest Pietists there. In Thomasius's view, scientific education should "shape men whom the world can use." In place of the "dusty pedant," Thomasius wanted a "lively, chivalrous, even courtly *homme du monde*."[63] With the new orientation toward practical, contemporary disciplines and the rejection of overarching systems with sharp profiles came a strong preference for eclecticism. One of the first members of the philosophical faculty at Georgia Augusta, Professor Samuel Christian Hollmann, embodied this perspective, which was eclectic more in what it chose to reject than in what it chose to accept. Hollmann, honored as the professor to open lectures at Georgia Augusta on October 14, 1734, expressed clear opinions about what was conducive to true philosophy. He described abstract speculation, democracy, religious enthusiasm and strife, and political upheaval as negative conditions, while commending the growth of the natural sciences, the Lutheran Reformation, the printing press, and the *Aufklärung*. Put in terms of representative figures, Hollmann preferred Cicero to Plato, the lettered statesman to the brilliant dogmatist.[64] One of Münchhausen's consultants, law professor Johann Jacob Schmauß, advised him to cultivate a modish, moderate intellectual environment. He called for the abandonment of scholasticism and the traditional disciplines of grammar, dialectic, rhetoric, and poetics. Instead, he suggested courses in newer disciplines like practical homiletics, *jus naturale et gentium*, European statecraft, German culture, and natural sciences such as anatomy and chemistry. The university as Schmauß envisioned it would draw its significance and its direction from contemporary political and social concerns. Usefulness, competence, and civic-mindedness would be the new virtues.[65]

In its first decade, Georgia Augusta was indeed known for being nontraditional, irenic, and eclectic. To critics, though, it seemed that Göttingen academics were eager simply to be *known* at all. There was some truth in this criticism. Münchhausen's ultimate goal was to secure for Georgia Augusta an international reputation that would make it the preferred university for nobility from all across Europe. In a careful and well-documented study of the social history of Georgia Augusta's founding period, Charles McClelland has shown that Münchhausen was successful in this regard. Two trends contributed to the convergence of noble interests and the rise of the university. The decline and constriction of Hanoverian estates caused nobles to turn to universities as a "surrogate source of honor," to regard education as a distinction of nobility. With the departure of the Elector and family to Britain, the indigenous nobility rose in power and asserted itself against the middle class, also coming to dominate the civil service.[66] It was in this context that Georgia Augusta was conceived and born; it would become the university of the elegant (*für die elegante Welt*), a school "irresistibly attractive to persons of standing."[67] McClelland notes that the university "clearly succeeded in attracting a disproportionate share of the nobles," contributing to an overall "rise of higher education qualifications among the ranks of higher civil servants, both noble and non-noble."[68] By 1760, one scholar observes, the century-long absence of the Elector and his family from Hanover allowed the Privy Council and the University of Göttingen to replace the Electoral court "as the centres of political and cultural life, respectively."[69]

But what were the academic implications of this bold experiment, this effort to provide cutting-edge higher education for bureaucratically oriented small-state nobility? As we have already seen, it meant a new curriculum that was shifted decisively away from the traditional model. Not only were there new disciplines in the curriculum, there were also a new orientation toward the goal of university education. Georgia Augusta would be a center for *Bildung*, education and formation for the whole person. The ideal of the *gebildete* man, early on, consisted of being competent, public-minded, knowledgeable, and, above all, socially adept. Alongside statecraft and the newfangled *Naturwissenschaften* in the curriculum stood fencing, dancing, art, riding, music, and foreign languages. The university riding master, in fact, walked ahead of associate professors in academic processions.[70] Professors were themselves expected to embody the ideal of the learned man of affairs who stands at the center of public life as a poet, jurist, or statesman—not at its margins as a cloistered, bookish purveyor of traditional knowledge. Vital public personae imbued Göttingen academics with a kind of social and cultural authority. This not only expanded the renown (*Ruhm*) of the university, it also helped professors to carry out what was perhaps their most important task: turning out moral, rational, and useful citizens. Whether they ended up in the pulpit, the civil service, or the cabinet, Göttingen products had to be tasteful and competent servants of state. Thus, early Göttingen professors did not emphasize research or seek to turn their students into scholars. Rather, their aim was to make the student "accustomed to scientific culture and to acquaint him in a positive way with [the professor's] own discipline, such as his future career and position might require."[71] This meant, of course, that the professor had to be a true scholar (*Wissenschaftler*) in his own right. Even so, with respect to the perennial question of how to balance research and teaching, there was at Georgia Augusta a slight but real preference for the latter.

This preference complemented another of Münchhausen's concerns: the negative effects of specialization. Academic specialization sometimes yielded territorialism, factionalism, and—Münchhausen's bugaboo—the destruction of consensus. Thus he forbade "scholarly monopolies." Professors were free in theory to teach outside their own areas of expertise (*Lehrfreiheit*).[72] Not only were (most) scholars free to teach on a range of subjects outside their disciplines, Georgia Augusta professors also enjoyed extensive academic freedom in conducting research. Scholars were encouraged not only to pursue nontraditional subjects such as statistics, ethnography, and German but to develop new approaches to traditional subjects as well. Professors enjoyed a level of academic freedom at Göttingen perhaps unprecedented in the history of universities. According to one scholar, what set Münchhausen apart from other educational reformers of the period was precisely the belief that the most effective way to cultivate social formation and professional training was "through the freedom and independence of *Wissenschaft*."[73] This became important to its reputation as an Enlightenment university, a venue for rational, open-ended inquiry. Indeed, the founders saw themselves, in this regard, as finishing what Halle started. It is important to note, though, that academic freedom was not a license to pursue scholarship for its own sake. Like everything else at Georgia Augusta, it had a practical and moral purpose. It allowed the university to avoid the kind of retrograde, censorious atmosphere of older universities. But it also created a miniature republic of letters within the university, in which professors were to be the model citizens. The General Statutes of the university (1736), for example, specify the proper procedure for a disputation between professors. The disputation as an academic practice (*Lehrform*) did not survive long at Göttingen, but it was initially retained for its moral-pedagogical value:

Beyond private exercise in question and answer, where professors try to stimulate their audience, they should also recommend practice in disputation. When a public disputation is held—and it is desired that these happen often—one professor should invite another professor to be his opponent (no one should ever participate if not invited); then the young people will learn that friends, both of whom are educated and honorable, can be of different opinions, that neither needs to hate the other, that neither resorts to screaming or ruthlessness to win, and that one can be gracious even in defeat.[74]

As the disputation served the goal of moral education, so would all of the activities of the Göttingen professor. Section 36 of the General Statutes stated that "all teaching, which scientific universities exist to produce, aims toward the public good." Here "the public good" is understood in moral terms, for professors, according to the Statutes, only fulfill their duty to uphold the public good when they have set "good wills in motion by good will, even as they also shape intellects with intellect."[75] The professor must thus be both knowledgeable and good. Goodness is defined in the next section of the Statutes, in circular fashion, as the aggregate of qualities which, when emulated, make the emulator a more useful citizen.[76] The circularity of this definition only shows how closely the founders connected morality to social usefulness and, more importantly, how the former served the latter.

Scholarship at Georgia Augusta

It is beyond the scope of this book to offer a full account of the scholars, disciplines, and methods that made Georgia Augusta a distinctive and, indeed, distinguished place.[77] Nevertheless, it is important for this study to draw attention to some of the scholarly paths charted by Michaelis's contemporaries. These shed valuable light on the nature of his work by setting it in an even richer institutional context. If the creation of a "new Athens" on the Leine River and the rise of an aristocratic "scholarship factory" at its center provide the deep background, it remains to identify some of the figures, ideas, and movements that shared the foreground with Michaelis.

The most important theologian in the early history of the university was Johann Lorenz Mosheim (1693–1755). He came to Göttingen as an older and already famous scholar—according to one historian, the most renowned theologian in the German-speaking world at that time.[78] Born in Lübeck, Mosheim studied at the theology faculty at the University of Kiel, which was characterized by Pietist leanings and the irenic legacy of Helmstedt theologian George Calixtus.[79] Mosheim made his reputation while on the theological faculty at Helmstedt, where he served from 1723 to 1747. In that time, he began a magisterial four-volume history of Western Christianity, *Institutiones historiae ecclesiasticae* (published in its completed form in 1755). It is largely on his reputation as a church historian and even as the "father of modern church history" that his fame rests.[80] Before coming to Georgia Augusta, Mosheim served as an advisor to Münchhausen, handpicking the first theology professors and helping to write the statutes for the Göttingen theological faculty while still at Helmstedt. Münchhausen wanted Mosheim to be the first chair in theology, but he was not successful in convincing Mosheim to come until 1747. Not only did Mosheim become the leading light of the theological faculty once he arrived at Georgia Augusta, he also served as chancellor of the university from the time of his arrival until his death. Mosheim also became one of Michaelis's most important mentors.[81] Though Michaelis and Mosheim worked in different fields, Mosheim reframed contemporary theology in ways that set the stage for Michaelis's reconception of biblical studies.

What is true of scholars in many disciplines is also true of theologians: to orient themselves, they must know who their enemies are. Mosheim identified a new enemy for his discipline and thus shifted the ground for theology. Mosheim circumscribed the discipline not by accounting for confessional boundaries (e.g., Lutheran theology versus Reformed theology) but rather by setting Christianity, taken as a whole, beside non-Christian belief. On Mosheim's expanded view of the theological task, the theologian operated on two fronts. Where earlier figures were preoccupied with defending confessional particulars against fellow Protestants, Mosheim also believed that the theologian had to address the criticisms of atheists and naturalists. Mosheim's scholarly work—even the "impartial," pragmatic history for which he later became known—had an apologetic cast.[82] In a brief treatise on theological training, *Kurze Anweisung, die Gottesgelahrtheit vernünftig zu erlernen* (published posthumously in 1756), Mosheim offered a concise description of the new situation faced by the eighteenth-century theologian:

> A theologian in our day who is worthy of the name finds himself in a very difficult position. In the days of our predecessors, it was far easier to bear the name with honor. In our times, religion is contested by almost every human science. That is why a theologian in our time must know something about practically every scholarly discipline so that, with this, he can fend off the objections of unbelief and defend religion.[83]

Believing that a new day had dawned, Mosheim drew the most significant dividing line between the broad categories of "religion" and "unbelief." This had an important consequence for theologians: it was not enough for them to be stewards of confessional traditions, they also had to be able to draw on all fields of knowledge to safeguard religion itself. The theologian had to be a philosopher, historian, and philologist as well if he was to defend belief against its enemies. As Mosheim himself demonstrated in his attack on John Toland,[84] the theologian must be prepared to maneuver on enemy ground. One sees in Mosheim's quotation the need for a broad education and a theology that extended well beyond the older mode of polemical or controversial theology. By taking skepticism and unbelief seriously as intellectual options, Mosheim opened university theology to methods and knowledge in an array of fields. He provided interdisciplinarity with a theological rationale.

If Mosheim believed that Christianity was threatened by the likes of Toland, he believed that it was threatened, perhaps even more gravely, by those *within* the Christian churches. Another leitmotif in Mosheim's work was theological irenicism.[85] Taking 2 Timothy 2:23–24 as a base text, Mosheim delivered a speech that was published in 1723, appropriately titled *De theologo non contentioso*. Mosheim resumed the theme in additional lectures the following year. In these speeches, Mosheim decried the vanity of wanting to seem brilliant in argumentation and of stoking controversy over unnecessary or unimportant questions. Charity, peaceableness, and intellectual humility were Mosheim's cardinal theological virtues. For his inaugural address at Georgia Augusta twenty-four years later, Mosheim chose the same theme, delivering an address entitled *De odio theologico*. Mosheim stressed that religion had much to lose from hypocritical theologians preaching love and peace while devouring their opponents. Too many believed that "what predators are among animals, theologians are among men."[86] Mosheim declared himself a bitter enemy of theological odium (*Theologenhaß*) and put all on notice that, as chancellor, he would not allow controversies, feuds, and rivalries to fester. In redrawing the boundaries of university theology, Mosheim darkened the line between religion and unbelief while at the same time blurring the lines that separated the Christian confessions.[87]

Apologetic and irenic impulses both found expression in Mosheim's scholarship. In his *Institutiones*, Mosheim's belief in the correctness of orthodox, trinitarian Christianity is clear. In this sense, his work was apologetic. However, in treating the history of churches after the Reformation, Mosheim remained true to his own irenic principle. Instead of offering judgments about which groups were in the right, Mosheim confined himself to an "external" history of the institutions, a factual description of ecclesial movements carefully divorced from normative theological judgments and appeals to divine providence. Yet Mosheim was no materialist. To accommodate the possibility of theological judgment, Moser distinguished between an "invisible" church, whose members were scattered among the various confessions and were known only to God, and the "visible" churches identifiable with specific persons and institutions. In his historical scholarship, Mosheim strove for fairness, declaring that whenever he took up his pen, he made every possible effort "to give constant attention to justice, impartiality, and truth."[88] Setting this rhetoric aside, it remains true that Mosheim exemplified a new approach to church history, one that has been described as "pragmatic."[89] His work in church history was characterized by narrative focused exclusively upon the "human dimension" of history, the course of events associated with the external, observable aspect of Christian institutions. For Mosheim, church history, in contrast to the partiality and *Tendenz* of earlier exemplar histories, must not reflect the scholar's personal enthusiasms and moral judgments. When the historian makes an assertion, then, he must do so on the basis of argument and direct appeal to reliable sources. The work of the Christian theologian, broadly conceived, was the defense of the faith. In setting forth the history of the churches, though, Mosheim believed his role was not advocacy but a scientific handling of the materials of religious belief.

Mosheim was one of Münchhausen's closest advisors. To Münchhausen, Mosheim was the ideal theology professor. Michaelis's success at Göttingen, then, no doubt had a great deal to do with his ability to import the Mosheimian ideal into biblical studies and make it productive there. Of the theologians associated with Göttingen, Mosheim was the most significant for the young Michaelis. After 1760, Michaelis had little to do with the theological faculty, and, as intimated above, he had poor or insignificant relationships with those who were there when he arrived. Christoph August Heumann and Georg Heinrich Ribov opposed Michaelis's efforts to offer *collegia* in dogmatics in the 1750s; after ten years of struggle, Michaelis gave up the fight. Setting school politics aside, though, it is important to note that the larger theological climate at Göttingen was, on the whole, conducive to the scholarly projects of Mosheim and Michaelis. The statutes of the faculty, as we have seen, made it clear that professors had to hold to historic Christian doctrines such as the trinity, the resurrection of Christ, and the revelatory character of the Bible. Theologians also had to adhere to the Lutheran confessional symbols. Yet, as we have seen, confessional identity was not emphasized at Göttingen; it was not essential to the mission and identity of the school. A commitment to a fairly minimal Protestantism was assumed, while anything that smacked of Protestant scholasticism or sectarianism was discouraged. One consequence of this was that theologians at Georgia Augusta looked increasingly toward other disciplines like philosophy to clarify, reinterpret, or bolster Christian doctrines. Joachim Oporinus (1695–1753), for example, wrote a dissertation defending the immortality of the soul and, later, a philosophical examination of biblical teaching on the existence of good and evil spirits.[90] Ribov, a Wolffian, was concerned to distinguish what in the Christian religion was provable by reason and what was not: thus his 1740 *Gründlichen Beweiß, daß die geoffenbahrte Religion nicht könne aus der Vernunft erwiesen werden*.[91] Later Göttingen theologians Karl Friedrich Stäudlin (1761–1826) and Christoph Friedrich von Ammonn (1766–1850) incorporated Kantian moral philosophy into their ethics and biblical theology, respectively.[92]

Theologians also looked to history. One vestige of Göttingen's somewhat distant Pietist heritage (via Halle) was a theological eclecticism. At Halle, theologians like Johann Franz Buddeus set theology on a different footing by embracing philosophical eclecticism. Because seventeenth-century scholastic theology was identified with Aristotelianism, figures like Buddeus scoured the history of philosophy to find alternative doctrines and conceptual frameworks that might be helpful to a revamped Lutheranism. This maneuver had parallels in philology and church history. To overcome the legacy of Lutheran orthodoxy, biblical scholars like August Hermann Francke and Johann Heinrich Michaelis (Johann David's uncle) embraced historical philology, while others like J. G. Walch turned to the history of the church.[93] Their goal, like Buddeus's, was to generate new theological resources through historical study. Without a robust confessional framework, their use of history to furnish ideas, vocabulary, and substance for contemporary theology was necessarily eclectic. In this way, a separation developed between "dogma," what was to be believed, and "history," a mixed bag of good and bad examples. History was no longer sacred on this view. It was not even sectarian.

The same separation characterized theological scholarship at Georgia Augusta. "Dogma," identified by pragmatic cameralists with a minimal Protestantism, was one thing. Mosheim and Michaelis, like the others, fell in line, embracing central Christian doctrines. But "history" was another. Mosheim eschewed confessional loyalties that might influence him to see the hand of Providence supporting or guiding his theological forebears. History was a human stage, a "closed, immanent frame,"[94] and he studied it as such. Michaelis, as we will see, also regarded history as something of a closed system of knowable causes and effects. To him, ancient Hebrew was a language like any other, the Israelites were an ancient people subject to the ordinary vicissitudes of history, and Moses was best understood as a statebuilder in a particular historical moment. Both Mosheim and Michaelis made the most of their freedom to investigate the historical dimensions of the Christian tradition without correlating their results to specific theological positions. All was well as long as they remained true to the dogma of the university. This dogma, as we have seen, was intended less to distinguish among denominations than to separate what was respectably Christian from what was not. Mosheim proved himself an able and energetic defender of mainstream Christian belief when he provided, in 1720, a thorough refutation of John Toland's audacious *Nazarenus* (1718). Michaelis also came to the defense of key Christian doctrines, perhaps most famously in 1783 when, after Reimarus's criticisms of the resurrection created enormous controversy, he argued for the historical veracity of the biblical accounts. Indeed, Michaelis's works, including the response to Reimarus,[95] enjoyed an extensive afterlife in English translation precisely because, to British admirers, he embodied German scholarship and erudition without forsaking important doctrines like the resurrection of Christ and

Mosaic authorship of the Pentateuch.[96] Many of Michaelis's explicitly theological writings were devoted to a defense of Christian theological concepts like atonement or, somewhat surprisingly, a form of typological interpretation; in each case, his goal was to defend the rationality of basic Christian doctrines.[97] Though it has become somewhat common to refer to Michaelis as a middling figure caught between orthodoxy and the new historicism,[98] it is more helpful to see Michaelis's work as an appropriate response to the dual emphases of Enlightenment university theology: first, an apologetic enterprise directed against atheism and skepticism, and second, an eclectic one invested in the refurbishment and modernization of Christianity.

It was not only theology that formed part of Michaelis's institutional context. Michael Carhart, in an insightful study of Enlightenment Germany, has shed valuable light on a group of loosely connected scholars associated in various ways with Georgia Augusta in the eighteenth century.[99] With appropriate qualifications, Carhart calls this group the "Göttingen School." Under this rubric, Carhart examines the scholarly programs of several Georgia Augusta professors whose careers spanned the second half of the eighteenth century: Christian Gottlob Heyne, Johann Gottfried Eichhorn, Johann Christoph Adelung, Christoph Meiners, and our own Michaelis. Examining the Göttingen School and its contributions to various disciplines within a wider European context, Carhart brings the scholarship of the German Enlightenment into focus as a nonideological mode of inquiry oriented toward what he calls a "collectivist particularism." The Göttingen School stood apart from other currents of thought associated with the Enlightenment: for example, radical republicanism, revolutionary thought, and the more speculative and abstract systems of the *philosophes*. Each of Carhart's main figures rejected "universal principles" in favor of "particularism in the study of real, historical, and unique nations."[100] Collective particularists were analytical, empirical, and suspicious of grand theories; they were sensitive, above all, to the peculiar genius of historical groups. Whether examining the origins of language, disentangling legal collections, or trying to understand societies in newly discovered lands, they did not turn toward timeless theoretical frameworks but rather worked to understand new data in terms of discrete groups with their own histories and conditions. This marked an important moment in Western thought: "The idea of *cultura animi* is as old as Rome. But the idea of culture is only as old as the Enlightenment."[101]

Conclusion

This "cultural" program corresponded closely to the social and political character of the university. It allowed historians, anthropologists, and philologists to cultivate critical analysis of received tradition, yet without embracing revolutionary thought or sharp political ideologies. By turning to the category of culture, Göttingen scholars created a mode of *Wissenschaft* that also accorded with political gradualism, conservative reform, and a deep interest in what makes societies strong and distinct. Though Michaelis was not a theorist of culture in any explicit sense, Carhart is correct to characterize Michaelis's interdisciplinary approach to the world of the Bible as "an expression of a cultural holism that existed before 1800."[102] Michaelis, in his approach to the Old Testament, assumed the cultural particularity of the ancient Israelites. Indeed, this was his primary interpretive lens, and it allowed him to integrate knowledge of botany, criminal law, climate, zoology, geography, and history into a coherent understanding of the Bible as the literary remainder of a lost Israelite civilization. In this sense, Michaelis contributed to the development of a Göttingen School of cultural inquiry. To place him in this context is to see a valuable trajectory arcing out of Michaelis's work and connecting him with the next generation—men like J. G. Herder and Michaelis's own students Eichhorn and Schlözer. It is also to do justice to the polymathic character of his work and to avoid a somewhat reductive understanding of Michaelis as a historical interpreter or a historical critic of the Old Testament. Though constantly engaged with the historical background of the biblical texts, Michaelis used historical knowledge to recover words, customs, and settings that aided contemporary appropriation of the Bible in moral, aesthetic, or philosophical terms. To call this interest "historical" is to obscure the expansive, contemporary interests that Michaelis brought to his work. However, "culture," as a category, fits nicely.

Scholars in all disciplines adjusted to the realities of the new university. Jurists, historians, and anthropologists at Göttingen turned to a study of culture consonant with the mild progressivism of the Hanoverian cameralists.[103] Mosheim, following an eclectic tradition from the preceding century, created an academic theology that faced away from the church and functioned as a bulwark against the intellectual perils and social evils of atheism. In this arrangement, the stewardship of confessional particulars so important to traditional theology diminished in importance, and in its place there reigned a carefully enforced irenicism. For Mosheim and Michaelis, this led naturally to an empirical theology strong enough to withstand atheist attacks and robust enough to meet the standards of a true university *Wissenschaft*. Though Mosheim and the historians associated with the Göttingen School shed valuable light on Michaelis's new program for biblical studies, the closest disciplinary parallel was not to be found in theology or history but in classical philology, the subject of the next chapter. For classicists faced an analogous problem: how to make old, authoritative texts matter not simply in a modern setting but also in a modish one. It was only right that J. M. Gesner, an old soul and a "new humanist," should provide guidance to a young Michaelis trying to find his way in Germany's new Athens.

3

The Study of Classical Antiquity at Göttingen

Among all peoples, the Greeks have dreamt life's dream most beautifully.
—Goethe, *Art and Antiquity* vol. 5, issue 3 (1826)[1]

"Life's dream," Goethe's dream, was wholeness. German thinkers throughout the eighteenth century sought avidly to integrate high moral purpose, social coherence, and the fullest possible cultivation of human capabilities into a compelling vision of life. Though the old Christian synthesis embodied in the traditional confessions had once been integrative and visionary, it now seemed, by the light of a new *Aufklärung* breaking over the German lands, to be unworkable, implausible, and outworn. Skepticism, indifference born from religious strife, and new currents filtering into the republic of letters created a new climate for political, philosophical, and religious thought. Early in the century, promethean Pietist A. H. Francke and his Halle cohort had worked to unleash a new Reformation upon Europe in the name of what Johann Arndt called "true Christianity." Personal conviction, moral discipline, and social activism—the very qualities that would eventually vault Halle's Prussian sponsor to its preeminent position among the German territories—characterized the Pietist movement.[2] For all of their energy, vision, and organizational savvy, though, the Pietists were not able to maintain their hold on the University of Halle, let alone remake Europe. With the triumphant return of Christian Wolff to Halle in 1740, the rise of rationalist hermeneutics under J. S. Semler (1725–1791), and the installation of neopagan F. A. Wolf (1759–1824) over the philological

Seminar in 1783, the old Christian synthesis, despite its new Pietist form, showed itself once more to be incapable of unifying intellectual life. In their zeal to undo the academic traditionalism of their orthodox forebears, the Pietists had enlisted the help of the new philosophy and the new criticism. By midcentury, it seemed that only these remained. The critical handling of traditional materials at the university gradually lost contact with Pietist moral aspirations and social activism. *Wissenschaft* was orphaned.

If the first half of the century belonged to the Pietists, the second half belonged to the philhellenists. German scholars, writers, and intellectuals looking beyond the Christian tradition turned to ancient Greece to recover an integrative vision of life. For several decades, Greek antiquity seemed to exercise a "tyranny" over these figures and over German literature, philosophy, and religious thought.[3] To Goethe, this liberative period of "tyranny," the age in which German thinkers tried to find themselves by estranging themselves, was in fact the "age" of art historian J. J. Winckelmann (1717–1768). In 1805, Goethe published an essay entitled "Winckelmann und sein Jahrhundert" honoring his life and legacy. A meditation on Winckelmann's life, the essay identifies the ancient Greeks with the unification of human capacities and the successful integration of the individual into a "great, beautiful, dignified, and worthy whole" encompassing nature and culture. If anyone in Germany embodied Hellenic wholeness, added Goethe, it was Winckelmann.[4] In describing Winckelmann this way, Goethe claimed him as a neopagan hero and forebear courageous enough to set aside the Christian past and tread a new path through Greek antiquity. Goethe may have been among the chief apostles of German philhellenism, but Winckelmann enjoyed pride of place as its greatest prophet. As the flame of Halle had burned bright and hot on the intellectual scene for several decades early in the century, Winckelmannian philhellenism kindled a flame in the second half of the century that drew the attention of leading intellectuals like Lessing and Herder and inspired the remarkable figures who converged on the court of Duke Carl August at Weimar and the University of Jena in the 1780s and '90s: Friedrich Schiller, August and Friedrich Schlegel, J. G. Fichte, and Friedrich Schelling. It also gave rise to the influential educational theories of Wilhelm von Humboldt and fueled the scientific, philological enterprise of scholars like Friedrich August Wolf.

Göttingen has an important place relative to the dual stories of Pietism and philhellenism in the eighteenth century. Both movements may be understood as far-reaching integrative movements oriented toward culture and belief. They stand, perhaps, as instances of the perennial ebb and flow of the Christian and classical traditions in Western thought. They are important here, though, as two sides of a frame that allow us to see the distinctiveness of Georgia Augusta's *via media* between Pietism and philhellenism, its middle path between Halle in the early part of the century and Weimar-Jena in the latter part. This path was opened at Göttingen by classical scholars Johann Matthias Gesner (1691–1761) and Christian Gottlob Heyne (1729–1812). Though Gesner and Heyne stood between these two movements chronologically and, in a certain sense, ideologically, Göttingen at midcentury was not merely a way station on the road from seventeenth-century pedantry to nineteenth-century *Wissenschaft*. Rather, Göttingen must be seen as the site of an academic program with its own account of culture and belief, one shaped by the realities of the Enlightenment university. Too often, Göttingen classical scholars are seen as precursors (*Vorläufer*) or transitional men: rationalists not courageous enough to disavow Christianity, preromantics not fully appreciative of historical incommensurability, historians not fully committed to historicism, or philologists not fully practiced in critical reconstruction. These sorts of judgments do little to illuminate the particular way that Gesner, Heyne, and, as we will see, Michaelis sought to recover and reappropriate the materials of traditional culture in a new irenic, pragmatic, and academic mode. Theirs was not an experimental, romantic (philhellenic) quest to reenter antiquity or a promethean (Pietist) effort to remake society in its image, but rather a conservative maneuver to reshape *antiquity* in light of contemporary social realities. Michaelis's attempt to reconstruct the biblical materials along these lines occupies the second half of this book. The similar, closely related attempts of Gesner and Heyne to do this for classical antiquity are a vital part of the background to Michaelis's biblical project. They are the subject of this chapter.

The Göttingen Classical Project in Eighteenth-Century Context

German philhellenism was not simply a movement: it was a "faith."[5] To its proponents, it entailed the monumental task of replacing Christianity with a new form of life derived from an imaginative engagement with Greek antiquity. To say this is to indicate the kind of personal, intellectual, and creative investment that characterized philhellenists and inspired them to create journals, pioneer new forms of literature, undertake Mediterranean pilgrimages, adopt looser sexual mores, and abandon respectable careers. Winckelmann, the father of this faith, found in Greek sculpture a powerful aesthetic and moral ideal capable of liberating Germans from both the Christian tradition and the stultifying effects of their own cultural impoverishment. The two keys to Winckelmann's discovery were the identification of *Greekness* as an abstract quality belonging to a people and arising from its particular climate and geography and, second, the isolation of the ideas, indeed the *spirit*, expressed by Greek art. On this basis, Winckelmann analyzed Greek painting and sculpture to great effect in his 1755 *Gedancken über die Nachahmung der griechischen Wercke in der Mahlerey und Bildhauer-Kunst* (*Reflections on the Imitation of Greek*

Works in Painting and Sculpture). Winckelmann found in the "noble simplicity and quiet grandeur" of the ancient Greeks a compelling alternative to the stifling morality and dim view of human capabilities he thought were inherent in Christian theology. To experience Greek sculpture in this collective and idealistic manner was to confront an incarnated vision of humankind as beautiful, strong, free, and noble. The paradoxical way forward, then, was to become "great" and "inimitable" by imitating the ancients.[6] By looking to ancient Hellas, the Germans would also be able to shed their dependence upon (contemporary) foreign intellectual capital: no more would Prussia need to look to France or Hanover to England. Winckelmann's *Reflections* called for cultural and religious emancipation by means of aesthetic renewal.

Emancipation and the attainment of an authentic German culture drawn from the inner resources of the individual provided philhellenism with its religious dimension. One of its most important features was its metaphysical ambition. Goethe, as we have already seen, hailed Winckelmann as the first great pagan of his time and, in this respect, a cultural and religious pioneer.[7] Goethe immersed himself in Greek literature and art and began the constructive enterprise of creating a pagan alternative to bourgeois Christian culture. In the course of his Italian journey, Goethe was, in a manner of speaking, "born again" as an artist. He came alive there to what he described as the wholeness of life.[8] Goethe's collaborator, Friedrich Schiller, also looked to antiquity to prepare the ground for aesthetic reawakening. He declared in his 1794 letters *Über die ästhetische Erziehung des Menschen (On the Aesthetic Education of Man)* that the Greeks put moderns to shame, combining "the first youth of imagination with the manhood of reason in a glorious manifestation of humanity."[9] The best hope of humanity, Schiller argued, lay in a new, hellenically inspired program of aesthetic ennoblement, the creation of a kind of "aesthetic state" to transcend the existing political and religious order. Philhellenic faith even extended as far as the hope that Germany's new Greeks would one day be able to produce a new scripture, a new Bible. Friedrich Schlegel's famous paean to poetry in *Athenaeum Fragment* 116, for example, claims for Romantic poetry the ability to fuse together all forms of literature, infuse life with sociability and wit, and gather up all forms of experience: "it alone can become ... a mirror of the whole circumambient world, an image of the age."[10] In another place, Schlegel maintained that all ancient poetry should be understood as a single poem and that "all books should be only a single book, and in such an eternally developing book, the gospel of humanity and culture will be revealed."[11] Novalis was also interested in creating a secular scripture. He admired the unifying, all-encompassing character of the Christian scriptures and proclaimed that the "highest task" of a writer was to produce a new Bible.[12]

Toward the end of the eighteenth century, the movement began to divide into two distinct but equally enthusiastic modes. On the one hand, it yielded a school of

Romantic poets and thinkers, for the most part, outside the university: for example, Goethe and Schiller in the Weimar "classical" period and, under their influence, Schlegel, Novalis, and Hölderlin. On the other hand, philhellenism took a distinct scholarly form, becoming a totalizing study of the ancient world based on philology, text criticism, and literary history. An important strain of philhellenism, already apparent in Winckelmann's systematic attempts to analyze and describe stages in the history of art, was historical scholarship. To appropriate antiquity, one had first to gain knowledge of it. F. A. Wolf, professor at Halle and later Berlin, was the leading figure in the creation of a science of antiquity (*Alterthumswissenschaft*) arising from the Greek cultural revolution. Though a founder, Wolf was not an innovator. As Anthony Grafton has shown, what made Wolf unique was the ability to make use of traditional scholarship, to join scholarly modes into a single program, and "to fuse materials from the divergent realms of philosophy and erudition."[13] Wolfian historical science, with its emphases on the reconstruction of textual history and the integration of written and antiquarian sources, defined the aims and methods of German classical philology in its nineteenth-century golden age. Thus Ulrich von Wilamowitz-Moellendorff, the greatest classicist of the late nineteenth and early twentieth centuries, maintained that the modern conquest of the ancient world found full expression not in the enthusiasms of Goethe, Humboldt, and the Schlegels but rather in the "comprehensive science of antiquity" set forth by Wolf.[14] Yet it is important to note that Wolf was no less enthusiastic in his philhellenic belief than Goethe and his good friend Humboldt. In his programmatic description of the historical science of antiquity, the 1807 *Darstellung der Althertumswissenschaft*, Wolf begins with a careful discussion of the contributions that philology and the study of material culture make toward developing a complete understanding of the ancient world. Yet Wolf's interdisciplinary program was also, in the philhellenic sense, deeply religious. By the end of the treatise, Wolf makes clear that *Altertumswissenschaft* builds toward the contemplation of what is "most holy," which, for Wolf, was the "genuine humanity" of the Greeks. Intense philological and historical study were ways to express and reinforce devotion to this ideal, as well as a means for building "patience" and "dogged industry" in the young.[15]

Like Wolf, Humboldt brought philhellenic ideals to the university context. And like Wolf, he did so out of a deep conviction of their superiority to Christian ideals. Humboldt began classical studies early in life, mastering Greek at a young age. Humboldt continued on in this vein at Göttingen, studying under Heyne. Between 1794 and 1797, Humboldt lived in Jena, where he established close working relationships with Fichte and the Schlegel brothers and also collaborated with Goethe and Schiller. Humboldt served as Prussian ambassador to the Vatican between 1803 and 1808. His time in Rome apparently had an effect on him similar to the effect their

Italian journeys had on Winckelmann and Goethe. Humboldt, a man of broad talents and interests, became absorbed with the Greeks. The 1806 "Latium und Hellas oder Betrachtungen über das classische Alterthum" is a fine example of this absorption. In a separate essay, "Ueber den Charakter der Griechen, die idealische und historische Ansicht desselben," Humboldt states plainly the significance of the Greeks:

> The Greeks are not for us simply a people in history about whom it would be useful to know something. Rather, they are an ideal. Their advantages over us are such that their very unattainability nevertheless makes it useful for us to imitate their works and beneficial for us to recall, in our own dull, narrow minds, their free and beautiful ones. They allow us to see our own lost freedom ... They are for us what their gods were for them: flesh of our flesh and bone of our bone; all the misfortune and unevenness of life but [also] a sensibility that transforms everything into play, and yet only wipes away the roughness of earthly existence while preserving the seriousness of the Idea.[16]

Like Schiller, Humboldt believed that the moderns had fallen from an original state of Hellenic grace. Like Wolf, he believed that the path of redemption lay in the study of the Greeks. Humboldt had a unique opportunity to act on his philhellenic ideals. Between 1809 and 1810, Humboldt served in the Prussian educational ministry. In this short period of time, he laid out plans for the new university at Berlin and set in motion a reform of primary and secondary education that continued well into the nineteenth century. Humboldt made his conception of *Bildung* the centerpiece of his reforms. *Bildung* consisted, for Humboldt, in the "sound formation of social morals" resulting from "the individual's self-transformative progress from natural immaturity to self-willed citizenship."[17] To this end, Humboldt devised a system of schools (*Gymnasia*), exams (*Abitur*), and philological gatekeepers designed to bring students into transformative contact with the ancient world.

The academic programs of Wolf and Humboldt exemplify the institutional reach and scholarly shape of German philhellenism in the late eighteenth and early nineteenth century. The value of an academic, religiously charged science of antiquity, though, was not apparent to everyone. To take only one example, Herder saw a basic contradiction in a mode of genuine historical study that privileged the Greeks. He certainly appreciated the Greeks, claiming that where "other nations debase the idea of God and make it monstrous," the Greeks "elevate what is divine in man."[18] Yet he regarded Winckelmann's investigation of Greek art as a brilliant but insufficient form of historical inquiry. Winckelmann had illuminated the Greek genius, but could not other ancient cultures be illuminated and praised for their genius as well? Herder was too deeply committed to historical particularism and the distinctiveness of cultures to make one group, however venerable, the ideal pattern for all the rest. Herder saw that the normative dimensions of philhellenism hindered historical inquiry by preventing the non-Greek civilizations in which Herder delighted from being understood on their own terms. Another difficulty with the academic philhellenism of Humboldt and Wolf was that it could not remain both *wissenschaftlich* and enthusiastic for very long. The more closely historians looked at ancient Greece, the harder it became to sustain the classical image of Greece as an ideal society populated by serene, beautiful, and cultivated individuals. As Suzanne Marchand aptly stated, "to investigate the wider history of philhellenism is . . . to describe the ways in which the triumph of historicized classical scholarship over poetry and antiquarian reverie gradually eroded the very norms and ideals that underwrote philhellenism's cultural significance."[19] By the end of his life, Goethe was already able to regard his generation's intense preoccupation with Greece as a kind of strange and distant but beautiful memory.[20] In Goethe's final years, classical scholarship at the university, by contrast, was thriving. No longer fueled by philhellenic faith, it had become a specialized academic discipline operating under the umbrella of *Wissenschaft*. It lived on without its effusive, romantic *Doppelgänger*.

It is possible, then, to draw a line from Winckelmann's aesthetic philhellenism to Wolf's *Alterthumswissenschaft* as we have done here. One can portray the history of philhellenism as an ironic tale of the unintended effects of scholarship or, perhaps, the corrosive effects of criticism on belief. When Göttingen and its most famous classicist, Heyne, are inserted into this narrative, they are usually placed somewhere in the middle, midway between Winckelmann and Wolf. Steven Turner, in an otherwise valuable study, does precisely this. Turner claims that Heyne reinvigorated the public image of classics and stressed its contemporary relevance; in this way he was "able to forge a temporary compromise between aesthetic neohumanism and classical scholarship as practiced."[21] As I will show, Turner is certainly correct to emphasize the social and contemporary quality of Heyne's scholarship. Yet to characterize it merely as a "temporary compromise" between "aesthetic neohumanism" (Winckelmann) and "classical scholarship" (Wolf) is to obscure the true nature of the Göttingen classical project. In one sense, Heyne surely was a transitional figure. He was a friend of Winckelmann's and a sympathetic, if also critical, reader of his works. Furthermore, it was Heyne's shining reputation that first drew Wolf to Göttingen, where Heyne also taught Humboldt and the Schlegels. It is also true that these same individuals regarded the scholarship of their aging teacher as shallow and outmoded.[22] Clemens Menze, for example, argues that Heyne's scholarship opened antiquity to Humboldt but did not ultimately determine how he would appropriate it. That is, he learned from Heyne but chose, unwisely, to reject Heyne's holistic, genuinely historical philology and adopt a dogmatic, amateurish, and idealized version of antiquity.[23] One could go on for some time clarifying the relationships of Heyne to figures like Humboldt, Wolf, and Schlegel.[24] That he mediated between the enthusiasm of Winckelmann and the classicism of Jena and Berlin is undeniable.

What has not been fully appreciated, however, is the character of Heyne's work as a university program dependent upon the innovations of his predecessor at Göttingen, J. M. Gesner. The point of this chapter is to shift the discussion of Heyne away from Winckelmann and Wolf and back toward Gesner and Georgia Augusta in order to describe the Göttingen classical project on its own terms. By doing so, we see it more clearly as a revivificatory academic enterprise, a distinctive mode of scholarly engagement with antiquity that was sociable, progressive, and modern. It remained relatively free of the dark *Sehnsucht*, fanaticism, and idolatry that fueled philhellenic dissatisfaction with the contemporary world. Instead, it made and kept peace with the generic Protestantism of the burgeoning *Bildungsbürgertum*. It ceded no ground to the ancient past, insisting instead on a fresh encounter with ancient authors on unapologetically contemporary terms. If Winckelmann, Goethe, and Schiller plunged headfirst into the depths of a lost Greek world, Gesner and Heyne chose rather to fish useful things out of it, feet planted firmly on the shore.

To distinguish between the classicism of figures on the Winckelmann-Wolf axis and the approach of Gesner and Heyne, we will refer to the former as "philhellenism" and the latter as "neohumanism." The division between the two, of course, cannot be taken as absolute. The overlaps are significant. Yet it is crucial to maintain a distinction. Gesner stood well outside the philhellenic trajectory. By the time that Winckelmann was born in 1717, for example, Gesner had already drawn up the guidelines for his philological seminar. When Winckelmann's *Gedancken* was published in 1755, Gesner had already been at Göttingen for over twenty years. Unlike Winckelmann's followers, Gesner did not show a strong preference for Greece over Rome. Nor did he ever question the basic tenets or usefulness of Christianity. He did not see classical antiquity and Christian faith as rivals but rather as complementary sources for *Bildung*. "What," he asked, "could be more wholesome for tender, young minds than to place in their hands, along with the books of religion, the writings of the greatest men of all time, of Cicero, Caesar, and the rest?"[25] In this respect, Gesner shared the easygoing Christian humanism of his teacher at Jena, Johann Franz Buddeus. Gesner believed that the study of classical antiquity reinforced Christian faith. Classical sources confirmed biblical teachings (Gesner's favorite example was the immortality of the soul), provided linguistic and historical background necessary to a fluent reading of the Bible, and provided the Christian pedagogue with a wider array of moral exempla. After all, Gesner challenged, did not St. Paul and the Fathers know the pagan authors well?[26] At the center of language instruction Gesner placed the reading of the New Testament in Latin and Greek. Heyne's commitment to Christian education, by contrast, seemed minimal. At Georgia Augusta, he steered classical philology away from Gesner's Christian humanism. He disparaged New Testament Greek and withdrew the Bible from the philological curriculum. Under his guidance, the philological seminar, as we will see, shifted focus from preparation for careers in ministry and teaching to interdisciplinary research in classics itself. Later in his career, Heyne became something of a Kantian in religious matters. In spite of all this, though, Heyne never went as far as his famous students did in criticizing Christianity or substituting Christian faith with philhellenic faith. He criticized the excessive and unscientific quality of Winckelmann's historical work, and he was, in general, more restrained than his students in seeking to appropriate the Hellenic past. If a less enthusiastic Christian than Gesner, Heyne nevertheless maintained a certain affection for the church throughout his life. As his son-in-law A. H. L. Heeren reported, the hymnal that Heyne kept by his bed was as worn from use as his copy of Homer.[27]

Like the older humanism of preceding centuries, the neohumanism of Gesner and Heyne aimed at a renewal of culture based on a return to classical sources in their original languages. They opened a path to antiquity at Georgia Augusta, a new university striving to be new. On the one hand, this meant that their work did not take explicit account of confessional boundaries or disputes. On the other hand, it meant that their teaching, programs, and research had to contribute to cameralist educational objectives: the cultivation of taste (*Geschmack*), the formation of moral judgment, a commitment to social utility, and social aptitude. Their work, moreover, had to reflect new standards for scholarship, which emphasized historical inquiry, empirical methods, and whatever contributed to academic celebrity. Under these conditions, philology emerged as the centerpiece of neohumanist education. In theory, the study of ancient texts in their original languages allowed greater immediacy with the author, his aesthetic vision, moral sensibilities, and historical setting. Like their forebears, Gesner and Heyne believed that the past yielded its treasures to linguists, fluent readers, and men of taste (poets like themselves!) and hid them from scholastic theologians and benighted philosophers. What made them *new* humanists was not only their location but also their position. Gesner and Heyne never forgot that they were employees of an Enlightenment state.

Johann Matthias Gesner (1691–1761)

Born in Roth (near Ansbach) to clergyman Johann Samuel Gesner and his wife Maria (Huswedel) on April 9, 1691, Johann Matthias Gesner began his life under difficult circumstances. He was the third of nine children in a family that lived on the modest income of his father, a pastor in Auhausen who endured a long illness before dying in 1704 and leaving the family strained. Maria remarried, and Johann Matthias's stepfather, Johann Zuckermantel, fortunately proved supportive. The young Gesner was accepted at the Gymnasium in Ansbach and, with the aid of benefactors and public funds, completed his studies there in 1710. At Ansbach, the talents of the precocious Gesner were noticed by Rektor Georg Nikolaus Köhler, who took a liking to the young student and kindled his interest in languages. Köhler loaned him copies of Greek texts, gave him additional work in Greek and Hebrew, and devised special exercises whereby Gesner had to reconstruct intelligible texts from fragments.[28] Gesner later called his Gymnasium years "the most pleasant" in his life and referred to his accomplishments as "violets on the burial mound of Köhler."[29] Gesner matriculated at Jena in 1710 as a theology student, completing work in metaphysics, ancient languages, and classical literature. In the theological faculty, Gesner studied under Buddeus, who would become his most important teacher. Buddeus befriended Gesner and even allowed the poor, struggling student to live in his own house. Though Buddeus provided material helps such as lodging, steady income as a tutor to his son, and access to his own fine library, it was his example as an educator that would have the most lasting value for Gesner. An orthodox theologian with Pietist leanings, Buddeus read widely in classics and in the newer philosophy. He thus modeled an easygoing Christian humanism, drawing eclectically and unselfconsciously on classical, Christian, and contemporary writings without fear of contradiction.[30] In doing so, Buddeus aimed at the reformation and reinvigoration of pedagogy. Buddeus had planned to start a Seminar for gymnasium teachers at Jena, and even had Gesner write up its founding principles and ground rules. These were published in a work entitled *Institutiones rei scholasticae* in 1715. Gesner, on Buddeus's recommendation, was to lead the Seminar. Much to his disappointment, though, Gesner was passed up for a position in Jena; he left, and the Seminar never materialized there.

Between 1715 and 1734, Gesner served as Rektor or Konrektor of three different gymnasia: at Weimar (1715–1729), at his native Ansbach (1729–1730), and at Leipzig (1730–1734). In these twenty years, Gesner built a reputation as an innovative reformer, an accomplished scholar, and an enthusiastic humanist. In this period, he published works on classical languages and literature, notably chrestomathies and textbooks for students of Greek and Latin, and he maintained a presence in the wider scholarly world. While Rektor at Weimar, Gesner also served as the librarian for Herzog William Ernst. Gesner took great delight in this work, making the most of access to such a fine collection and building contacts with scholars who visited the library.[31] This happy period in Weimar, though, ended badly, as William Ernst's successor, Herzog William August, dismissed Gesner as librarian in 1729; Gesner resigned from the Gymnasium in protest. After a brief stint in his native Ansbach, Gesner accepted a call to the renowned Thomasschule in Leipzig in 1730. He found it in a poor condition: facilities were run-down, the classical languages were neglected, the quality of teaching was low, truancy was a problem, and all was characterized by a general disorder.[32] With the help of Johann Sebastian Bach and Johann August Ernesti, though, Gesner turned the school around and strengthened his reputation as an effective reformer. Gesner received and rejected many calls from reform-minded schools in this period (Gotha, Dresden, and Heilbronn) and one to a prestigious position as the superintendent for all of Prussia. An otherwise happy period in Leipzig, though, was tainted by the fact that faculty at the University in Leipzig refused Gesner teaching privileges.[33] When Münchhausen called him to Göttingen in 1734, Gesner was ready to accept.

One of the first professors to arrive in Göttingen, Gesner came to Georgia Augusta in 1734 as the Professor of Poetry and Eloquence (*Professor der Poesie und Beredsamkeit*). To this title he would add many more. In his twenty-seven years at Göttingen, Gesner would remain very much a public figure, and one who maintained the same passionate interest in general education that he had demonstrated as a gymnasium Rektor. It is important to note that Gesner was not a professor of classical philology but rather a kind of scholar-poet in residence whose responsibility was not merely the study of ancient literature but also the composition of new Latin poetry.[34] Gesner's poetic work was oriented, first and foremost toward the life of the university; he who once sold occasional poems in order to eke out a living in Jena was now composing them for a single, larger client. Gesner's role also included public relations and propaganda. For example, Gesner, with Münchhausen's approval, drafted an anonymous letter addressed to an English baron which praised the university lavishly and created a sensation; the origin of the letter remained a mystery for years.[35] Gesner also served as librarian. He was a natural choice for the job, given his experience at Weimar, and he led the library successfully during his tenure. In addition to teaching and serving as *Bibliothekar*, Gesner served as the leader of two scholarly societies, the Deutsche Gesellschaft and the Academy of Sciences. The former, founded by Gesner in 1738, was devoted to the advancement of German literature, a subject to which Gesner confessed he had come too late to master but which he innovatively believed was crucial to the future of German academics. Gesner served as secretary of the historical-philological division of the Academy of Sciences in 1751 and then as Director in 1753. The cordial, high-spirited Gesner, by all accounts, was well suited for the job. Far from being an isolated and solitary academic, Gesner was the consummate university man. With one eye on his Cicero and the other on the fortunes of the young university, Gesner saw that its future depended on a successful reappropriation of the past.

Language, Literature, and *Bildung*

At the center of Gesner's long, productive career—whether at various gymnasia or at Göttingen—was a single, overriding concern: to make the ancient world a living power in cultural transformation. His principal interest was in the achievement, through classical studies, of a fully humane *Bildung*, a comprehensive shaping of the intellect, will, and faculties of judgment. This guided all his efforts as a teacher, administrator, and finally as a teacher of teachers. Even his scholarly work, which might have reached beyond the classroom, has been justly said to show "a strong didactic interest."[36] His chief contributions to the discipline of classical philology—his editions of Greek and Latin authors and his lexicographic work—were quickly superseded. This perhaps explains Gesner's total or virtual absence from leading histories of scholarship.[37] Yet it is a conspicuous absence. For it was Gesner who provided the impetus for a burgeoning neohumanist critical philology at the university.

For a man whose entire professional life was bound up with the study of the past, Gesner remained firmly oriented toward the present. This impulse to realize the value of the past in and for the university context is no clearer than in his pragmatic view of language and language instruction. The languages of classical antiquity were arbitrary historical vessels for the noble thoughts of the great souls of antiquity. The goal in language instruction was simply to enable intelligent reading, to remove barriers to the content of literature. The Latin language, for example, was of little concern to Gesner in and of itself; rather, the goal was "a command of the Latin language sufficient for understanding ancient and modern writings without hindrance."[38] Unlike Herder, who regarded the diligence (*Fleiß*) and discipline necessary for language study as important components of *Bildung*, Gesner saw no inherent value in the rigors of language study. The content of ancient literature took priority over its form. The real goods of classical philology were not linguistic competence but "intellectual independence, decency, intelligence, and moderation in thought, speech, and conduct."[39]

Gesner had little regard for the pedantry (*Pedanterey*) of many of his contemporaries and little patience for the zeal of others for a systematic grasp of the language. The former, he commented, ultimately proved unhelpful; they were mere "word-collectors" who were content to:

> spend days, months, and years on nothing other than the most serious disputations over letters, pronunciation, orthography, word choice,

phrases, periods, and expressions, and thus to waste their entire lives on things of no consequence so that nothing truly useful either for the higher sciences or for life comes of it.[40]

Language was instrumental to the discovery of things useful to "life" and "the higher sciences," presumably law and theology. Those who insisted on a fully systematic understanding of language undermined themselves. Failing to keep social realities in view, they taught ancient languages to their students as though they intended to become scholars. The disastrous result was to engender a loathing (*Ekel*) for Latin and formal study that would prevent students from gaining, through the study of classics, qualities that might be "indispensable or useful in civic life, in the arts or in the professions, in service at court and in the military."[41]

In place of pedantry and formalism, Gesner favored an empirical approach that centered on fluency and reading comprehension. In implementing such an approach, Gesner streamlined or invented tools designed to focus the efforts of the student upon a single object: the transformational content of ancient literature. He published new editions of ancient works that, while failing to meet the critical standards even of his day, yet succeeded in their single aim: readability.[42] He pioneered the use of chrestomathies, which were used to enable students to read actual (simplified) texts as quickly as possible. Along with these, he wrote and used handbooks (*Handkommentare*) for poetical works that dispensed with detailed background information and indicated briefly all that would deepen appreciation for what is "beautiful, worthy, and truly poetic."[43] Gesner is perhaps best known for a new method of instruction that blended language instruction with literary appreciation: so-called *kursorische Lektüre*. This was developed in conscious opposition to what Gesner called *statarische Lektüre*, in which a small quantity of text is read thoroughly. Gesner described a typical scene from the university this way:

> One and the same passage is typically read aloud two or three times and analyzed two or three times by students, according to their understanding.... so that a quite ordinary passage is handled for an hour. Years may be spent on a single book of Cicero's letters.[44]

Statarische Lektüre succeeded only in deadening the mind of the student to the actual meaning and content of literature. For the student's efforts, in this setting, were dissipated by endless discussions of trivia and grammar. Beneath the unbearable load of learning, there was little energy left to devote to meaningful interpretation. In Gesner's *kursorische Lektüre*, the goal was "to concentrate all interpretation on the understanding and internalization of what the author intended to do and say." After students attained a basic knowledge of Latin and Greek grammar, the teacher would take up a discrete work (*ein klassisches Buch*) and read the entire work in class before setting it down again. In the course of such cursory reading, he paused only to point out exceptional passages and clarify obscurities—all else was left aside.[45] Ernesti, Gesner's close friend and colleague, later reported the goals of this method as he understood them; in Paulsen's summary, they were: "first, right understanding; second, a feeling for the excellence and beauty of the language and thought; above all ... that students understand the context of the whole and how to handle it."[46] Cicero's letters were read in a mere six weeks.[47]

Gesner offered a memorable formulation of the value of ancient literature in a 1738 document devoted mostly to school reform, "Schulordnung vor die Churfürstlich Braunschweigisch-Lüneburgischen Lande." In the midst of an extended discussion of Latin instruction, Gesner pauses to reflect on its ultimate value:

> Still, the teacher above all takes care to shape, on the part of the people, a good opinion of antiquity and of the usefulness and convenience that familiarity with its literature can bring. In this, the teacher says to them that most ancient writers were the most excellent people of their time and wanted to write not out of base motives but from the one and only motivation to leave to posterity a lasting monument to reason and other good qualities. Who, therefore, reads and understands their writings enjoys the company of the greatest people and noblest souls that ever lived and, through this, takes to himself, as happens with all conversation, beautiful thoughts and forceful words: thus will modern writers perceive that they will enjoy yet greater and broader renown, the closer they come to their ancient forebears.[48]

Here language instruction goes hand in hand with a cultural imperative to commend classical antiquity. To read the works of the ancient Greeks and Romans is, above all, to encounter the West's greatest moral exemplars. Gesner's program is reverential but not overly so: the goal is to surpass the ancients. Nevertheless, doing this hardly seems possible without first sitting at their feet. The way back, which is also the way forward, then, requires linguistic competence and the guidance of teachers who will keep the philological task centered on content and oriented toward a readerly ethic of qualified reverence, expectation, and personal transformation.

It is not surprising, then, that Gesner set out to train teachers by qualifying them in a seminar on, of all things, classical philology. The Philological Seminar, founded by Gesner at Göttingen in 1738, began as a new initiative to train gymnasium teachers. Modeled explicitly on the seminar which Buddeus had hoped to start with Gesner at Jena some twenty years earlier, the Philological Seminar would advance the notion of *Bildung* and classical study that Gesner had worked out early on and applied in his years at various gymnasia.[49]

In Gesner's day, prospective teachers typically enrolled in the theological faculty. Gesner's plan included public support for nine theology students planning on careers as educators to enroll in the Seminar. The Professor of Eloquence stood at the head of the Seminar ex officio as its "Inspector." He oversaw the work and progress of the members, reporting to prospective employers and to the government (*die Geheimte Rath-Stube*). Seminarists were required to complete studies both in the arts faculty and in traditional theological curriculum in addition to the Seminar itself. Within the Seminar, which met for two hours every day, the Inspector supervised work in a broad curriculum that included nine collegia: 1) general instruction in ancient literature; 2) Latin grammar with emphasis on German translation; 3) Greek grammar, also with emphasis on translation; 4) readings in Greek using Gesner's own chrestomathies; 5) rhetoric, with emphasis on independent composition and anonymous peer criticism; 6) general introduction to poetry (German, Latin, and Greek); 7) *kursorische Lektüre* of Latin authors; 8) *kursorische Lektüre* of "excellent poets," with emphasis on proper aesthetic judgment; 9) general study of antiquity with emphasis on all information necessary to read ancient books.[50]

Gesner's approach was multifaceted. The collegia on grammar and poetry introduce a distinctly comparative element by considering Greek and Latin together, and the innovative inclusion of German translation and poetry suggests a broader, more contemporary line of inquiry. The ninth collegium on history immediately recalls the sweeping interdisciplinarity of later neohumanist *Alterthumswissenschaft*, and indeed represents its beginnings. A notable and significant omission among the collegia is text criticism, the traditional centerpiece of humanist philology. Gesners's own editions, as we have seen, achieved readability at the expense of critical rigor: they were largely reproductions of *textus recepti*. Literature, not texts, lay at the center of Gesner's Seminar. Seminar work, then, had a decidedly oral character, including exercises in reading aloud, poetic analysis, and rhetoric, with emphasis on individual performance and practical demonstrations of competence. This contributed to a "general, dialogical method" aimed "especially at emphasizing the independent contributions of seminarists."[51] Yet Gesner did not allow the pursuit of individual scholarly interests to overshadow training in pedagogy.[52]

Something new emerged in Gesner's new *Lehrform*. Much grew directly out of Gesner's experience as a gymnasium instructor: the centrality of reading, immersion in the ancient world, and a fluid pedagogy aimed at understanding and internalization. Yet the collegia of the Seminar—which were built around the independent, interdisciplinary contributions of seminarists—represented not simply a new form but also a new method. The Seminar would change classical philology in profound ways that Gesner himself would not live to see.

Christian Gottlob Heyne (1729–1812)

Heyne was Gesner's successor in the fullest sense of the term. He inherited the formidably broad range of posts which Gesner had occupied: leader of the Philological Seminar, Professor of Poetry and Eloquence, university librarian, and director of the Academy of Sciences. A proper sense of what Heyne shared with Gesner, rather than with Winckelmann and Wolf, is essential to a full understanding of the Göttingen program. As will be clear, Heyne differed from his predecessor in important ways. What differences there are, though, are not to be found in their biographies, which were similar. Each began inauspiciously, in circumstances pressed by poverty and apparent lack of opportunity, and each served Georgia Augusta loyally and in socially prominent ways for decades after his initial call. The life of Heyne may be divided into two totally distinct periods separated abruptly by Münchhausen's invitation to come to Göttingen: youth and young adulthood troubled by poverty and war, and a stable, highly successful career as a university professor and public figure.[53]

Heyne's father, a linen weaver, forsook a more secure life in Silesia and moved to Saxony to maintain his Protestant faith. Conditions for linen weavers, though, were poor there, and the family was thrust into a state of "misery and need" from which they never fully escaped.[54] It was into these conditions that Heyne was born in 1729. With the support of his godfather, Heyne was able to attend the Latin School in Chemnitz. Early school experiences, though, were marked by bullies who preyed on the awkward and incompetent teachers who subjected their students to "senseless and pointless" drilling in grammar and vocabulary.[55] In 1748, Heyne began studies at the University of Leipzig. Heyne later looked back on this period, in which he was still destitute, as nearly hopeless:

> In this way I came to the point in life when I fell prey to despair. Raised without basic principles, with an entirely unformed character, without a friend, guide, or counselor—I still do not understand how I lasted in this helpless circumstance! What kept me going in the world was not ambition, youthful imagination, or the ability or desire to have a place among scholars. My constant companion was the bitter sense of lowness and of my lack of a good education and external development, as well as a consciousness of my awkwardness in social life. Mostly what affected me was a defiance of Fate. This gave me courage not to give in.[56]

Heyne's years at Leipzig, while difficult, also included positive experiences that shaped him in important ways. The first to reach out to Heyne was professor and classicist Johann Friedrich Christ. The professor loaned Heyne editions of Greek and Latin texts and encouraged the young student, who was by his own admission still aimless, simply to read the ancients. Heyne followed the advice zealously and said later that his desire to read became so consuming that he scarcely stopped to rest, sleeping only two nights out of seven for a six-month period until he fell ill.[57] In 1750, Christ also arranged a position for Heyne as a house tutor in Magdeburg, while Heyne was midway through his studies. Despite his destitute condition, Heyne turned it down because, he reasoned, failure to complete his studies would have had ruinous, lifelong consequences. Heyne later marveled at his own asceticism.[58] As his studies progressed, though, Heyne gravitated toward the teaching and work of philologist Johann August Ernesti. In place of Christ's "web" of philological "excesses," Heyne found Ernesti's "practical brevity, thoroughness, and orderly lectures" much more to his liking.[59] Yet it was ultimately law professor Johann August Bach who awarded Heyne a master's degree in 1752. From Bach Heyne learned how to interpret ancient laws according to a thorough grasp of their conceptual meaning and historical circumstances.

After completing his studies, Heyne went to Dresden at the behest of the Count of Brühl in the hope of obtaining a position in his service. This did not immediately materialize, and Heyne found himself destitute again. The following year, in 1753, Heyne was hired as a copyist at the Count's library and remained there for three years. In that time, Heyne published editions of the works of Tibullus (1755) and Epictetus (1756), upon which his reputation as a philologist was first established. With the onset of the Seven Years' War and the destruction of the library, though, Heyne was once again without means. During the war, Heyne survived by taking temporary positions as a translator or house tutor, at one point enduring the loss of all his positions during a bombardment.[60]

It is not difficult to imagine the extent of Heyne's satisfaction, then, at being chosen to succeed Gesner in 1763. Leiden philologist David Ruhnken recommended the relatively unknown Heyne to Münchhausen, who liked Heyne's cooperative nature. Heyne's winsome personality and skill in public affairs engendered the loyalty of friends such as Herder, who said of Heyne that he was most unusual among classicists in possessing the "noblest, finest, and most pleasant soul."[61] To critics of Heyne like Wolf, though, Heyne's public-spiritedness was a sign of mediocrity: Wolf quipped that Heyne was the "greatest politician among the philologists and the greatest philologist among the politicians."[62] Heyne was an effective "man of affairs" (*Geschäftsmann*) in the republic of letters. As Professor of Poetry and Eloquence, Heyne produced 135 "Programs and Prolusions," 47 academic treatises, and 20 orations, in addition to an impressive array of historical and philological works: a translation of a four-volume world history, editions of Virgil (1767–1772), Pindar (1773), Apollodorus (1782), and Homer (1802), and numerous smaller works.[63] Heyne also reorganized and reinvigorated a faltering Academy of Sciences and broke new ground as *Bibliothekar* by expanding the collection from 60,000 to 200,000 volumes and making it the first university library to house a collection of sculpture and other realia such as maps, engravings, coins, and gems.[64] Finally, Heyne as editor of the *Göttingische gelehrte Anzeigen* (from 1770) made the journal a vital tool in making scholarly research useful and accessible to the wider world. Heyne himself wrote between seven and eight thousand reviews and chided colleagues for being content to remain "mere teachers," indifferent to the growth of science.[65] Like Gesner before him, Heyne raised the profile of the University and sought to increase its usefulness to the world beyond its walls.

Propaideia Old and New

Heyne is best known for the profound and influential way that he reconceived the study of the ancient world.[66] What was once a discipline focused narrowly on texts and authors became under Heyne a remarkably broad, far-reaching area of study. Nowhere is this clearer than in Heyne's own definition of "literature":

> "Literature" encompasses many things: a general overview of the culture of both nations [i.e., Greece and Rome]; how and why they rose, grew, and fell; the derivation and development of language; knowledge of myths and ancient literature according to their stages of development; and an integrated understanding of individual writers and the periods to which they belong. Special attention should be paid to the value and use of the most important writings, along with a discussion of the work that has already been done and an account of what still needs to be done.[67]

The passage is remarkable for several reasons. It demonstrates, first of all, that Heyne's vision was steadfastly holistic. Former students and philologists in subsequent generations criticized Heyne's lack of critical acumen, his discomfort with aggressive modes of textual analysis, and his unwillingness to pronounce on difficult historical issues. Though the criticisms have some validity, they also belie a fundamental misprision: it is the culture *in toto* that, for Heyne, forms the ground for understanding, not individual facts created by critical judgments. Ancient texts reveal far more about the cultural milieu of the authors than they do about a putative *wahrliche Geschichte*, or indeed of the idealized urtext behind or beyond the texts. Language, according to Heyne, is the gateway to this cultural understanding, and the philologist is the gatekeeper. After language, it is "myth" that must occupy the philologist. Heyne's reputation as a founding figure in the modern study of myth is richly deserved. He created a new approach to myth that concerned itself not with anachronistic judgments concerning the irrationality, religious perversity, or unhistorical character of myths, but rather with the ways that myths function as keys to the worldview and self-understanding of the societies that create them.[68] In applying himself to this kind of holistic analysis, the philologist must remain cognizant of the history and organic nature of the culture to which myths bear witness.

Heyne demanded that classical philology encompass the totality of ancient life—art, literature, politics, geography, religion, and economics—and that, far from exhibiting "mere enthusiasm," it be thorough, orderly, and founded on a scientific treatment of ancient realia and texts.[69] Werner Mettler, in an influential discussion of Heyne's philological method, maintains that Heyne's distinctive contribution did not consist in specific discoveries but in a new perspective on the nature of the philologist's task: to cultivate receptivity (*Hörenkönnen*) to the inner reality of ancient societies by examining their cultural forms in a holistic manner. The result, as Heyne envisioned it, would be a new proximity to the *Geist* of ancient Greece that allowed the philologist to unify antiquarian and literary methods in his own vital, empathetic sense of the past.[70] The philologist, then, employs epigraphy, political and legal history, mythology, religion, art history, archaeology, and numismatics in penetrating the ancient world. Heyne guided philology toward the *Geist* of classical Greece while enlarging the scope of philological inquiry to include new goals and methods. Wolf brought this enterprise fully into its own in the early nineteenth century, but its beginnings lie with the appropriative strategies of Heyne and Gesner before him.

This strategy for vitalizing ancient literature is clear, for example, in Heyne's treatment of Homer. Notes taken by Humboldt in the summer semester of 1789 during Heyne's course on the *Iliad* were published as an appendix to an edition of Humboldt's letters to Wolf.[71] The notes shed valuable light not only on Heyne's philological method but also on his pedagogy. Roughly a third of the notes are taken up with general introduction: the age and dating of Homer, the historical background of the Trojan War, and the linguistic and compositional history of Homeric epic. Heyne gently shapes an impressive array of obscurities and disputed matters into a clear and coherent picture of Homer and the events behind the *Iliad*, with emphasis on the raw, uncultivated nature of the great poet's age. In one brief paragraph, for example, Heyne explains the peculiarities of Homeric Greek not as a later admixture of dialects but rather as marks of the language in a time before grammar itself had stabilized.[72] To take a second example, a rhapsodist, Heyne argued, was not one who stitched (*rhaptein*) odes (*aoide*) but rather one of a guild of performers, originally a single family in Chios, who sang (*aidon*) short pieces (*rhapta*). In this way, Heyne stressed the lively, oral, and performative origins of the epic and located them in a traditional environment closer to Homer's own preliterate situation; the written form came much later.⁷³ The last part of the general introduction lays out the topography of Troy and surrounding territories in a way that allows the students to visualize the action, to place themselves, as it were, in the battle itself. The final lines leading into the line-by-line commentary were calculated to create suspense:

> The Achaeans landed between Rhoeteum and Sigeum, in an area two and one-half miles long. They pulled their ships to land, not in one line but, because it was too narrow, in more than one line. Before and between the ships stood their huts . . . The left flank of the Achaeans ran north toward the Hellespont. There stood Achilles. Since the shore was slanted, the right flank ran more inland, closer to the city and to war. At the farthest edge stood Telamonian Aias.⁷⁴

Heyne's subsequent commentary on specific words and phrases in the *Iliad* indicates an interest in syntax and lexicography and in the larger cultural and historical situation of the epic—the kind of information that facilitates a learned, sympathetic encounter with the *Iliad*. As Mettler has pointed out, Heyne showed comparatively little interest in the textual obscurities and difficult passages that occupied philologists like Ruhnken and Bentley.⁷⁵

Like Gesner, Heyne had little feel (or use) for certain aspects of linguistic and textual analysis, which would later figure prominently in the work of nineteenth-century philologists. According to his biographer Heeren, Heyne was never content with what he called "mere linguistic erudition" (*bloße Sprachgelehrsamkeit*).⁷⁶ Heyne's teaching lacked extensive instruction on grammar and meter. When a writer was discussed, linguistic issues receded into the background. Heyne would treat linguistic issues quickly before moving on to the vital step of "making the poetic element sensible and knowable."⁷⁷ Heyne possessed no real genius or enthusiasm for the Bentleyan tradition of textual criticism. Like grammatical analysis, textual criticism for Heyne threatened to foreclose or crowd out more important tasks. This tendency to smooth over critical problems in the interest of providing a more congenial atmosphere for poetic interpretation is evident in the case of Heyne's edition of Pindar, which, like Gesner's editions, achieved clarity at the expense of accuracy. Heyne believed that an overly aggressive mode of criticism belied an incorrect interpretive posture. He thus referred repeatedly to the "vanity of wanting to seem brilliant through emendations."⁷⁸ Heyne's students and successors became rigorists, while Heyne remained ever cognizant of his role as a scholar with a public profile. Heyne's philology was not "esoteric like the methodological, grammatical, narrower, and more severe scientific philology that belonged to the next generation." Rather, it was "pedagogically extroverted," aimed at winning "insightful admirers and lovers of the greatest and noblest souls of ancient poetry."⁷⁹

In this respect, Heyne was closer to Gesner than to his successors. Gesner had succeeded in setting classical philology within a more contemporary, humanistic conceptual framework, such that it became a key nonecclesiastical resource in the replenishment of cultural values. In this way, philology was well suited to serve the University's sociopolitical ends with a degree of independence, that is, without recourse to theological justifications for the value of classics and ancient languages. Gesner had argued that the study of ancient literature could be culturally relevant in its own right; it could make its own unique contribution to *Bildung*. Without Gesner, classical studies in Germany might well have lain beneath the dust of pedants, antiquarians, and schoolmen.[80] Yet with Gesner, philology, if relevant, still remained essentially propaedeutic. Gesner's seminarists were required to matriculate in the theology faculty, and Gesner's Seminar was oriented, above all, toward vocational training. A requirement of admission under Gesner was the desire to serve as *Schullehrer* or *Hauslehrer* after graduation. The purpose of the Seminar was to form the will, intellect, taste, and judgment of the seminarists so that they could do the same for their students. Gesnerian philology served the purposes of civic-minded pedagogy.

Heyne, by contrast, is said to have overseen the transition of philology from a propaedeutic discipline to an independent one.[81] This claim must be understood carefully. Heyne's approach to classical studies was decidedly more expansive than any followed by his predecessors or contemporaries. Under Heyne, classics became less dependent, intellectually and institutionally, on law, theology, and pedagogy. Despite the well-known but misleading *legenda* of Wolf,[82] which indicts Heyne for failing to maintain the independence of classics, Heyne did preside over a change in the status of the discipline. The nature of this shift is evident in Heyne's own description of the Philological Seminar that he inherited and adapted from Gesner. In 1788, Heyne took stock of changes in the Seminar during his tenure and noted that it no longer conformed to the original vision of Gesner:

> To the Philological Seminar was given, in its first arrangement in 1737, the task of training good house tutors and schoolteachers. For this only nine theology students were accepted . . . But now the Philological Seminar has gradually come to resemble a nursery for humanists, who are considering studying for themselves the humanities proper, whether for the school, the academy, or simply as scholars.[83]

Classical philology, no longer a theological or pedagogical propaideia, was coming into its own as a discipline and field of inquiry. As Inspector of the Seminar, Heyne cultivated new humanists in the "nursery" he had built on the foundations that Gesner laid.

The Seminar in Heyne's time did not cycle through distinct collegia as it did under Gesner. Both Heyne and one-time seminarist Heeren report that the Seminar was a venue for practice and active demonstration (*Übung*) and not for lectures. Sessions had two parts: *Interpretieren* and *Disputieren*. In the first, a student would hold forth on a difficult passage from a Greek or Latin text, acting as the teacher and drawing on linguistic and historical information to make its meaning clear. Heyne himself would then lead a short discussion of the effort afterwards, in which he evaluated the student. In the disputation, students were free to choose any subject pertaining to the humanities and to argue for or against a specific position.[84] All was conducted in Latin. In everything, a robust academic freedom was observed: students were not required to maintain specific positions on linguistic or historical issues. Nevertheless, the Seminar, despite Heyne's denial of a Heynian school of thought, had a distinct character: all learned Heyne's method of studying the ancient world. This method lent the Seminar its basic shape: the use of information gained from text and realia to identify with the mind of the author and the context of the work; the announcement of the unique contribution of the author (as in his trademark proclamation, *Nun kömmt der Tichter!* or *Now comes the poet!*); and, finally, the exploration of the text's relevance to the present. The threefold program of historical contextualization, textual interpretation, and contemporary application not only integrated literary and antiquarian studies, it also allowed classical philology to take its place among the modish, practical disciplines characteristic of the Enlightenment university. Heyne did not accomplish this by a polemical recasting of philology's role vis-à-vis other disciplines. Instead, he broadened philology's own methods and concerns in a way that allowed the philologist to bring the study of antiquity into contact with *Wissenschaft* and modern culture.

The study of the ancients, according to Heyne, had a great deal to teach moderns about aesthetics. In a programmatic description of the study of antiquity, *Einleitung in das Studium der Antike, oder Grundriß einer Anführung zur Kenntniß der alten Kunstwerke* (1772), Heyne maintained that true art is not arbitrary. It operates according to rules that coordinate external images and internal perceptions of themes, ideas, and topics in rational ways. Ancient studies, then, constitute the effort to understand the "internal" products of a past society (e.g., morals, religious ideas, myths) in terms of its "external" remnants (e.g., art, artifacts, monuments). By moving between ideals and their particular historical forms, the student of antiquity becomes a skillful interpreter of art, architecture, and literature. He acquires "sensitivity to the beautiful, the shaping of taste, love, the duty to enjoy, and the possibility of enjoying nobler pleasures."[85] The more rigorous one's actual engagement with the empirical and historical dimensions of ancient artifacts is, the deeper his aesthetic insight extends. Heyne criticized Lessing and Winckelmann, for example, for using the famous Laocoön sculpture as a touchstone for theoretical discussions of art and aesthetics. Winckelmann's failure to base his conclusions on a thorough examination of the sculpture exposed him, Heyne believed, to charges of dilettantish enthusiasm and, worse, of engaging imaginary objects in the manner of Don Quixote.[86] Taken to its logical conclusion, Heyne's insistence on particularity suggests that no work of art could ever be idealized in the way that Winckelmann idealized the Laocoön group: it is and must remain a historically contingent expression of a cultural notion. Yet this does not preclude a normative aesthetic dimension. Heyne believed that disciplined encounters with the past— whether through texts or objects—strengthened the taste and aesthetic judgment of the individual. For Heyne, the cultivation of taste, a key element of *Bildung*, did not follow from the a priori adoption of the right aesthetic ideals but rather through an experience of "estrangement" (*Entfremdung*) that allowed the individual to experience the past, to partake of its spirit.[87] Historical study, then, prepares the ground for a mode of aesthetic appreciation.

Heyne also remained sensitive to the political reflexes of the ancient past. Jacob Bernays, in a classic study, examined Heyne's involvement in a dispute with fellow Göttingen professor August Ludwig Schlözer over the significance of Phocion of Athens.[88] Schlözer's associate, Duke Ludwig Ernst of Braunschweig, had been forced to leave the Netherlands in 1784, during the Dutch Patriot Revolution. The Duke returned home and paid Schlözer to write his biography. In 1786, Schlözer published a hagiographic account of the Duke's life. The book, which included a picture of Phocion on the cover, implicitly compared the Duke to the Athenian statesman and the Dutch burghers who expelled him to the rash Athenians that turned on Phocion. Heyne delivered an address on Phocion to the Academy of Arts and Sciences in 1787, shortly after the publication of Schlözer's book. In it Heyne did not mention either the Duke or Schlözer by name, but it seems likely that Heyne's address, later reported in the *Göttingische Anzeigen von gelehrten Sachen* (Jan. 15, 1787), was aimed at Schlözer. According to the *GAGS* report, Heyne questioned the wisdom of relying on Plutarch's one-sided, reverential account of Phocion's life, noting that other sources like Nepos and Diodor allow a different understanding. Heyne also adduced historical arguments of his own, claiming that the real danger to Athens was not the petty hypocrisies of the Athenian leadership (which Phocion self-righteously denounced) but rather the rapid rise of the Macedonians. In accommodating the Macedonians and underestimating the threat they posed to Athenian sovereignty, Phocion acted foolishly if not treacherously. His death, on this account, was just. By criticizing Phocion, Heyne implicitly questioned the wisdom of Schlözer's involvement with the Duke. The Phocion episode illustrates well the connection of classical studies to political discourse at the university: at that time "one clothed views on parties and personages of the present in the form of judgments concerning the men and affairs of Greece and Rome."[89]

As classical studies under Heyne mattered to politics and aesthetics, they also played a useful role in contemporary thinking about culture. An excellent example of this comes from a 1763 speech entitled *De genio saeculi Ptolemaeorum*.[90] Heyne's aim in this speech was to examine Hellenistic Alexandria in the time of the Ptolemies. Heyne promised to "hold forth on the spirit of the Ptolemaic era" as a function both of the cultural mindset and historical circumstances of Alexandrians in this period. He then went on to paint a comprehensive portrait of Alexandrian thinkers and writers as capable scholars, gatherers of information who lack genius, "stormy enthusiasm," a "wealth of ideas," and any sense for what is "lofty, high-minded, or exalted." They were instead more likely to be "informed than inspired."[91] Citing economic and cultural factors such as prosperity and its unfortunate tendencies to produce a hyperrefined cultural elite and a polished system of education that saps inborn genius and talent, Heyne explained how external conditions shaped and expressed a historically distinct Alexandrian intellectual culture. In the end, Heyne believed that Göttingen, which possessed a similar profile, could become a "new Alexandria" capable of outshining the old.[92] Heyne thus modified the popular "new Athens" moniker often applied to Göttingen, offering what was, given Georgia Augusta's aristocratic atmosphere, arguably a more appropriate analogy.

Heyne's method, then, may be described as a totalizing mode of inquiry that begins with an orderly examination of realia and proceeds, through sensitive interpretation of contextualized literature, to connect the ancient world to the present. The totality of the ancient past was Heyne's overriding concern. The past existed in its totality, just beyond his grasp: "I possess neither the powers nor the knowledge, nor leisure enough, to elaborate the Whole, of which a dark image sometimes hovers before my eyes."[93] By uniting philological, literary, and antiquarian studies, Heyne sought to encounter the totality (*das Ganze*) of the ancient world in an empathetic way. Put differently, the point of bringing the disciplines together was not so much to unite them as to make them disappear, to make use of them until they gave way to a unified encounter with the ancient past as a seamless and elusive reality. The goal was to understand it as one experiences the present, to gaze upon it as a unified Whole just beyond reach. For Heyne, the path to the Whole was the path of the well-trained humanist. On this Heyne and Wolf were agreed. If the humanist is to avoid the fate of Winckelmann's quixotic followers, he must first journey to the university and become, through solemn commitment, *studiosus philologiae*.

Conclusion

Heyne was clearly an important and influential innovator. Yet even he was not immune to the oedipal dynamics of academic life. By the time of his death, his most famous students regarded his work as outdated and his method as shallow, credulous, and superficial. Dissatisfied with the "indecisive and uncritical" musings of

Heyne, Wolf enlisted stringent textual criticism in the service of vivid, precise historical reconstruction.[94] Contemptuous of Heyne's airy humanism, Humboldt the reformer turned Heynian holism into an institutional program animated by what Clemens Menze has characterized as a reductive, dogmatic philhellenism.[95] The temptation to understand Heyne principally as a transitional figure between scholarly modes or as a precursor to more illustrious successors has been hard to resist. One scholar refers to the prevalence of an "already—not yet" (*schon—noch nicht*) schema in assessing Heyne's place in the history of scholarship.[96] Even if he is credited with innovations in the study of history, archaeology, and myth, he is, by this light, seen as the last representative of an outmoded approach to the ancient world. Within a generation, classical scholars not only dismissed his legacy, they pitied him as an individual. Thus the great Roman historian B. G. Niebuhr assessed Heyne's legacy in the following way a mere fifteen years after Heyne's death:

> Heyne does not deserve disdain, but his works for the most part all have the same failing: they were written too hastily. Heyne was overloaded by his affairs and his own projects; it is sad that such a truly wonderful talent was so mediocre in his production ... Despite good intentions, his memory is lost to the world he left behind, for it asks not "how large is the collection of his works?" but rather "*what* are his works?" His fate recalls the scripture: "he went away and there is no longer a trace of him."[97]

Niebuhr's scriptural reference is telling. By paraphrasing Wisdom 5:11, which is set in the middle of a larger discourse about the great reversal of fortunes in the final judgment, Niebuhr likens Heyne to members of a wicked generation that, though impressive in life, did not ultimately endure when their true merits were weighed. To Niebuhr, who had shown brilliantly in his own work what Heyne's approach could achieve, Heyne's output seemed modest, even negligible.

Despite the eschatological pretensions of his judgment on Heyne, Niebuhr was not yet in a position to weigh the true merit of Heyne's legacy. In time, it has become clear that Heyne's disciplinary innovations brought the study of the past into a successful and sustainable academic form. With Heyne, the study of the deep past became a coherent discipline characterized by empiricism and methodological rigor and reoriented toward the social realities of the university. For Heyne, classical literature was "the center out of which everything flowed and to which he brought everything back."[98] The vision of a full and independent humanism centered on classical antiquity was Heyne's constant guide. It was a vision that was realized institutionally, in the creation of new venues for humanistic scholarship: a massive library, an innovative journal (*Göttingische gelehrte Anzeigen*), the Academy of Sciences, and the Philological Seminar. It was also realized in Heyne's own method, as he connected scattered branches of antiquarian learning to literary and aesthetic studies, organizing all into a single *Studium der Antike*. Classical philology at Göttingen need not be characterized merely as a halfway house between rhetoric and history, pedantry and *Wissenschaft*, classical aesthetics and romanticism. Instead, it may be understood on its own terms as an outgrowth of an institutional Enlightenment.

In the eighteenth century, there developed at Göttingen a well-worn path connecting the ancient world to the modern university. This path was shaped in particular ways by conditions at Georgia Augusta. The desire of the founders to outstrip rival universities, attract students from among the European nobility, and have renowned, pedagogically effective specialists had consequences for all aspects of university life. The decline of academic theology and a cultural shift away from Lutheran confessionalism also played a role. Münchhausen's vision created the conditions for a reconception of the humanities oriented toward social utility and irenicism. This allowed Gesner and Heyne, new humanists, to salvage classical philology. Whether it would allow an enterprising Hebraist to do the same for the Bible Michaelis was determined to find out.

4

Michaelis and the Dead Hebrew Language

The exactitude of a language diminishes its richness.
—Johann Gottfried Herder, *Fragments on Recent German Literature* (1767–1768)[1]

Like so many modern academic disciplines, philology as it is practiced and understood today took shape largely at the hands of German-speaking scholars in the late eighteenth and early nineteenth centuries. Though the study of Hebrew continued without interruption through the late antique, medieval, and Renaissance periods, the modern academic study of Hebrew philology (*Hebräistik*) was formalized at various venues within the context of the modern European university. In the German lands, this program was both a component of and a response to intellectual and religious currents related to the *Aufklärung*. Hebrew study had retained a place at the early modern university largely because of its role as an ancillary discipline to theology. In a period when German university reformers stripped theological faculties of their historic primacy, the survival of Hebrew seemed precarious—all the more so, given the negative trajectory of attitudes toward Judaism in German Protestant theology of the eighteenth and nineteenth centuries.[2] Remarkably, the study of Hebrew at the university did not die out. It flourished. Its flourishing depended upon the prestige it gained from a new academic rigor (*Wissenschaftlichkeit*) and a new cultural rationale. These did not efface the role of *Hebräistik* as a theological propaedeutic; rather, they helped scholars assimilate the

Johann David Michaelis (1717–1791)

study of "sacred languages" to an academic environment oriented holistically toward the study of language, culture, and religion. The most important figure in the establishment of an academic study of Hebrew in this period was Johann David Michaelis.

Michaelis was the leading Orientalist scholar of his generation, but his contributions were not confined to that field. In addition to numerous articles on various points of Near Eastern language and history, Michaelis published influential works on ancient law, theology, and the philosophy of language. Furthermore, his tenures as head of the Academy of Sciences at Göttingen and the important journal *Göttingische gelehrte Anzeigen* solidified his position as a leading figure in the European republic of letters. His writings and letters show contact with the leading lights of his day. He corresponded with Winckelmann and Lessing, disputed with Mendelssohn, and received a backhanded compliment when he was chosen to serve as a rhetorical punching bag in Hamann's withering attacks on biblical criticism. To English scholars like Robert Wood and Robert Lowth, Michaelis was the leading representative of a burgeoning critical German tradition. Michaelis, for his part, became an important mediator of English scholarship to the German-speaking world.[3] Michaelis was a *Macher*, a first-rate intellectual entrepreneur. In 1756, he convinced the king of Denmark to support an expensive (and ill-fated) scientific expedition to southern Arabia, a mission that would be headed by Michaelis's own student, Carsten Niebuhr. To his peers and to the remarkable generation of Goethe, Michaelis was the very embodiment of Orientalist erudition. Though ultimately critical of Michaelis, Herder nevertheless appreciated Michaelis's learning and his important role in opening the ancient Near East to thinkers who were turning increasingly to culture and history to find distinctively German paths into Europe's postconfessional future.[4] Goethe himself confessed that "on men like Heyne and Michaelis rested [his] full confidence; [his] dearest wish was to sit at their feet and experience their teaching."[5] Though a physically small man, Michaelis cultivated a larger-than-life teacherly persona. Like other professors, Michaelis received the honorary title of "knight" (*Ritter*). In what must have seemed like a caricature of Georgia Augusta's aristocratic personality, though, Michaelis used to stride into the lecture hall in full riding attire, complete with boots and spurs, with his Bible under his arm.[6] By all accounts an animated teacher, Michaelis held forth on the Old Testament, employing a mix of jokes, sarcasm, and role-playing. As his reputation grew, students from all over Europe came to his crowded lecture hall. A man to be reckoned with both in the classroom and in the republic of letters, Michaelis did not so much become famous because of his *Hebräistik* as university *Hebräistik* became famous because of Michaelis.

One of the reasons that Michaelis has endured in scholarly memory, then, is that he was better attuned than most to the nature of the university. The son of a Halle professor, and the grandnephew of one of Halle's founding fathers, Michaelis understood the institutional realities of the university and was well suited to bring his discipline into line with them. What Gesner and Heyne did for classics, Michaelis did for the study of Hebrew. The neohumanistic context of the development of a Hebrew philology at Georgia Augusta, however, has received little or no attention in histories of scholarship preoccupied either with a crisis of orthodoxy provoked by rationalism or with the triumphant emergence of an abstract "critical method."[7] Neither perspective, though, adequately explains Michaelis's project on its own terms. Far from being an effort to promote abstractions like "rationalism" or "criticism," Michaelis's recovery of Hebrew was an attempt to move beyond confessional interpretation and to render the Bible relevant as a new but old sort of cultural authority. And for Michaelis and many of his contemporaries, the attempt to understand culture began, above all, with language.

The Unfinished Renaissance

When Michaelis came to Göttingen in 1745 as a twenty-eight-year-old assistant professor of Oriental languages, Gesner had already established himself as one of the university's most influential and articulate leaders. Gesner reached out to Michaelis, who reported that friendship with Gesner was one of the few bright spots in his early years at Georgia Augusta.[8] Their friendship deepened over time, and when Gesner died in 1761, it was Michaelis who offered the public eulogy on behalf of the university.[9] In it Michaelis surveyed Gesner's professional achievements, commended his pedagogical contributions, praised his poetic ability, and reviewed, from the vantage point of a close friend, Gesner's final battle with a painful illness. It reads throughout like the poignant tribute of a knowledgeable admirer.

When Heyne succeeded Gesner as Professor of Poetry and Eloquence in 1763, it was Michaelis, now an established scholar in his own right, who was faced with the task of welcoming a newcomer. Since Michaelis had taken over, in an interim capacity, Gesner's duties as university librarian and head of the Philological Seminar (jobs which would later fall to Heyne), the relationship between the two men was especially important and complex. Intimations of rivalry and even hostility between Michaelis and Heyne have obscured connections between the two men. A closer examination, though, reveals a cordial and cooperative relationship. In his autobiography, Michaelis emphasized that he did not want to continue permanently in either job. He also worked carefully to deflect the charge, given the fact that Michaelis had recommended someone else for Gesner's post, that he had actively opposed Heyne's candidacy.[10] When Michaelis was compelled by the government at Hanover to resign as Director of the Academy of Sciences in 1770, a post of Gesner's which he *did* want to occupy, it was Heyne who was installed in his place. Though this was, by all accounts, a severe blow, it is not clear from this that the proud Michaelis subsequently singled out Heyne for special enmity. It appears rather that the scholars' families, who lived in closely situated houses, remained friendly.[11] There is evidence from the same year that Michaelis and Heyne were conferring on a scholarly project: a German translation of Robert Wood's *Essay on the Original Genius of Homer*.[12] Finally, it was Heyne who offered a warm, laudatory eulogy for Michaelis to the Academy of Sciences when he died in 1791.

Thus Michaelis's career, which straddled the tenures of Gesner and Heyne and was intertwined with them, fits squarely in the middle of a period of momentous change associated with both classical scholars. Without attempting to delineate overly specific lines of influence, I take this fact as highly suggestive. Shared affinities among the three men, though obscured by disciplinary boundaries, illuminates the development and direction of an underlying philological method. In the case of Gesner and Michaelis, something like direct influence of the former on the latter is demonstrable, as will be clear. In the case of Heyne and Michaelis, it is Heyne who bears witness to the fact that Michaelis drew directly and successfully on methodological developments in classical studies, developments which were shaped for much of Michaelis's working life by Heyne himself. This testimony comes in Heyne's eulogy for Michaelis. After describing the state of both classics and biblical studies at the beginning of Michaelis's career as stringently grammatical, philosophically imprecise, and diffuse, Heyne credits Michaelis with reforming the study of Hebrew literature along Gesnerian lines:

> And therefore because Gesner and Ernesti were acknowledged with success and acclaim in profane literature, Michaelis, kindled by their brilliant examples, presently resolved to transfer and apply the same [methods] to the study of Hebrew literature and authors. However, he brought to his studies some things that were lacking in his equals, very renowned men; for if in full and accurate knowledge of Roman and Greek doctrines he yielded to Ernesti and Gesner, he surpassed them in a proper understanding of how histories pertain to life and affairs.[13]

Heyne's testimony indicates that Michaelis was well apprised of currents in classical philology and eager to show their relevance to biblical studies. Not only did Michaelis learn from earlier classicists, he surpassed them.

Heyne characterized Michaelis as a disciplinary pioneer, one who skillfully appropriated methods from classics. Johann August Ernesti (1707–1781), Gesner's colleague at the Thomasschule and later professor at Leipzig, drew on classical philology to formulate rules for grammatico-historical exegesis of the New Testament. The Dutch scholar Albert Schultens (1686–1750) was a strong advocate for comparative Semitic philology, especially of Hebrew and Arabic, and an opponent of "metaphysical" approaches to the study of Hebrew. Michaelis, following their example, became, in Heyne's judgment, the standard-bearer for a new kind of inquiry. Like Ernesti and Schultens, Michaelis placed philology at the center of biblical interpretation. However, Michaelis surpassed his predecessors in widening the scope of comparative philology, refining its methods, and placing biblical studies on a new academic course.[14] This course, moreover, bears important similarities to the one marked out by Heyne himself, as the two university men who inherited a vibrant neohumanist tradition sought to make the study of antiquity an attractive and socially relevant enterprise.

In invoking Heyne's testimony, I do not want to suggest that Michaelis was the first Hebraist to borrow models from the study of Greek and Latin literature. In this connection, one may point to Johannes Buxtorf (1564–1629) of Basel. As Stephen

Burnett has pointed out in his thorough study of Buxtorf's scholarship, Buxtorf was a "pedagogue who followed the example of Latin and Greek teachers on liberal arts faculties." In setting Hebrew language and Jewish learning on a new foundation, Buxtorf aimed at making biblical and rabbinic literature accessible to humanists "in much the same way that Greek and Latin teachers pressed classical literature into the service of Christian education."[15] This is not surprising, given the fact that the formal foundations for classical learning such as printed texts, patronage systems for scholars, and organized collections were already in place by Buxtorf's time. It would have been natural for sixteenth- and seventeenth-century Hebraists to organize themselves and their work in ways that resembled those of their better-established counterparts.

Yet, unlike Buxtorf, Michaelis and company distanced themselves from confessionally oriented Hebrew studies and aimed instead at a broadly cultural recovery of the past. If Heyne aimed to be a "full humanist" for whom classical antiquity was the "center out of which everything flowed and to which he brought everything back,"[16] then Michaelis, his Orientalist counterpart at Göttingen, was a humanist centered on ancient Near Eastern antiquity. Greek and Latin scholars may have initiated the first recovery of the sciences (*Auferstehung der Wissenschaften*), but the restoration, according to Michaelis, was not yet complete:

> The other half is still lacking: and if the writings of the Orient that are available in Syriac and Arabic were to become known, or even just those writings among them that concern the things in natural science and history that are more relevant to us, there would have to be a new recovery of the sciences. A hopeful view, which will please not only theologians and philologists, but all scholars, provided they do not measure knowledge according to bread.[17]

Here the third culture, identified with the civilizations of Hebrew's sister languages, is the basis for the final part of an unfinished Renaissance. At stake in a proper understanding of Hebrew is not, above all, a correct knowledge of the Bible, but rather, on this view, a valuable opportunity to enrich European intellectual culture.

The Deadness of the Hebrew Language

When Michaelis took up formal Hebrew studies as a university student at Halle, he did so, by his own admission, without any genuine enthusiasm for the subject.[18] His father, Christian Benedict Michaelis (1680–1764), taught Hebrew at Halle, and his granduncle Johann Heinrich Michaelis (1668–1738) was a key figure in Halle's founding generation. A close associate of Francke, J. H. Michaelis was a Pietist who, like Francke, was deeply committed to biblical philology and the study of Hebrew. One example of the connection between Pietist conviction and careful philology comes from J. H. Michaelis's 1720 treatise on the accents preserved in the (Masoretic) Hebrew Bible, *Gründlicher Unterricht von den Accentibus prosaicis u. metricis oder Hebräischen Distinctionibus der Heil. Schrift A.T.* The work was designed as a student-friendly guide to the Hebrew accents that would also show how careful philological study leads one more deeply into the meaning of the text. The basic premise of the work is that the various accents can be divided into two categories: conjunctive accents, which join words, and disjunctive accents, which set them apart from one another. In Gen 1:1, there is a disjunctive accent on the last syllable of the first word (בראשית)[19] which stops the reader and forces him to ponder the nature of the beginning: how, out of the "unsearchable depths of His eternity," God revealed Himself and His "wisdom and goodness" toward creatures. On the second word (ברא "he created"), there is a conjunctive accent that joins it to the third word (אלהים; "God"). According to J. H. Michaelis, the conjunctive accent joins the two words and prompts the reader to understand that this verb is the special activity of God and God alone, forcing questioners to content themselves with this revelation and to "rest with us in the omnipotence and wisdom of God." But there is also an unexpected disjunctive accent (*atnah*) on the third word, which forcefully marks off the phrase containing the second and third words from the words that follow. In this case, the second word of the phrase is a singular verb (ברא "[he] created") and the third word is a plural noun (though it functions semantically and syntactically as a proper, singular noun most of the time אלהים is morphologically plural). Thus, the disjunctive accent emphasizes the *plural* character of the *one* divine being. In short, it foreshadows the doctrine of the Trinity.[20]

Christian Benedict Michaelis also worked in the Pietist-philological vein. Though not as well published as J. H. Michaelis or his son, Johann David, Christian Benedict was an effective teacher at Halle, supervising scores of Hebrew dissertations and furthering his uncle's work on accents. Largely because of J. H. and C. B. Michaelis, Halle became a vital center for Hebrew scholarship. The "Halle School" was further distinguished by the innovative use of cognate languages, especially Arabic and Syriac, to clarify Hebrew grammar, morphology, and syntax.[21] As a student at Halle, Johann David studied several cognate languages, gaining exposure to the works of the great Ethiopic scholar Hiob Ludolf and, for Arabic, Schultens. After initial hesitation, Johann David decided, finally, to join his father and become a scholar of Hebrew and Old Testament. It is not surprising that Michaelis, who had inherited a vibrant scholarly tradition, denied that he was in any sense a pioneer in Hebrew studies. In addition to innumerable smaller studies, Michaelis published two larger works on the Hebrew language: *Hebräische Grammatik* (1745) and *Beurtheilung der Mittel, welche man anwendet, die ausgestorbene Hebräische Sprache zu verstehen* (Judgment of the means by which to understand the dead Hebrew language; 1757).²² These two works will form the basis for this chapter.

In the prefaces to both of these works, Michaelis disclaimed originality. He acknowledged influential predecessors like Schultens, who helped him to "use Arabic to discover what is hidden in the dead Hebrew language," as well as his own father.²³ Pointing to the abundance of Hebrew grammars already available, Michaelis justified the writing of his own by a desire to have a "convenient guide" to use in university teaching, one which reflected his own judgments and pedagogical style. The main shortcoming of existing grammars, according to Michaelis, was a disorganized or illogical presentation, not a gross deficiency in understanding.²⁴ Michaelis's substantive changes were modest, amounting to discrete, relatively brief discussions of "new" topics: Masoretic markings, Qere and Kethib, short and long vowels, and the method of finding root meanings.²⁵ The grammar's most significant innovation, according to Michaelis, was its presentation of the "indispensable theory of nominal forms" developed by Matthaeus Hiller (1646–1725) and Johann Simonis (1698–1768).²⁶ Finally, Michaelis again denied originality in the preface to his *Beurtheilung*, the work in which he offered the most comprehensive version of his program for Hebrew study:

> No one who is occupied with Near Eastern languages can properly be unaware of what is stated here [i.e., in this entire treatise]: if it seems strange to some, though, I gladly renounce any claim to originality. Others have shown us the way that I too am commending. Yet the way only became obscure because there were very many teachers of Hebrew whose reputations and followings might have suffered if the right method of study, long demonstrated by the greatest Christians and Jews, were to become known.²⁷

A polemical interest is discernible in this quotation, as Michaelis alludes to unnamed scholars who, like linguistic charlatans, cynically staked their livelihoods on novel theories about the Hebrew language. Roughly the first quarter of the *Beurtheilung* is devoted to criticisms of rival systems of Hebrew study, and these, in turn, shed further light on Michaelis's contexts and aims.

Yet it is appropriate to begin with Michaelis's own key assumptions. Many of them can be discerned in a telling passage that contains the opening lines of Section 1 of the *Beurtheilung*. It deserves to be quoted at length:

> It is *the* important question, worthy of serious, impartial investigation: is it possible for us at present to understand the Hebrew language reliably? Are we able to determine the meanings of its words and expressions with that high degree of probability which philologists tend to call "certainty"?

> The language died out roughly two thousand years ago, and we have nothing more of it from the period in which it was alive than a single book, or, actually, a very modest collection of books, namely the Hebrew Bible. Is it possible from this alone to learn a language with certainty? ... How many words [in the Hebrew Bible] occur but once? How few are so fortunately situated that one can, with certainty, learn their meaning from the context?[28]

This important passage reflects two key assumptions. First, Michaelis assumed that Hebrew was a dead language and that it had been that way since before the Common Era. To emphasize "deadness" in this way was to deny that Hebrew was a vital linguistic medium for any living community. And when Michaelis dated its death to "roughly two thousand years ago," he created a separation between ancient Hebrew and the religion of Judaism. It was Israelite and not Jewish Hebrew that counted. Whatever Hebrew remained in use from the late Second Temple period to the present, according to Michaelis, was no Hebrew at all. Michaelis called Rabbinic Hebrew a "Euro-Hebrew" that was enriched by Aramaic and Arabic loanwords. He contended, above all, that it was a medieval scholarly language and never, like a living language, "imbibed with mother's milk." It remained a written language, subject to scholarly neologisms and caprices, which never entered into common life and was thus never learned "perfectly and readily." It was "more than a thousand years removed" from the time when Hebrew was both a common and learned language and was thus only a degraded language: "What a decline from the old and what a swarm of new meanings!"[29] Second, what remains of biblical Hebrew is only a modest, problematically small collection of texts. In order to reconstruct a dead language, one must have a large enough corpus with which to work. In the case of biblical Hebrew, the corpus is a corpse, and a partial one at that. For Michaelis, the most significant indication of its inadequate size is the formidable number of *hapax legomena*, or words that occur once in the Hebrew Bible. Since only a "few" are "fortunately situated" so as to be clear from context, it is necessary to enlarge the corpus, to extend artificially the field of data by consulting cognate languages.

The *Beurtheilung* bears further witness to Michaelis's program and its context. This is clear in the early sections, where Michaelis addressed his opponents. The first group that he addressed was the Jews. In the sixteenth century, Christians had to learn Hebrew from Jews, but instead of revering them simply as "first teachers" Christians lent them more credibility than they deserved, making Jewish teaching a *principium cognoscendi* in the study of Hebrew. Despite acknowledging the valuable contributions of medieval Hebrew grammars, in which Michaelis found "much that is good and true," he did not judge Jewish teachings differently than he did the work of Christian scholars.[30] Michaelis argued further that the advantages which Jews were supposed to have had in the study of Hebrew amounted to very little. Hebrew was not, as some have thought, a "mother language" for them, as their Hebrew was tainted with European languages and subject to changes occurring under successive periods of foreign imperial rule and rootless wandering. More significantly, the Jews did not possess the *spirit* of the ancient Israelites:

> This people [i.e. the Jews], whose learning, untouched by the pleasant Muses, was scholastic to the highest degree, and who are now distant from the beautiful sciences, have not, for hundreds of years, felt the impulses of that spirit which inspired the poets of old. They are distant from the golden age of the Hebrew language which yielded the songs of Moses, the poignant laments of Job and Jeremiah, the psalms of David, and the poetry of the prophets.[31]

Here Michaelis also introduced what became an important element in his program of study: the periodization of Israelite and Jewish history. A separation between the pre-exilic and subsequent periods, especially the modern Jewish one, allowed Michaelis to dispense with the latter. In suggesting that modern Jews were aesthetically impoverished and centuries removed from a poetic tradition they no longer bore, Michaelis denied both that Jews had an advantage in Hebrew study and that their work was indispensable to it. Instead, the state of Jewish learning, according to Michaelis, was characterized by internal contradictions, guesswork, and appeals to oral tradition that do not count as legitimate proof in linguistic argument. Though he acknowledged that Jewish tradition has preserved the correct meanings of a number of ancient Hebrew words, he points to woefully imprecise botanical knowledge to prove that much had been lost.[32] Thus Jewish learning deserved no special authority, and students of Hebrew should, as with any other source, consult it discriminately.

The most common method of Hebrew study in Michaelis's day was what he called the Bohl-Gousset system, after its founders and chief representatives Samuel Bohl (1611–1639), onetime professor of theology at Rostock, and French scholar Jacques Gousset (1635–1704). By this method, one gathered all occurrences of a Hebrew word in which the meaning of the word was clear. From this, one posited a generalized "first meaning" (*erste Bedeutung*) and used this as a basis for determining its particular meanings in specific cases, with context being the chief aid in this task. Michaelis, referring to lexicons which sometimes contained a bewildering array of meanings for a single word, described Bohl's system as an understandable response to this poor state of affairs.[33] Yet the method is deficient because "first meanings" are not general and abstract, as Bohl thought, but rather, Michaelis asserted, "simple and external." The real proof of its inadequacy, though, was in its practical inferiority to

Michaelis's comparative Semitic approach. For example, Michaelis indicated that the Hebrew root נחם had a variety of apparently incompatible meanings: "to be vengeful," "to regret," and "to comfort." Faced with this, Bohl posited a broad meaning: "to change one's idea." Michaelis, though, asked why this word would be associated with these changes of mind and not others. What communicative value could such an abstract idea have had for early speakers? The confusion is dispelled, though, when one realizes that the single root נחם is the equivalent of two Arabic words, *nahhima* and *nachhama*, which shows that the Hebrew word is of two origins and thus has two *separate* meanings: "to breathe forcefully or deeply" (*nahhima*) and "to play, thus cheer up or comfort" (*nachhama*).[34]

Gousset, in adapting Bohl's system, made a virtue out of ignorance, for he justified a willful rejection of cognates on theological grounds, claiming loftily that the Hebrew language "is a sun that needs no foreign light."[35] In doing so, Gousset narrowed the study of Hebrew even more than Bohl had, for he did not even allow the positing of first meanings that were not attested in the Bible itself. Thus Hebrew was, for Gousset, a language to be "deciphered" with only the aid of its own internal resources, as all first and secondary meanings were said to be discoverable within the biblical text.

Against Gousset and Bohl, Michaelis argued that proper nouns alone attest a "wealth of unused Hebrew root-words," which suggests that the Hebrew language is much richer than expected. Moreover, the idea of *deciphering* a language of modest size, let alone one that is potentially very rich, is mathematically impossible.[36] Most devastating, though, was a series of empirical observations concerning the general behaviors of languages. Some words that are common in one language will be rare in another. A language may also lack a word for a certain thing or use a foreign word to signify it. Languages may have structural differences (e.g., Latin lacks definite articles where German has them). Languages may also have a preponderance of synonyms or of words with several meanings. Individual writers are distinguishable, manifesting peculiarities of making characteristic errors. All of these factors render the prospect of *deciphering* any foreign language, armed merely with knowledge of one's own language, absurd. Finally, Michaelis asked with reference to a perpetual object of concern: how can this method yield the meanings of the numerous names for trees and plants in the Bible?[37]

Another rival system, dubbed the "hieroglyphic," was connected by Michaelis to pastor Friedrich Christian Koch (1718–1784), Caspar Neumann (1648–1715), and a certain Professor Engström.[38] It begins with the assumption that each letter of the Hebrew alphabet has a specific meaning and that the definitions of words are constructed from the *meanings* of the letters. The example that Michaelis gives is אב or "father." א, in such a system, stands for "activity" because it is the "soul of letters," and ב suggests the image of a cube or three dimensions. These two come together to signify "father" in the following way: "activity" and "cube" recall a "space, out of which an inner impulse is spread." This image is identified with love, "for when love surges and seethes in the heart, one cannot avoid noticing it: by this love is a father known."[39] Michaelis identified several assumptions that contributed to the plausibility of the system: cabbalistic affinity for finding symbols in scripture; "Jewish" belief in the special character of Hebrew as a divine language that expresses "the essence of things"; and the notion that Hebrew is a changeless language that is also the oldest in the world. This led all too easily, for Michaelis, to the superstitious idea that Hebrew was not an ordinary human language but rather one that expressed mysteries and profundities in its very letters.

If there was one idea associated with the "hieroglyphic" system that Michaelis found most troubling, it was the idea that Hebrew was an exceptional language subject to its own rules and methods of inquiry. This sort of exceptionalism, in his view, harmed theology by reducing the study of Hebrew to metaphysics, mystery-mongering, and superstition.[40] A close examination of the Hebrew language shows that it has features common to all languages. In this connection, Michaelis cited the existence of archaisms and defunct verbal forms (for example, the older form of the Qal perfect second person feminine singular קטלתי shortened to קטלת). Once exceptionalism is abandoned, the empirical difficulties of the hieroglyphic system become clear: no real human language could develop in a way that would allow an inquiry based on symbolic letters to be of any use. Because languages are spoken before they are written, and as children's acquisition of language teaches us, syllables and not letters come first in linguistic development. It makes no sense to proceed as though the meanings of words were determined by letters.[41] Far from being a changeless, primeval, and hieroglyphic language, Hebrew is a language like any other, bound to time and place and subject to ordinary vicissitudes.

For this reason, Michaelis supported the use of other languages to improve knowledge of Hebrew. Yet, as he reported, not all languages are equally useful in this regard. Many of this contemporaries proceeded on the assumption that Hebrew was the oldest human language; as a result they clarified obscure words by comparing them to similar sounding words in European languages, for example German *Schilde* ("shields") for שלטי (šilṭê) instead of *Wurfspieße* ("javelins"). Given the extreme diversity in the grammatical structure and sounds of words in existing languages, it would "require the greatest amount of etymological patience to derive them from a single language."[42] This scheme also invites haphazard comparison, gross speculation, and superficial examination. Comparisons must instead be informed by historical, geographical, and structural-linguistic factors. Michaelis discussed favorably the attempt of theologian Hermann von der Hardt (1660–1746) to derive Hebrew from Greek, or rather an early ancestor, "Scythian," thought to be prevalent in the eastern Mediterranean. Ultimately, though, Michaelis dismissed the attempt on historical grounds: the climate and location of Scythia were too harsh to allow that the Scythians would have written epics or chronicles older than those in the Bible.[43] More plausible, though still unsatisfactory, were attempts to clarify Hebrew by recourse to other Oriental languages such as Armenian, Persian, and Egyptian. But despite the fact that there are, for example, Persian loanwords in the Bible, the structures of the languages were too dissimilar.

In Michaelis's view, the most important resource for understanding Hebrew was the use of cognate languages from the ancient Near East: "the still living Arabic language clearly belongs to this group, then the two dead languages for which we have many writings, Syriac and Aramaic, and then those for which we have less, Ethiopic, Samaritan, and finally Talmudic—but not Rabbinic."[44] Along with other languages discovered after Michaelis's time (Ugaritic, Akkadian, Moabite, etc.), the group identified here still represents the languages that comprise modern comparative Semitic philology. For Michaelis, Arabic was preeminent because it was the only language "still living." Unlike Schultens, though, Michaelis consulted other Semitic languages as well in his lexicographic and exegetical work. To explain the value of consulting these languages in the study of Hebrew, Michaelis compared his method to the attempt of a scholar to understand Gothic by drawing on Danish and Icelandic, or of a German speaker who finds he can communicate with people from Switzerland, Bavaria, and Swabia once he accounts for differences in pronunciation and inflection. Michaelis went as far as to deny that Arabic, Syriac, and the rest were separate languages at all. Rather, he referred to them as "dialects."

That Michaelis overestimated the relatedness of these languages is clear.[45] Yet this judgment raises an important question: *why* did he overestimate their closeness? Ignorance is not a sufficient explanation. Michaelis was an accomplished linguist who wrote grammars and published chrestomathies in Arabic, Syriac, and Hebrew, in addition to countless specialized studies. He was aware of evidence in favor of and against his position.[46] Michaelis was not simply defending a traditional or inherited position. Though Schultens and his teachers at Halle also advocated the use of Semitic cognates, Michaelis never hesitated to express disagreement with their work. He cherished his independence. Michaelis drew on his background and influences to advance a theoretical framework that was not self-evident to his contemporaries. Michaelis emphasized the closeness of Arabic to Hebrew because Arabic was a living language with a large literary corpus. As he put it, "the dead Hebrew language lives on in its relative Arabic." Michaelis, then, located Hebrew in a family of languages, as a "daughter" of "Canaanite" and as a "sister" of Syriac, Aramaic, and Arabic. This genealogical maneuver allowed him to overcome the paucity of extant biblical Hebrew and the troubling effects of *hapax legomena*. It also allowed him to experience Hebrew as a living language through its sister Arabic, while ignoring Jews, the most obvious living speakers of Hebrew.

The task of the Hebraist was not merely to understand Hebrew grammar, vocabulary, and syntax and to produce intelligible translations (though these were necessary) but rather to regain a sense of the full vitality and expressive power of biblical language, to come to know it as the actual language of a fully functioning society. Much was at stake in a historically minded recovery of language. In 1759, Michaelis wrote for the Royal Academy of Sciences at Berlin a prizewinning essay on an assigned topic: the influence of language on opinions and of opinions on language.[47] In it Michaelis articulated an underlying philosophy of language which takes as its starting point the fundamental arbitrariness of words. As Michaelis put it, "their laws are democratic: use is decided by the majority, and what is used becomes, as Horace has said, correct and standard."[48] In this way, notions common to a group are embedded in language and exercise an undetected influence on speakers. Words become a repository of cultural information. Etymologies are "a treasury of sound reason, of sayings that escape even philosophers," even as languages as a whole become "a collection of the wisdom and genius of whole nations, to which each individual has made a contribution."[49] The philologist, then, gains access not only to a group's texts but also to the ethos, the mind-set, and the collective wisdom of the culture. He encounters its history and its *Geist*.

Propaedeutic work was aimed at removing barriers to this understanding. The ideal was to approximate the fluency of biblical authors for whom Hebrew was a "mother language." To understand Hebrew in this way was to do so with naturalness, immediacy, and sensitivity to special vocabulary (especially botanical), idioms, and rare meanings of common words.[50] This, of course, was not possible for the modern scholar. Yet it was useful to keep this in view as a goal, an indication of what is required to understand a language fully and in ways that an ancient audience might have understood it. This sense was expressed throughout Michaelis's work both as a preoccupation with "mother language" and, failing this, a serious attempt at "thoroughness" (*Gründlichkeit*) and "certainty" (*Gewißheit*). Thoroughness and certainty, then, were scholarly surrogates for the higher ideal of natural, native ability. By striving to understand Hebrew as a living language and not as a sacred, inert linguistic code, Michaelis opened the way for a naturalistic mode of inquiry amenable to scientific investigation.

This mode of inquiry included "philosophical" principles, which Michaelis emphasized in the Appendix to *Hebräische Grammatik*. The Appendix bears the title "Appendix, consisting of an attempt to determine what a thorough knowledge of Hebrew grammar requires" (*Anhang. Bestehend, in einem Versuch, dasjenige zu bestimmen, was zu gründlicher Erkenntniß der Hebräischen Grammatik erfodert werde*). It is a brief treatise of fifty-three pages that moves briskly through a straightforward argument. Michaelis argued that the grammarian must reckon above all with a single feature of human language: mutability. Hebrew owes its forms to a long process of change, and the grammarian must not only recognize the meanings of various forms, he must also understand in a systematic way the changes which produced them: "I understand grammar to be nothing other than a system of rules according to which changes in the language take place."⁵¹ Despite the fact that there is an unlimited number of *possible* changes that a language can undergo, the changes that one observes are, for the most part, regular, such that one can recognize patterns, posit the existence of "common principles," and bring these together systematically in order to create a grammar.⁵² Michaelis qualified this procedure in an important way: in order for it to be properly thorough, the grammarian must "be in a position to prove that [the rules he has observed] are actually customary changes in *our* language."⁵³ Here Michaelis rejected exceptionalism. In order to understand Hebrew, one must know it as an ordinary language in terms of present-day experience, common sense, and universal human concepts (*die allgemeine Denckungs-Art der Menschen*).⁵⁴

No instance of linguistic change, however, is *necessary*. Therefore, grammatical rules cannot be predicted or reasoned deductively from first principles. They must be observed in the biblical text, "the only book that remains to us from the period in which Hebrew was alive."⁵⁵ This did not mean, however, that the grammarian should consult only the biblical materials. The paucity of linguistic data in the Bible, as we have seen, was axiomatic for Michaelis; thus it was necessary to draw on cognate languages, especially Aramaic, Syriac, Ethiopic, and Arabic, to develop more reliable grammatical rules. Recourse to these languages, which are closely related to Hebrew, allows the grammarian to discern rules not fully evident in the Bible: "Many rules that are difficult to discern in the Hebrew Bible occur in these languages clearly and more frequently."⁵⁶ The final step was to examine putative rules gathered from the Bible and cognate languages in the light of "philosophical grammar." By philosophical grammar, Michaelis meant a "science of possible linguistic changes." This amounted to an inherently probabilistic system of rules that acknowledged physiological factors and, in Wolffian fashion, the law of noncontradiction and the principle of sufficient reason.⁵⁷

Two examples illustrate the use of philosophical grammar and cognate languages in clarifying features of the Hebrew language. The form ילדתיך (*yəlīdtīkā* "I have begotten you") in Ps 2:7 is difficult; the expected form, with an a-vowel (*patah*) and not an i-vowel (*hireq*) under the *lamedh*, is *yəladtīkā*. Michaelis points out that many commentators, noting the unusual pointing in a crucial line of a messianic psalm, understood the unexpected vowel to be an indication that "supernatural," as opposed to ordinary, human procreation is in view in the psalm. To which Michaelis replies: "one can hardly grasp what the replacement of A with I has to do with supernatural procreation." Citing the same unexpected I-vowel in suffixed forms of ילד elsewhere in the Hebrew Bible (Jer 2:27 and Num 11:12), Michaelis invoked a physiological factor: the higher position of the tongue required for the pronunciation of *lamedh* and *daleth* influenced the articulation of the vowel. Since the position of the tongue is higher when pronouncing the I-vowel than when pronouncing the A-vowel, the I-vowel replaced the A-vowel in suffixed perfect forms.[58] Many elements of Michaelis's method are clear in this example. He identified an instance of linguistic change and explained it in a way that accords with present-day linguistic experience. The rule he posited is not only possible but universalizable; that is, it was meant to apply to all instances of the same change in like circumstances. Finally, by invoking physiological factors, the explanation is also a positive example of the constraints that "philosophical grammar" can place on rule-making.

A second example illustrates how cognate languages can also inform the rule-making procedure. It begins once again with an unexpected letter: the preformative *he* in the Niphal infinitive (הִקָּטֵל *hiqqātēl*). Why not rather a preformative *nun*? Michaelis noted, first of all, a regular correspondence between Arabic and Hebrew: where there is a preformative *he* in the Hebrew C-stem (Hiphil), there is an *aleph* in the Arabic C-stem. Given an original Arabic N-stem infinitive *nəqātālā, Michaelis suggested that this form was difficult to pronounce and that a prosthetic *alif* was added to the beginning to yield *'inqātālā*. The Hebrew form, then, was the product of a similar change. An original but awkward *nəqātēl received a prosthetic *he* and became *hinqātēl, just as the Arabic form received a prosthetic *alif* and became *'inqātālā*. But in Hebrew, the assimilation of *nun* before a consonant is a regular change; thus, *hinqātēl became *hiqqātēl*.[59] In this example, Michaelis drew on what he perceived to be a similar change in a cognate language. He posited a rule for this change (a prosthetic syllable is prefixed to a word that begins with two consonants joined by a shewa), which he then applied to the Hebrew form with appropriate modifications (use of *he* instead of *aleph*; assimilation of the *nun*). Though the data used to support the rule were drawn in this case from Arabic and Hebrew, the rule meets the same standard of sufficient reason, regularity, and observability.

In approaching Hebrew above all as a dead, ancient, and poorly attested language, Michaelis sought to overcome gaps in linguistic knowledge that result from these characteristics. In doing so, he rejected rival attempts to understand Hebrew as a language that was exceptional either for its sacred or hieroglyphic qualities or for its ability to survive conquest and captivity via (Jewish) tradition. By dividing sharply between pre-exilic Israel, when the Hebrew language flourished, and subsequent periods, when it declined and finally died, Michaelis isolated the Hebrew literature of a distinct period and made it the object of his recovery efforts. But he insisted that the language of this period be understood in a lively and realistic way, as the vehicle of expression for a robust civilization of shepherds, poets, warriors, and kings. To achieve this, the modern scholar must attain a certainty and thoroughness in language study that comes from an understanding of philosophical grammar and a mastery of Hebrew's cognate languages. The final and most important step, though, was to encounter the Israelites anew in related civilizations, to transform one's understanding by seeing precisely how the Hebrew language, despite succumbing long ago to the fortunes of time and history, yet lived on in her Semitic sisters.

Judaism and the Classicization of Hebrew Antiquity

It was not only the Arabic language that interested Michaelis but also the way of life of the Arabs themselves. Arabic studies helped him to approach more closely the ideal of knowing Hebrew as a "mother language" while providing, at the same time, imaginative access to ancient Israelite society. Michaelis regarded Arab culture as primitive and essentially unchanged from ancient times. It thus shed valuable light on the closely related culture of the Israelites:

> Had we not some knowledge of Arabian manners, we should very seldom be able to illustrate the laws of Moses, by reference to the law of usage. But among a race of people, living separate from other nations, and who have rarely been subjected to a foreign yoke, ancient manners have maintained themselves so perfectly, that, in reading the description of a wandering Arab, one might easily suppose one's-self in Abraham's tent.[60]

Michaelis shared with his mentor Albert Schultens the belief that the peoples of the Arabian Peninsula, inhabitants of *Arabia felix*, preserved an ancient and traditional way of life because they were never successfully incorporated into the Persian, Greek, or Roman empires. Untouched either by war, imperial conquest, or trade, Arabian nomads endured as living relics out of their own forgotten past, a past shared by the pre-exilic Israelites. The systematic effort to interpret the Hebrew Bible ethnographically, in terms of present-day Arab language and culture, then, was one of the most distinctive features of Michaelis's program for Hebrew study and biblical interpretation. He is rightly seen as an innovator in this regard. Michaelis incorporated information from Near Eastern travel literature into his exegetical work, even translating and editing in 1776 the historical and geographical writings of the medieval Muslim writer Abulfeda (Abu al-Fida, 1273–1331). Michaelis is best known for the influential comparative six-volume work *Mosaisches Recht* (1770–1775), which shed light on biblical laws by comparing them, among other things, to Bedouin customs. Convinced of the importance of ethnography, Michaelis convinced the Danish foreign minister, Count Bernstorff, to secure royal support for a scientific expedition to Arabia, which would shed light on biblical antiquities and Near Eastern languages.[61] A state-supported scholarly enterprise, the foreign expedition was the first of its kind. It was a highly publicized (and ill-fated) venture that earned Michaelis wide renown, bolstering his reputation as Europe's leading Orientalist and exemplifying the shift of biblical studies from exegetical theology into what Sheehan has aptly called a Near Eastern "philology of things."[62]

In emphasizing the importance of ethnography and Near Eastern antiquities for the study of the Bible, Michaelis moved decisively away from what had been for centuries an obvious and important resource in biblical interpretation: Jews and Jewish literature. Christians had been learning Hebrew from Jewish teachers since the Middle Ages. What was a fairly obscure branch of learning associated with notables like Nicholas of Lyra or with the Spanish conversos, though, gave rise to a veritable Hebraic republic of letters throughout Europe in the decades after the Reformation. In the sixteenth and seventeenth centuries, confessional disputes and theological polemics enlarged Christian appetites for Jewish learning, as Lutheran, Catholic, Reformed, and freethinking interpreters ransacked Hebrew philology, Talmudic tracts, and kabbalistic texts for ammunition in their attacks on one another. The uses and abuses of Jewish learning among these so-called Christian Hebraists were manifold.[63] Even though Christian attitudes toward Judaism varied widely, however, the triumph of humanism and philology assured that Judaism and Jewish learning would remain, in one way or another, relevant. This situation lasted well into the eighteenth century, as even Michaelis's native Halle suggests. For at Halle, the center for Orientalist scholarship, Francke's *Collegium orientale theologicum*, existed side by side with the *Institutum Judaicum*, a center for outreach to Jews that incorporated knowledge of Judaism into missionizing efforts.[64] It is striking, then, that Michaelis, who became the most eminent Orientalist and biblical commentator of his generation, flatly denied the relevance of Jewish learning to a *historical* or *philological* understanding of the Old Testament.

As we have seen, Michaelis took pains in his programmatic writings to marginalize Jewish scholarship, discredit rabbinic exegesis, and sever any connection between the language of the Old Testament and the degraded "Euro-Hebrew" of contemporary Jews. Frank Manuel has discerned in this effort a Protestant disparagement of tradition, a German Lutheran desire to recover "the true Mosaic law, scraped of the encrustations of the benighted rabbis."[65] Pulled from the wreckage of Jewish interpretation, the "true Mosaic law," when compared favorably with Israel's ancient barbaric neighbors, shone forth in Michaelis's writings as a rational, humane, and progressive achievement. In this way, Michaelis defended the prestige of the Bible against its cultured despisers by divorcing it from a benighted Judaism and explicating its uniqueness in historical and cultural terms. One consequence of this "brazen reappraisal," however, was a denigration of the *religious* value of the Old Testament and thus of Judaism.[66] In an important treatment of Michaelis's scholarship, Jonathan Hess has argued along similar lines that Michaelis used an ethnographic approach to the Bible to isolate the Jews from their biblical forebears:

> [Michaelis] presents contemporary Jews as a dispersed group that fundamentally lacks a sense of its own history. Bound together only by a far-reaching network of Rabbinic perversions of Mosaic law, contemporary Jews are neither authentically Oriental nor truly European, neither trustworthy remnants of ancient Judaism nor connected to the modern world.[67]

In identifying the ancient Israelites with the Arabs and not with Jews, Michaelis, as Hess points out, also created separation between contemporary Jews and "true Europeans." In this arrangement, the common ground that Jews and Christians shared for centuries, namely the Old Testament, effectively disappeared: it no longer belonged to Jews and, as a partial remnant of an extinct culture, it had no spiritual authority over Christians. Cutting them off from their biblical past and their Christian contemporaries, Michaelis stranded the Jews.

This maneuver was not politically innocent. As Hess has shown, Michaelis's ethnography provided scholarly reinforcement to anti-Jewish attitudes and ideas. In 1781, Christian Wilhelm Dohm (1751–1820) published a short but ambitious treatise entitled *On the Civic Improvement of the Jews*. In it, Dohm argued that it was in Prussia's best interests to grant citizenship to the Jews, a small and poor segment of society, and to integrate them fully into society. The little book created a sensation.[68] Michaelis opposed Dohm's proposals, writing an extensive review and publishing it in his own influential journal, *Orientalische und Exegetische Bibliothek*. Though Michaelis was highly critical of Dohm, Dohm was pleased to have a review from an eminent scholar. He paid Michaelis the compliment of publishing the review in its entirety in subsequent editions of the treatise. Michaelis thus became a key figure in the long, consequential debate begun by Dohm. Michaelis and Dohm agreed that contemporary Jews had fallen into a poor and degraded condition, bereft of learning, sound morality, and social utility. Dohm believed that this was a result of centuries of oppression and poor living conditions in countries throughout Europe and that, under better conditions, the Jews could be remediated. Michaelis denied that Jews could ever be fully integrated into society, citing a number of factors, including the Jews' dishonesty (Jews, he noted, made up a disproportionately high number of convicted criminals) and disloyalty (their ultimate desire is for a homeland of their own in Palestine, not equal status in a European nation). Above all, Michaelis feared that assimilation and inclusion of the Jews would weaken the military and economic power of the state. Jews could not become reliable soldiers because Sabbath and dietary laws would hinder full participation in fighting and training. He also believed that the physical and racial profile of Jews made them ill suited for war. Among Jews, few, he wrote, are "well-developed men."[69] Instead of incorporating Jews into society, German governments would be better off, Michaelis argued, creating a colony on an island with a southerly climate where Jews could produce a useful crop like sugar. With his "vision of sugar island Jews," Hess argues, "Michaelis articulates a racial antisemitism that marks the ultimate embodiment of German Orientalist fantasies of both intellectual hegemony *and* colonialist power."[70]

It is not surprising, then, that Michaelis has garnered attention as a purveyor of anti-Jewish attitudes and an anti-Semitic scholar. Anna-Ruth Löwenbrück, for example, has produced a thorough study of Michaelis's role in the history of modern anti-Semitism.[71] According to Löwenbrück, Michaelis broke new ground when, in his review of Dohm, he deliberately avoided theological arguments against the Jews. The issue for Michaelis was not the relation between "Jews and Christians," as it had been framed for centuries, but rather the relation between "Jews and *Germans*."[72] Michaelis did not enter the debate over the status of the Jews as a theologian or religious partisan of any sort. Rather, he asserted that the Jewish question was in essence a political one.[73] Thus, Michaelis based his anti-Jewish arguments on his own status as an expert on the history and nature of the Jewish people, "scientific" factors having to do with race and climate, and issues of statecraft and governance. In doing so, he made the inferior status of the Jews a national question framed by objective considerations, one which superseded traditional, religious opposition to Judaism. Once the Jews, separated from their biblical heritage by Michaelis's Orientalism, were stripped of religious relevance, their status as a contemporary group had to be assessed in relation to the state. As the history of racial theory and German National Socialism demonstrates, this was a consequential development indeed. An early representative, then, of modern anti-Semitism, Michaelis occupies an important position on the trajectory sketched by Löwenbrück. Another scholar sees Michaelis's work in theological terms, as part of a larger Protestant movement to document (and perhaps facilitate) the "death of Judaism."[74] And, finally, according to Hess, Michaelis did not merely reflect an unconscious "deep-seated Jew-hatred"; rather, he "epitomized a mode of colonialist thinking" in which Orientalist scholarship was activated to exercise "intellectual authority over the modern Arab world" and, at the same time, put "the ancient Israelites and contemporary Jews in their proper places."[75]

That Michaelis deserves a place, even a prominent one, in the histories of modern anti-Semitism, Lutheran anti-Jewishness, and Saidian Orientalism is clear. The question for this study, however, is the *role* that Michaelis's anti-Jewish attitudes played in *his* larger scholarly project. Though perhaps an exemplar of colonialist thinking, Michaelis's interventions in contemporary politics, as he indicated in the Dohm affair, were tentative and occasional.[76] Michaelis was not a pastor, and he never held a position in the theological faculty. He had no role in any religious community that would have required or allowed him, in any formal or official capacity, to guide Christian relations with the Jewish community. Though his writings reflect a disparaging and even contemptuous attitude toward elements of Judaism and modern Jewish society, he had no programmatic interest in prescribing attitudes or policies regarding contemporary Jews. To say this is not to diminish or excuse Michaelis's anti-Jewish attitudes. It is rather to suggest that theoretical frameworks oriented primarily toward Michaelis's cultural chauvinism or his anti-Semitism have more to do with our interests in ideological critique than with the full range of aims and interests associated with Michaelis's scholarly project. Eurocentrism and anti-Jewishness, though real, do not fully encompass this.

By contemporary reckoning, Michaelis's project seems disappointingly ordinary: to offer a new understanding of the Bible. In discussing the celebrated Arabian description, which was the culmination of all his ethnographic inquiries, Michaelis was careful to point out that its goal, above all, was to obtain information that would aid biblical interpretation. In a 1762 document, *Fragen an eine Gesellschaft gelehrter Männer, die auf Befehl Ihro Majestät des Königes von Dännemark nach Arabien reisen* ("Questions for a society of learned men who travel to Arabia by command of His Majesty the King of Denmark"), Michaelis drafted dozens of questions pertaining to botany, geography, language, and manners which the learned expeditioners were supposed to look into while in the Near East. Michaelis was clear about their purpose:

> The questions are taken up almost entirely with the clarification of the Holy Scriptures. I can foresee that this will displease some and appear all too theological. But they will not take offense when I confess to them that it seems all-important to me to illuminate that which pertains to a true understanding of a book on which our entire religion is founded.[77]

For a list of questions taken up with philological minutiae, the claim made by Michaelis here is grand. At stake in the expedition was a "true understanding of a book" that would allow scholars to explain the basis of "our entire religion" in a way that critics weary or suspicious of theology would find compelling. Though his concerns perhaps appeared "all too theological," the goal was to recover the ancient world of the Bible in a way that would supersede outmoded confessional understandings and allow it to speak to moderns.

For a variety of reasons having to do with Michaelis's social, religious, and scholarly views, traditional Judaism, then, became a casualty of his project. The point here is that, for some of the same reasons, confessional Christianity became a casualty as well. Michaelis's attitudes toward Judaism, though colored distinctively by his views on race and politics, were of a piece with the broader realization that a scriptural Bible, one understood by the light of particular religious traditions (whether Jewish or Christian), no longer had a place in modern intellectual inquiry. For academics like Michaelis, though, this did not mean that the Bible itself had become obsolete; it meant rather that a new approach to the Bible was needed. The point was not to create invidious comparisons between modern Jews and ancient Israelites. Rather, the centerpiece of his scholarly program was the positive reevaluation of ancient Israel as a *classical civilization*. Michaelis's rejection of Judaism and Christian confessionalism highlights the fact that his primary interpretive lens was historical and philological, or, more accurately, civilizational. Though he retained theological interests throughout his life, Michaelis took pride in the fact that he never joined the theological faculty at Göttingen. One of his greatest scholarly projects, a new German translation of the Bible to replace the revered, "national" translation of Luther, was conceived in distinctly nonconfessional terms, as a nonchurchly Bible.[78] Michaelis translated, as he put it, for all German-speakers: "Lutherans, Reformed, Catholic . . . Socianans, even for those who did not believe in revealed religion."[79] The extensive notes attached to the translation were designed to vindicate the antiquity, aesthetic richness, and cultural interest of the Bible. It thus amounted to a nontheological apology for the relevance of the Bible. Michaelis sought consciously to avoid traditional constraints on interpretation in order to create the conditions for a neohumanistic encounter with ancient Israel, one characterized by philological rigor, philosophical interest, and aesthetic insight.

As Gesner and Heyne had reformulated the study of ancient Greece and Rome in a new effort to reinvigorate modern life, Michaelis presented ancient Israel as a culture with its own distinct genius. By treating it as a classical civilization, he imposed a nontheological framework on the biblical materials, which allowed him to investigate the history and literature of the Israelites in a way that was at once profane and reverent. Michaelis consistently upheld the divine character of the Bible and the peculiar status of the Israelites as God's people. Yet this did not prevent him from inquiring into Israelite culture and society exactly as one would inquire into any other civilization. The Bible was simply a source of evidence for this inquiry. But the mode of inquiry was marked, above all, by the implicit assumptions that the study of ancient Israel was capable of enriching modern culture and that the Bible, ancient Israel's literary remains, contained ideas foundational to Western culture: monotheism, the immortality of the soul, the rule of law, and the quest for the sublime. On this view, the Bible replenishes contemporary life by returning it, in part, to its sources. In this sense, Michaelis's Israel was *classical*. Israelite civilization was accessible to the humanist, the philologist, and the ethnographer. These possessed the skills and expertise to understand the Bible apart from confessional frameworks.

Michaelis was no different from Gesner and Heyne in attempting to understand the poets, sages, lawgivers, and chroniclers of the ancient past.

The effort to restore ancient Israel as a classical civilization was expressed first of all in the attempt to reform the *discipline* of biblical studies and to import methods and standards from classical studies. As Heyne himself noted, Michaelis drew inspiration for this move from Gesner and Ernesti. Yet an awareness of classics' higher disciplinary standards is evident as early as 1745:

> It is certain that if all who undertake [the study of Hebrew] also had a comprehensive understanding of Latin and were as advanced in this mother language of scholars as one expects schoolchildren to be, then the scholarly world would remain free of many Hebrew fantasies.[80]

The *Beurtheilung*, written in 1757, years after Michaelis arrived in Göttingen, shows a deeper familiarity with classical studies and a desire to show their value for biblical studies. In this work Gesner is held up as a model for his careful differentiation of periods in the development of language, his appropriate concern for botanical lexicography, and for a wise use of empirical models of language acquisition.[81] Gesner and Heyne subordinated grammatical analysis and textual criticism to reading and interpretation, preferring to use handbooks, chrestomathies, and streamlined reader editions in their teaching. These reflected an instrumental view of language, according to which the mastery of Greek and Latin allowed access to the great minds and souls of antiquity. Like Gesner, who invented a method of rapid reading (*kursorische Lektüre*) to facilitate the comprehension of the whole, and Heyne, who was famously impatient with grammatical analysis, Michaelis focused on developing fluency, comprehension, and readerly competence. These were, in his view, connected with a rapid reading process not burdened by premeditation:

> The true interpretation is the one which occurs immediately and automatically to a reader who is competent in the language and yet has not seen the text before, one who reads quickly and in context. More often than not, he is incorrect who labors long over it.[82]

Michaelis believed that the slow, plodding analytical method adopted by grammarians was inferior to the fluent style of a skilled reader guided by intuition and insight. He thus made *kursorische Lektüre* an essential part of his program for the study of Bible and Near Eastern languages.[83]

Michaelis was also concerned, like his classicist colleagues, to deflect accusations of pedantry and to emphasize the content of ancient literature. To this end, Michaelis recommended that aspiring Hebraists learn Arabic and Syriac, because curiosity about the exotic and extensive literatures in these languages would keep interest high. Similarly, he complained that familiarity with the contents of the

Hebrew Bible, coupled with bad habits acquired by students who begin Hebrew prematurely, engendered a loathing for Hebrew studies.[84] Gesner had lodged a similar complaint about the disgust (*Ekel*) that more traditional methods of Latin instruction produced in his students. Interestingly, Michaelis, who wrote grammars for four different languages, declared that he actually disliked grammar.[85] This somewhat disingenuous claim may be understood as a reflection, late in life, on the virtues of his own pedagogy. It allowed Michaelis to imagine that he had succeeded in gaining the skills and knowledge of a grammarian without actually becoming one. By focusing on content, he gained technical knowledge as well. Like his neohumanist colleagues, Michaelis developed a rigorous philology but one ultimately focused on reading and comprehension.

If classicists provided models of language instruction, they also provided models of scholarship. Throughout the *Beurtheilung*, Michaelis complained that philological work carried out by Hebraists could not meet the standards upheld in classical studies. In an important section on lexicographic method, Michaelis described a set of rules and procedures that distinguished between the primary meaning of a word—which was concrete and external—and its secondary meanings, which were metaphorical or affective. He also claimed that primary meanings were simpler and rarer, while secondary meanings were more specific, technical, and common.[86] Michaelis faulted Hebraists for spurning basic principles like these and refusing to learn from classics.

The attempt to recover ancient Israel as a classical civilization also included an important historiographic concept taken from classical studies: the notion of a Golden Age. Michaelis introduced a clear if somewhat crude periodization of the history of Israelite literature. Its purpose was to evaluate the artistic achievements of Israelite civilization by identifying biblical authors who were sufficiently representative of the literary genius of ancient Israel. He specified the content and parameters of Israel's Golden Age as follows:

> The languages of which I speak [i.e. Hebrew and Arabic] have already outlasted their Golden Ages by hundreds of years: now is not the time to seek the Muses among the Jews or Arabs. We do these peoples an injustice if we desire to judge their taste above all according to present-day standards. The most beautiful monuments of Hebrew poetry were extant before the Babylonian calamity, and the periods of oppression between Joshua and Samuel themselves yielded sublime poetesses. But none among the Hebrew poets rises above Moses in taste or majesty; the books of Job and Isaiah are next after Moses, and David himself is a distant fourth after these three. Good taste and all the ornaments of language, though, perished in the Babylonian activity.[87]

Thirty-four years later, Michaelis circumscribed Israel's Golden Age in a similar way, but with the inclusion of Jeremiah and stronger emphasis on the characteristic of beauty as a mark of the Golden Age:

> Before the Babylonian captivity the language has beauty. Job is a masterwork of poetry, and good poetry continues until the time of Jeremiah, whose Lamentations, especially in the first chapter, are beautiful. But after the Babylonian captivity no further trace of the beautiful is to be found. It seems that the entire genius of the language changed under the Chaldeans. Even the writers who have great and beautiful images, both Daniel, who lived at court, and Zechariah, whose genius no reader can mistake, yet have, because of their forms of expression, nothing of the beauty that we admire in the ancients.[88]

The crucial division for Michaelis was between the literature of pre-exilic Israel and literature produced after the Exile; indeed, it appears to be the only real boundary in the scheme. The choice of the Exile as the great milestone in the history of Israelite literature is significant. It accords, first of all, with Michaelis's vision of irreversible decline that is supposed to have marked the history of the Jews from the time of the Exile to the present. Secondly, it shows the connectedness in Michaelis's thinking of literature on the one hand and the cultural and political fortunes of Israel on the other. That post-exilic Hebrew literature lacks beauty is certainly open to dispute, and there is, in any case, no necessary link between national calamity and the loss of "good taste" or "ornaments in language." It seems rather that the ability to produce what Michaelis considered good literature depended in some measure on the viability of the civilization from which it came. In the case of Israel (and later of Judah), the destruction of the capital, the loss of national sovereignty, and the effect of mass deportations weakened state and society to such a degree that they could no longer sustain the conditions necessary for great artistic expression.

Conclusion

In turning to the poets of Israel's Golden Age, Michaelis hoped to encounter what he called the "Near Eastern Muses" (*die morgenländischen Musen*). He claimed that to read the Bible profitably and to appreciate its "sublime and beautiful poetry," one had to be aided by the Muses.[89] Not only does this show Michaelis's debt to classical thought, it also indicates what was at stake in the appropriation of a classical Israelite literature. It was not a Greek Muse or a universal human Muse that Michaelis identified but *Near Eastern Muses*. To understand the Bible, then, one had to reckon with the particular genius of the Orient. For Michaelis, it is this conception of a classical, ancient Near Eastern Israel, and not the churchly construct of an exceptional, suprahistorical race, that ultimately opens the literature of the Hebrew Bible to the interpreter. The Muse is known in the Hebrew Bible; she allows the Hebrew Bible to be known. Michaelis's "third culture" was not merely the Hebraic but rather the larger complex of Near Eastern thought and literature of which the Hebrew was only a part. He confronted the Hebrew language as the dead relic of an antique past, challenging the time-honored claims of traditionalists that what made the Bible the Bible was precisely its religious afterlife. Like Gesner and Heyne, Michaelis set himself the task of encountering classical civilization through a rigorous philological *propaideia* that included a scientific examination of language, an emphasis on readerly competence, and the careful use of nontextual ancillary disciplines. And like the classicists, Michaelis connected the greatness of Virgil to the greatness of Augustus. The tiny kingdoms of Israel and Judah never sponsored a worldwide *pax Israelita*. Nevertheless, their brief periods of autonomy yielded the psalms of David, the poetry of Moses, and the lyrical power of the prophets—just enough of a literary trail, perhaps, to follow back to a classical past.

5

Lowth, Michaelis, and the Invention of Biblical Poetry

Where private interpretation is every thing, and the Church nothing...
realities will be evaporated into metaphors.

—Samuel Taylor Coleridge[1]

American novelist William Faulkner declared famously that the "past is not dead." In fact, he added, "it isn't even past." In the eighteenth century, Europe's classical past was very much a part of the present. Ancient Greece and Rome nourished the early modern social, political, and cultural imagination in manifold ways. Whether preserved carefully in humanist scholarship or invoked breezily by *philosophes*, the heroes, texts, and ethos of antiquity shaped art, literature, scholarship, and belief. Rome featured prominently in the works of French writers like Montesquieu and Voltaire, who praised the virtuous republic and decried imperial expansion,[2] and in the enthusiasm of the revolutionaries who believed that, like those who brought down Tarquinius Superbus, they could raise a republic from a fallen monarchy.[3] By the end of the eighteenth century, even the old rivalry between Greece and Rome seemed to have reappeared, as Goethe and the *gebildete*, philhellenic Germans watched Napoleon and the worldly, imperial-minded French gain world dominance.[4] In his obsession with the proud, militaristic Romans, Napoleon fancied himself a Caesar and a Roman. In a certain sense, he was a Roman. Rome was the foundation of Europe: its laws, infrastructure, language, religion, and political boundaries. There was no escaping its influence. Even Hellenic Göttingen attested the enduring power of the Roman political and cultural gestalt. When the university opened to great fanfare in 1737, the French instructor Antoine Rougemont delivered an oration comparing the rule of George II to the *pax Romana* and promising that new Horaces and Virgils would arise from the fledgling *Académie;* his German counterparts, as we have seen, preferred to look to Athens.[5] Ancient Greece reemerged powerfully in the academic, literary, and educational circles at Göttingen, Weimar, Jena, and Berlin. There neohumanists and philhellenists showed that modern culture had as much to do with Athens as with Rome. Their forays into Greek antiquity proved no less fruitful or consequential than earlier humanists' preoccupation with ancient Rome. In turning to the Greeks, though, the Germans were simply taking their part in an extended intramural debate concerning the appropriation of a shared European Greco-Roman antiquity. By Goethe's time, the classical afterlife of the Greek and Roman civilizations already stretched across five centuries of late medieval and early modern European cultural and intellectual history.

The question for Enlightenment biblical critics, then, was the place and purpose of ancient Israel on a landscape already crowded with ancient exemplars. Michaelis sought to make ancient Israel a classical civilization, but what did the Israelites have to offer? They could boast no Plato, no Demosthenes, no Augustus, no Virgil of their own. To borrow from St. Paul, who was himself an "Israelite" contending with Greeks and Romans, Israel appeared not to be "wise according to worldly standards ... not powerful ... not noble" (1 Cor 1:26). The Israelites had mattered, of course, because of their centrality to the Old Testament, which foreshadowed Christ and served as the foundation of Christian scripture. Just *how* the Old Testament did this and what, exactly, was its contemporary valence were among the divisive doctrinal issues that irenic interpreters were trying to avoid. To focus upon the Israelites principally as scriptural actors was to revive rancorous confessional debates regarding typology and figuralism. Even apart from the context of Christian confessional debates, though, the Israelites clearly exemplified something not found in Greece and Rome: a totalizing vision of life ordered and sanctified by divine law. This is nowhere clearer than in a comparison of biblical and classical texts. To quote from Erich Auerbach's seminal discussion in *Mimesis*: "The Scripture stories do not, like Homer's, court our favor, they do not flatter us that they may please and enchant us—they seek to subject us, and if we refuse to be subjected we are rebels." The Old Testament, "fraught with background," does not enrich our understanding of reality, it rather "seeks to overcome our reality."[6] Ancient Israel's most obvious bequest was not only moral law, narrowly construed, but a way of life organized around a communal, historically rooted obedience to the divine will. Yet, by eighteenth-century Protestant lights, the New Testament offered moral teaching in a purer form than in the Old, and social realities were predicated on the unifying power of the state, not ancient biblical narratives. To appropriate the Israelite legacy normatively, then, was unnecessary. Moreover, it brought one too close to Judaism.[7] The Jews were nothing to Michaelis and many of his contemporaries if not living examples of the stultifying and debilitating effects of a normative appropriation of the Hebrew Bible. If the Israelite contribution to modern culture could not be understood in theological or normative terms, then surely, they reasoned, the value of the Old Testament lay elsewhere.

As we have seen, Michaelis gravitated toward the aesthetic, cherishing the hope that biblical interpretation would be absorbed into a new scholarly appreciation for a Near Eastern antiquity ruled by Oriental muses. He shared the zeal for the "beautiful sciences," the deep preoccupation with taste (*Geschmack*), that characterized German literary and academic life of the period. Acknowledging the poor reputation of Near Eastern poetry, Michaelis sought to rehabilitate its image and make it appealing to Westerners. He commented on Arabic poetry and Syriac exegesis appreciatively, and he drew attention to striking images that he found.[8] For all of his efforts and good intentions, though, Michaelis lacked a clear understanding of what made this literature distinctively Near Eastern. His mind tended to work in the opposite direction, making what was strange or obscure in the Bible intelligible and familiar. Bridging gaps created by history and language was his strong suit; isolating and articulating the specific genius of foreign cultures, as Herder complained, was not. Michaelis sensed that if ancient Israel were to earn a place among Europe's classical cultures, it would have to do so by its aesthetic, literary merits. Exactly what these merits were, though, Michaelis the philologist could not say. For this task, Michaelis needed the help of someone with keener poetic sensibilities.

Robert Lowth and the Sacred Poetry of the Hebrews

As a young university graduate on a tour of Europe, Michaelis traveled to England, where in 1741 he heard Robert Lowth (1710–1787) deliver the second in a series of lectures on Hebrew poetry. The experience was revelatory. When Michaelis encountered the work of Lowth, he found both an interpreter and an interpretive program that laid bare, with penetrating insight, the operation of poetic genius in the literature of the ancient Israelites. He wrote later that in Oxford he felt immediately that he was "bound to appreciate and love" Lowth.[9] This encounter was the beginning of Michaelis's lifelong association with Lowth. It yielded, years later, the unusual picture of the proud Michaelis, the most learned man in Germany and the foremost Orientalist of his day, making himself the eager and humble annotator of Lowth, a seemingly dilettantish clergyman. To Michaelis and Lowth's considerable German following, Lowth was the discoverer of Hebrew poetry. Michaelis was determined to bring his discovery to light, improve upon it, and introduce the scholarly world to Lowth and thus to Israelite poetic genius.

When a thirty-year-old Lowth was appointed professor of poetry at Oxford in 1741, he did not face the burden of high expectations. Past occupants of the poetry chair were not noted for groundbreaking research, and the position was regarded as a "sinecure" or a venue for "general literary criticism."[10] Lowth had only three weeks to prepare his inaugural lecture. Alluding to this unusual situation, the good-natured Lowth nevertheless promised to "cheerfully embrace the opportunity" though it had come "rather earlier than [he] could have wished."[11] In spite of these inauspicious circumstances, the lectures were an enormous success. The opening lecture delivered by Lowth became the first of thirty-four on a single topic, given over the span of ten years. Taken together, the lectures mark a watershed in the history of biblical interpretation.[12] Known collectively as *De sacra poesi Hebraeorum praelectiones* (Lectures on the Sacred Poetry of the Hebrews), the lectures were offered by Lowth at Oxford between 1741 and 1750.[13] A clergyman known for wide classical learning and elegant speech, Lowth lectured in Latin. The *Praelectiones* divide into four parts: on poetry (Lects. 1–2); on meter (Lect. 3); on Hebrew poetic style (Lects. 4–17); and on different types of Hebrew poetry (Lects. 18–34). Examples of these types include prophetic, elegiac, didactic, lyric, hymnic, and dramatic poetry. After providing a detailed examination of Lowth's general comments on poetry from the first two lectures, I will move to a thematic discussion that ranges across the remainder of the lectures.

Lectures 1 and 2 contain introductory remarks in which Lowth provides a general discussion of poetry and its relation to religion. Lowth begins conventionally, by locating the study of poetry among the disciplines. Poetry, he claims, is superior to philosophy and history; it is the supreme liberal art:

> Thus far Poetry must be allowed to stand eminent among the other liberal arts; inasmuch as it refreshes the mind when it is fatigued, soothes it when it is agitated, relieves and reinvigorates it when it is depressed; as it elevates the thoughts to the admiration of what is beautiful, what is becoming, what is great and noble: nor is it enough to say, that it delivers the precepts of virtue in the most agreeable manner; it insinuates or instills into the soul the very principles of morality itself.[14]

The last characteristic of poetry, its efficacy as a medium of moral truth, is crucial for Lowth. Echoing Horace, Lowth says that poetry does not simply delight and instruct; it delights in order to instruct.[15] In doing so, it addresses the will, intellect, and emotions. The origin of poetry is in religion; as he puts it, its "original occupation was in the temple and at the altar." Though religions vary in many respects, they all agree "that the mysteries of their devotion were celebrated in verse."[16] This type of poetry was characterized by "the more violent affections of the heart," a "vehemence of expression," and passionate language that is "pointed, earnest, rapid, and tremulous."[17] What underlies this account is a developmental view of culture that makes religion the site of humanity's earliest attempts at expressive language. It also identifies raw feeling and uncontrolled emotion with this early stage, creating an image of a pure religious poetry imbued with primitive power.

Lest his refined audience look contemptuously on such violent and tremulous language, Lowth informs them in Lecture 2 that this is precisely the kind of poetry one finds in the Bible. If religious poetry ranks first among poetic subjects, he reasons, then the religious poetry found in the Bible is surely the greatest of all. The ancient Greeks may have claimed divine origins for their poetry, but Lowth dismisses them as "most groundless and absurd." Is it right, he asks, to pore over Homer, Pindar, and Horace while the literary achievements of Moses, David, and Isaiah "pass totally unregarded?" He continues:

> Or must we conclude that the writings of those men, who have accomplished only as much as human genius and ability could accomplish, should be reduced to method and theory; but that those which boast a much higher origin, and are justly attributed to the inspiration of the Holy Spirit, may be considered as indeed illustrious by their native force and beauty, but not as conformable to the principles of science, nor to be circumscribed by any rules of art?[18]

This is a key passage, one that sets up Lowth's most significant methodological maneuver. If, as he argued in Lecture 1, poetry is the highest of the arts, one deserving careful study, then the inspired poetry of the Bible a fortiori ought to receive greater attention. In this way, Lowth makes the doctrine of inspiration ensure the literary excellence and reinforce the prestige of the biblical writings. In Lowth's scheme, the unrefined, expressive religious language described in the first lecture has become, by virtue of its presence in the Bible, the apotheosis of human language. The proper response to biblical poetry, then, is study and analysis. If study of Greek poetry yielded proper "method and theory," then one should expect no less of Hebrew poetry. Hebrew poetics is also "conformable to the principles of science" and "circumscribed" by "rules of art."

Lowth was sensitive to theological objections to this implicitly profane mode of biblical criticism. He had subtly shifted the purpose and method of biblical study on the basis of a belief in the "inspiration of the Holy Spirit." But the claim that "inspiration" could be identified legitimately with literary excellence and critical acclaim was not self-evident to all. Christian tradition, from the patristic era onwards, taught that the chief function of the Hebrew Bible, the Old Testament, was to foreshadow the coming of Christ, to point ahead to His redemptive work, and to illuminate the relation of God to the Church. The traditional scheme of Christian interpreters recognized four senses—the literal, the allegorical, the moral, and the anagogical—according to which the relation of the Old to New could be worked out. In time, the allegorical came to predominate, whether in its Augustinian mold or in the more qualified typologies of the Reformers. The result was that the Old Testament was rarely understood on its own terms: its value lay in its churchly, Christological character. To seek in the Old Testament literary exemplars, "principles of science," and "rules of art" was, in traditional terms, to distort its purpose and character. As Roston points out, traditional and critical modes of interpretation were not compatible:

> So long as the Old Testament was regarded merely as the harbinger of the New, as a dark prophecy pointing forward to the Christian Messiah, it could not be judged as the divinely inspired literature of the primitive Hebrews, wrought out of the vivid experiences of a nation almost obsessed by its consciousness of right and wrong. And until it was so regarded, it could not serve as a literary model for later poets seeking the more exotic writings of 'oriental climes.'[19]

To address this objection Lowth shifted attention away from the divine nature and telos of the writings, which, he acknowledged, ultimately place them beyond the reach of human criticism. Allowing that the Old Testament has a transcendent character, Lowth nevertheless maintained that the biblical writings have a striking effect on readers that is an essential element of their sacredness:

> It is indeed most true that sacred Poetry, if we contemplate its origin alone, is far superior to both *nature* and *art*, but if we would rightly estimate its excellencies, that is, if we wish to understand its power in exciting the human affections, we must have recourse to both ... Since then it is the purpose of sacred Poetry to form the human mind to the constant habit of true virtue and piety, and to excite the more ardent affections of the soul, in order to direct them to their proper end; whoever has a clear insight into the instruments, the machinery as it were, by which this end is effected, will certainly contribute not a little to the improvement of the critical art.[20]

In this way, Lowth opens the path for an examination, a "right estimation" of Hebrew poetry that makes use, above all, of the "critical art." The sacredness of Scripture is precisely what qualifies it to function as an object of critical study. His goal was not to supplant a churchly exegesis. Rather, he hoped, like Michaelis, to develop a mode of interpretation that took full account of "critical art" and brought the study of the Bible into academic form. Lowth argued that this could exist alongside theological interpretation by an academic division of labor between theology on the one hand and poetics on the other. He does not deny that the Bible contains "the oracles of divine truth" but rather explains that, in his capacity of professor of poetry, it is his task to address the "youth who is addicted to the politer sciences and studious of the elegancies of composition."[21] He aims to navigate between two disciplines, careful not to "wander too much at large in the ample field of Poetry" and "imprudently break in upon the sacred boundaries of Theology."[22] On this view, theological and literary interpretations are fully separable. The poetry of the Hebrews may stand alone as an object of study. In a subtle shift, the inspired words of the Old Testament have become for Lowth the sublime poetry of the Hebrews.

Lowth was not an innovator in this regard. English writers, from Milton to Dryden and Pope, had affirmed the literary excellence of biblical poetry.[23] Unlike his precursors, though, Lowth offered a full, critical account of what made it unique and superior. The identification of parallelism, as we will see, was central to this account. Also important was the concept of the sublime. The eighteenth century was the century of the sublime in English literary criticism. The word was nearly ubiquitous in the works of religiously minded literary critics. In the lectures, Lowth emphasized the sublimity of Hebrew poetry, making it a by-product of divine inspiration.[24] He devoted four lectures to the topic, acknowledging, at the outset, his dependence on (pseudo-)Longinus's *Peri hupsous* (On the Sublime). The Longinian concept of the sublime included five elements: grandeur of thought, passionate feeling, use of figures, noble and graceful expression, and dignified structure. The first two concern sublime *nature*, and the other three characteristics have to do with sublime *expression*.[25] Lowth's definition of the sublime reflects the same dual emphasis on content and style, but he was more interested in the subjective effects of sublime style on the reader: "that force of composition" that "strikes and overpowers the mind, which excites the passions . . . not solicitous whether the language be plain or ornamented, refined or familiar."[26] Charting the development of eighteenth-century conceptions of the sublime, Samuel Monk marked a clear shift from an objective understanding (whatever is grand or awesome) to a subjective one (whatever produces a feeling of sublimity). According to Monk, Kant finally brought clarity to a "century of fumbling aesthetic speculation" when he made sublimity entirely subjective, "not a quality residing in the object, but a state of mind awakened by an object."[27] Though indebted to the Longinian tradition, Lowth was close to Kant in his understanding of the sublime. The lectures do not deal with the "great objects" of Hebrew poetry but rather with the way that the Hebrew poets attained an unrefined, overpowering "force of composition."

Lowth stood at a point of transition between the neoclassical and preromantic periods of English literary criticism.[28] Neoclassical canons, derived from Aristotle, Horace, and Longinus, demanded strict meter and favored the use of witty circumlocution to discuss topics of universal human interest. Their influence is evident,

112   THE DEATH OF SCRIPTURE AND THE RISE OF BIBLICAL STUDIES

for example, in the critical and poetic works of Pope, Dryden, and Addison. Preromantic poetry, by contrast, made use of direct, heartfelt language to express emotions connected with individual experience. It tended to be emotional, direct, and earnest where neoclassical compositions were impersonal, balanced, reserved, sophisticated, and allusive.[29] The work of Thomas Percy, including his translation of Song of Songs (1763) and his *Reliques of Ancient English Poetry* (1768), and the rhythmic "translations" of Ossian (1765) by James Macpherson are preromantic examples from Lowth's context. Roston describes the transition from neoclassical to preromantic:

> Poetry was the gentleman's pastime, aiming at expressing general truths with charm and taste, often in the garb of classical mythology. The new road branching off from this was the road of passionate individualism, which scorned stylistic embellishments and demanded the language of the heart. It was a road in which nature was to become glorious and yet awesome, in which the broad daylight and the company of human society was often to be exchanged for mysterious darkness and romantic solitude.[30]

Just as Lowth himself was a transitional figure, one may observe the shift in sensibility in the lectures themselves. Lowth begins with Horatian and Aristotelian assumptions about poetry.[31] In Lecture 1 he illustrates his points exclusively with examples from ancient Greece (e.g., Aristotle, Aeschylus, Pindar) and Rome (e.g., Varro, Virgil, Cicero). While he was also aware early on that Hebrew poetry differed in important ways from classical poetry, the full import of this only became clearer to Lowth as the lectures, which were delivered over a ten-year period, progressed. Lowth's greatest assets were a strong foundation in neoclassical poetics, on the one hand, and, on the other, a willingness to abandon this foundation when neoclassical conceptions proved ill suited to Hebrew poetry. The progressive realization that Hebrew poetry could not be adequately described according to neoclassical critical canons was a light that gradually spread over the lectures. It freed Lowth from formalism and allowed him to see the features of the psalms and prophetic oracles with new clarity. What emerged was a groundbreaking conception of what makes Hebrew poetry distinctive. The shift away from classical conceptions toward what he came to see as an authentically Hebraic one yielded insights into the character of biblical literature. I will look at four examples: meter, eloquence, figurative language, and poetic genres.

In Lowth's time, the idea of a poetry that failed to exhibit meter was inconceivable.[32] Lowth says this explicitly when he confesses in Lecture 3 that meter "appears essential to every species of poetry" and that it is "absolutely necessary to demonstrate" that what we call Hebrew poetry is "metrical in form."[33] Though committed to the existence of meter, Lowth was unable to identify a clear metrical scheme. He had publicly criticized an earlier attempt to scan Hebrew poetry: Francis Hare's 1736 analysis of the Psalms.[34] When Lowth spoke of the "shipwreck of many eminent persons" who had tried to identify meter, he was no doubt thinking of Hare.[35] Nonetheless, several things suggested the existence of meter to Lowth: the presence of alphabetic acrostics, the use of "poetical particles," and a "certain conformation of the sentences, the nature of which is, that a complete sentence is almost equally infused into every compound part, and that every member constitutes an entire verse."[36] For all this, though, Lowth was forced to admit that an insuperable difficulty, in the end, renders Hebrew meter totally obscure: uncertainty about the true pronunciation of Hebrew. At this point in the lecture, Lowth shifts away from the question of meter to a more general—and more fruitful—observation about Hebrew poetry. Instead of the carefully constructed, "copious, flowing, and harmonious" verse of the Greeks, Hebrew poetry is characterized by simplicity, "dignity and force."[37]

Second, Lowth's belief in the importance of eloquence in poetry led him in Lecture 4 to discover another essential attribute of Hebrew poetry: "sententiousness." Just as Hebrew fails to exhibit a clear metrical scheme, it also fails to manifest classical eloquence. Instead, it is characterized by terseness. He notes that in Hebrew poetry tersely expressed sentiments are regularly "amplified" by a second, complementary sentiment that echoes the first. The use of this amplificatory technique distinguishes Hebrew from other poetry:

> Each language possesses a peculiar genius and character, on which depend the principles of the versification, and in great measure the style or colour of the poetic diction. In Hebrew the frequent or rather perpetual splendour of the sentences, and the accurate recurrence of the clauses, seem absolutely necessary to distinguish the verse: so that what in any other language would appear a superfluous and tiresome repetition, in this cannot be omitted without injury to the poetry.[38]

The discussion of the "recurrence of the clauses" in Lecture 4 foreshadows Lowth's most important discovery: parallelism. In this quotation, Lowth establishes that in the repetition of clauses lies, somehow, the peculiar genius of Hebrew poetry. He defends blunt repetition, which would be "tiresome" by neoclassical standards, as the source of "perpetual splendour." In Lecture 19, Lowth offers a full description of parallelism. There he revisits the religious origin of poetry, suggesting that Hebrew parallelisms developed out of ancient practices involving "alternate or responsive chanting" such as one finds in the acclamation of David by the women in 1 Sam 18:7 and the choruses of men and women in Ex 15:20–21.[39] A form consisting of a pair of lines, corresponding distichs roughly equal in length, became more or less standard. Lowth also posited a *parallelismus membrorum* or "parallelism of the members." He claimed that individual words in the first distich had direct counterparts in the second distich, with "things" answering to "things" and "words" answering to "words" as if "fitted to each other by a kind of rule or measure."[40] Finally, parallel lines, according to Lowth, were related to one another in one of three ways: synonymously (the second echoes the first); antithetically (the second is contrasted to the first); and synthetically (the second complements the first). As Kugel has pointed out, Lowth's presentation of parallelism, including the three types of parallelism, has proven extraordinarily tenacious despite important flaws.[41] From the time of Lowth onwards, parallelism has been seen as the literary marker par excellence of Hebrew poetry.

In discussing a third aspect of Hebrew poetry, the use of figurative language, Lowth again begins with neoclassical canons. Lecture 6 opens with an extensive quotation from Aristotle's *Poetics*. According to Aristotle, the proper use of figures requires "perspicuity without meanness"; the poet should use terms neither too low and vulgar nor too grand and obscure. He should use them moderately to enliven his writing, taking care not to use too much figurative language. Figures should also not be sustained for too long, and an elegant variation of images should be employed.[42] Lowth notes that the Hebrews violated Aristotle's canons, using "mean" images, making immoderate use of figures, and sustaining metaphors over vast poetic stretches. Hebrew poets, for example, use metaphors of "light" and "dark" readily and intemperately.[43] Though they may offend classical tastes, Lowth maintained that the Hebrew poets achieved by their intemperate use of figures an unmistakable perspicuity. They made their poetry bold, forceful, and clear. In examining figurative language, Lowth created a contrast that once again allowed the "genius" of Hebrew poetry to be made manifest.

Fourth, Lowth employed classical headings to sort specimens of Hebrew poetry, for example, the elegy, ode, and idyllium. As we have seen, Lowth often began with classical categories and then gradually abandoned them. He did not force Hebrew poetry into classical genres. He posited equivalences where he could, identifying the elegy and the *qinah* didactic poetry with the *meshalim*, and the ode with the *shir*. Yet he found that two major neoclassical categories, the epic and the drama, were not truly represented in the Hebrew Bible. After carefully examining the book of Job and the Song of Songs, he concluded that Job was not a true epic and the Song not a true drama. And what was perhaps Lowth's most important category, prophetic poetry or *nebu'ah*, had no classical analogue at all.

In these ways, Lowth worked to identify the peculiar, nonclassical genius of Hebrew poetry. His success had much to do with his background in classical poetics. This enabled him to probe Hebrew poetry in a sensitive, thorough, and insightful manner, and it provided him with a wealth of critical tools and concepts. Yet, in the end, Lowth was not beholden to neoclassical categories. Unlike so many English translators in the eighteenth century, he did not Hellenize or Latinize Hebrew poetry. Neoclassical translators normally reserved the right, for example, to alter the style of the original language to conform to contemporary literary standards. This meant that biblical poetry, when translated, was inevitably made to suit neoclassical tastes.[44] Lowth, by contrast, considered it necessary to preserve the terse, direct, and repetitive character of the Hebrew. Lowth was determined to understand Hebrew poetry on its own terms and in a way that was psychologically penetrating, historically sensitive, and culturally particular:

> [W]e must even investigate their inmost sentiments, the manner and connexion of their thoughts; in one word, we must see all things with their eyes, estimate all things by their opinions: we must endeavor as much as possible to read Hebrew as the Hebrews would have read it . . . hearing or delivering the same words, at the same time, and in the same country.[45]

Here the full scope and central concern of Lowth's ambitious project are expressed. One must understand the literary characteristics of Hebrew poetry: parallelistic expression, use of bold figures, vivid style, profuse imagery, and language that is direct and unrefined. But historical knowledge and literary appreciation are not enough. One must enter imaginatively into the Hebrew past in order to penetrate the Hebrew mind. The psychic interior of the Hebrew poets, then, was the true touchstone of Lowth's work.

Lowth's quest to recover the ethos of Hebrew poetry was rooted in the sacred status of the Bible. However, Lowth reanalyzed sacredness, making it the functional equivalent of a literary excellence capable of arousing feelings of sublimity. A subjective understanding of sublimity allowed Lowth to identify in Hebrew poetry an unrefined, parallel path to the sublime. He saw in the raw, primitive, and tremulous effusions of the Hebrews a shortcut to the ultimate object of Longinian awe. Theirs was a path that led straight through the psyche, in effect tunneling under the royal road of Aristotelian balance and moderation. This brought the Israelites into focus as a primitive people closer to nature and more deeply in touch with the divine. Even before he introduced Lowth to the Germans, Michaelis was already determined to restore the Israelites as a people of flesh and blood. Lowth's poetics allowed him to restore their souls as well.

Michaelis in English Context

Lowth's *Praelectiones*, in the words of one historian, was "a British work whose influence upon the German Old Testament scholarship of its day has probably never been equalled."[46] It influenced Old Testament scholars like Eichhorn, but also a wider circle of figures including Goethe, Mendelssohn, and Herder. Lowth's renown in Germany had less to do with the lectures than with the form in which they reached German scholars. To them, the *Praelectiones* were not simply the words and ideas of Lowth. They were a compendium of biblical and ancient Near Eastern erudition organized around Lowth's lectures. It was not Lowth alone, but Lowth and Michaelis, his formidable German editor, whose scholarly voice is heard in the lectures. Without Lowth's knowledge, Michaelis published the lectures in Germany five years after they were published in Britain. Michaelis mistakenly believed that Lowth had died and thus made no effort to contact him before reissuing the lectures.[47] In publishing the lectures, Michaelis made an inexpensive edition widely available to Continental readers. Lowth's lectures had been published in their original Latin at Oxford by the Clarendon Press in 1753, but the Clarendon edition was expensive: an impressive quarto volume, generously spaced with quotations in Hebrew, Greek, and Latin.[48] Michaelis's edition, a more modest octavo, was published at Göttingen and appeared in two installments, with volume one appearing in 1758 and volume two in 1761.

Noted historian of scholarship Rudolf Smend has criticized the editorial work of Michaelis. Though he acknowledges the pivotal role that Michaelis played in introducing Lowth to German scholars, he claims that Michaelis, failing to understand Lowth's objectives, merely used the *Praelectiones* as a venue for his own work. Michaelis appended a long editorial preface, 139 editorial notes, and four extensive *epimetra* (appendices); together, they are the equivalent of about half of Lowth's text. Noting the scope of Michaelis's additions, Smend observes correctly that they do not always contribute to a "properly critical understanding of the text"; they seem instead to provide opportunities for Michaelis to "show off his own knowledge and thoughts."[49] Smend notes with approval Michaelis's attempts to supplement the text with his knowledge of Semitic philology and to draw out the exegetical implications of parallelism. Yet he finds Michaelis's extensive notes on Job excessive, and he judges most of Michaelis's notes to be the unseemly additions of a pedantic know-it-all.[50] Smend divides author and editor in stark terms. Though "thoroughly appreciative" of Lowth, Michaelis is "hostile and insensitive to all that is new in Lowth's work" and is hindered by an "embarrassing failure to understand the great thrust of Lowth's design." To Smend, Michaelis is "neither a poet nor a judge of art."[51]

The portrait of Michaelis as a man of great learning and a pioneer in biblical science, on the one hand, and a frustrated poet and aesthetician on the other was a common one.[52] It is partly responsible for shaping the view of Michaelis as fundamentally out of touch with what Lowth was trying to accomplish in the lectures. This view has also found support in an unusual circumstance arising from the publication of the second edition of Lowth's lectures at Oxford in 1763. By this time, both volumes of Michaelis's edition had been published. Lowth notes, though, that he only received the Göttingen edition after the second edition had gone to press

Nevertheless, he took the opportunity in an authorial preface to acknowledge gratitude and admiration for the "learned and ingenious" Michaelis, by whom the lectures were "greatly improved and illustrated." He then informed the reader that he had taken the unusual step of issuing Michaelis's editorial preface, notes, and *epimetra* in a separate volume. He did this for two reasons. The first was to allow those who bought the first edition to benefit from the notes. The second was to deal with the fact that Michaelis criticized Lowth in many of his notes. Lowth then "thought it better to submit them in this form to the judgment of the reader, than . . . to divert his attention into a controversy, unpleasant, and probably fruitless."[53] He respected Michaelis's erudition and appreciated his enthusiasm. Yet he separated Michaelis's work from his own, and in the second Oxford edition he added the notes of a *different* Semitic philologist, Thomas Hunt (1696–1774), professor of Arabic and also Regius Professor of Hebrew at Oxford. Smend calls the move "generous" yet "skillful," because it allowed Lowth to avoid taking on Michaelis and to preserve good relations with his *de facto* German representative.[54] It is true that Lowth was ambivalent toward Michaelis. The Göttingen edition was indeed a showcase for Michaelis. That Lowth and Michaelis differed on some points is clear. That Lowth had reservations about Michaelis's editorial work is very likely. But it does not follow from these observations that Michaelis, for his part, remained insensitive or hostile to Lowth's objectives, or that his work on the *Praelectiones* was merely opportunistic and self-serving.

I maintain, rather, that Michaelis had clear insight into the true value of Lowth's work and that, as far as he knew, he was fully sympathetic to it. The argument requires that the influence of English thought on Michaelis be properly understood. At twenty-four, Michaelis spent eighteen months in England (1741–1742). Scholars acknowledge that the trip was formative, but the exact significance of the trip and its connection to Michaelis's scholarship is not well understood. The consensus is that Michaelis, raised and educated in a strict pietistic environment at Halle, finally threw off the bonds of conservative Lutheranism while in England, embracing critical and rationalistic ideas associated with deism and latitudinarianism.[55] If this is the case, Michaelis, at the very least, does not say so. In his autobiography, Michaelis discussed various aspects of his time in England. Most important here are his comments on the transformation he experienced there:

> In England, my perspective on theology changed for the better . . .
> Despite the fact that I was half-Pelagian in school, the doctrine of supernatural grace was pushed in such a way that I thought it biblical; if I had objections to it that were philosophical or, at least, came from my experience—which I suppose included religious emotions—I could find nothing that seemed to me supernatural. This changed entirely in

England, since I learned to explain the biblical texts, which were
supposed to be speaking of supernatural grace, in a different way.[56]

A semiconvinced Wolffian in his youth, Michaelis was no stranger to rationalistic theology or its Pelagian corollaries before coming to England. That English influences should suddenly have broken the spell of a Pietism to which Michaelis had been naively loyal seems unlikely. The issue rather was the presence of "supernatural grace" and how to "explain" it.

Michaelis was known for basing the truth of the Christian religion on the historicity of biblically attested miracles and for proudly denying that he ever needed or experienced in his own right the "inner witness of the Holy Sprit."[57] Despite his objective and empirical bent, Michaelis did not discredit the category of the subjective, but only the category of the *supernaturally* subjective. An interesting clue in this regard comes from a note that Michaelis appended to Lowth's twelfth lecture. In discussing the use of similes, Lowth cites Is 55:10–11 as an example of a "fuller and more diffuse" comparison by which "the divine grace and its effects are compared with showers that fertilize the earth."[58] To this brief interpretive comment, Michaelis attaches an extensive note on the meaning of grace. Michaelis does not reject the relevance of "grace" to this passage, even though the word does not appear in it. Rather, Michaelis aims to strip grace of its explicitly Christian theological overtones and to show that it had for the Hebrew prophets a definite meaning:

> The passage of the prophet loses much of its poetical beauty if it be
> not rightly understood. He is not speaking of that *grace*, which the
> school divines treat of, and which has been celebrated since the time of
> Augustine in so many controversies, nor of the virtue and efficacy of the
> Gospel in correcting the morals of mankind, but of the certain accomplishment of the prophetic word.[59]

In an irenic move, Michaelis leaps over centuries of confessional debate and seeks to establish a new meaning of grace. Drawing on parallel uses of the same likeness between rain and the unfailing character of the prophetic word (Deut 32:2; Ezek 21:2; Mic 2:6; Job 29:22–23), Michaelis qualifies Lowth's discussion by emphasizing the conventionality of this simile, its significance as a kind of stock phrase in Hebrew poetry. Given, then, that the basic meaning of the simile is the utter reliability of prophetic utterance, its "gracious" character may then be understood in terms of God's faithfulness to Israel, His ability and intent to do for them what He promised, however unlikely or improbable His promises may seem. Thus Michaelis explains God's fidelity to the Davidic covenant (Is 55:3–5) as "the accomplishment of that perpetual and permanent *grace* which he had sworn to David, namely, that an eternal and immortal King should sit upon the throne; and that he should rule and direct the heathen."⁶⁰ Grace, for Michaelis, is "accomplished" when the prophetic word is fulfilled. Yet Michaelis does not leave it there. It is not his intent merely to give grace a definite historical meaning; rather, it is to show how a more concrete understanding of a previously vague notion can be reclothed in poetic language. The fundamental trustworthiness of the prophetic word becomes the subject of poetical elaboration: its effect on weary, defeated, and disillusioned hearers will be as "refreshing" and life-giving as rain which fertilizes the earth. The prophetic word is as likely to fail as rain is likely to return to heaven without watering the ground.⁶¹ Michaelis's project is not naturalistic reduction; it is rather a kind of aesthetic criticism. Michaelis's claim that he learned in England how to interpret "supernatural grace" in a "different way," far from attesting a newly found rationalism, indicates the beginning of a new sensitivity to the poetic dimension of Hebrew literature. It was in England that Michaelis began to understand the power not of rationalistic interpretation but of aesthetic.

Michaelis's sensitivity to currents in English literature and scholarship has received remarkably little attention.⁶² Most works on Michaelis acknowledge his contact with Lowth, but they rarely, if ever, place his interest in Lowth in the wider context of his enthusiasm for English literature, specifically poetry, novels, and criticism. The failure to recognize Michaelis's broader and deeper understanding of English preromanticism has contributed to the view that Michaelis neither understood nor appreciated Lowth. Yet, as will be clear, Michaelis sustained a productive interest in English works that spanned decades.

Michaelis's formative experiences in England, including the learning of English, became the basis for extensive professional involvement with English literature and scholarship. In the eight years after his return from England, Michaelis's enthusiasm for Lowth and other English authors stimulated a number of translation projects. The first were Latin translations of English biblical paraphrases by two authors: George Benson (Epistle of James; Halle, 1746) and James Peirce (Epistle to the Hebrews; Halle, 1747). He has thus been credited with introducing the genre of the biblical paraphrase into German scholarship.⁶³ Next, Michaelis produced German translations of works from two leading lights of the English preromantics: Samuel Richardson (*Clarissa*, parts 1–4; Göttingen, 1748–1749) and James Thomson (*Agamemnon*; Göttingen, 1750). Michaelis also read Richardson's *Pamela* and was so inspired by it that he petitioned Frederick II of Prussia to found a university for women.⁶⁴

Apart from Michaelis's work on Lowth's *Praelectiones*, the most important evidence of his contact with English scholarship comes from his dealings with Thomas Percy and Robert Wood.⁶⁵ Thomas Percy (1729–1811) was the author of the influential *Reliques of Ancient English Poetry* (1765) and an English translation of Song of Songs (1764). Percy's translation was marked by literalness, vividness, and a keen interest in the Song's ancient aesthetic. It drew heavily on Lowth's ideas. Though he had not been introduced to Michaelis, Percy sent a copy to him and invited his comments. Lowth, Percy, and Michaelis interacted in a period when enthusiasm for a historical, aesthetic, and "Hebraic" approach to the Bible united scholars from England and Germany.[66]

As Lowth showed the way toward a historical and aesthetic treatment of Hebrew poetry, so Robert Wood (1717–1771), author of *An Essay on the Original Genius and Writings of Homer* (1769), produced an analysis of Homer that aimed to vindicate the artistic brilliance of Homer by placing his epic poetry in social, geographical, and historical context. Wood traveled to Greece and Asia Minor in order to see firsthand the natural environments which serve as the backdrop for the *Iliad* and the *Odyssey*. Throughout his *Essay*, Wood argues that Homer's epithets and descriptions are faithful representations of the natural environment, particularly as they manifest what he maintains was Homer's "Ionian" point of view. He judges Homer to be a faithful historian:

> If we examine the Iliad, as a journal of the siege of Troy, stripped of its poetical embellishments, we shall find it, in general, a consistent narrative of events, related according to the circumstances of time and place, when and where they happened: our map of Troy is proposed as the truest test of this matter.[67]

Wood is also concerned to show that the manners, religious ideas, and literary style of Homer are consistent with a primitive and illiterate society, which nevertheless enjoyed unparalleled closeness to nature. Interestingly, Wood offers as support for a primitivized reading of Homer the ethnographic study of Arabia, which, he claims, also illuminates manners and customs in ancient Aegean society. In terms reminiscent of Michaelis, Wood describes Arabia, unconquered and unchanged for millennia, as "a perpetual and inexhaustible store of the aboriginal modes and customs of primeval life."[68] It is in proximity and fidelity to nature, moreover, that the genius of the uncivilized Homer consists. According to Wood:

> Poetry is found in savage life; and, even there, is not without ... magic powers over our passions ... [Homer's] business is entirely with Nature; and the language, which belongs to imperfect arts, simple manners, and unlettered society, best suits his purpose.[69]

Gifted with the ability to imitate nature, Homer uses primitive poetry to convey events with directness, immediacy, and truth. Wood characterized the direct representation of nature, which had been deemed by neoclassical standards to be low and vulgar, as "valuable realism."[70] Wood was typical of the midcentury shift in literary tastes, which increasingly acknowledged the ingenious quality of primitive, culturally specific, and unadorned composition.

Wood's new aesthetic, an affirmation of beauty and genius arising from historical and natural immediacy, appealed to the Göttingen philologists. Like Percy, Wood knew Michaelis through Lowth's *Praelectiones*. He sent Michaelis a copy of the *Essay*, one of only seven copies made of this first 1769 edition. As Wood explained, this initial printing was only meant for "particular friends" and was intended to prevent Wood from "los[ing] the thread of the subject" while attending to other duties. Michaelis received it with gratitude and enthusiasm, and he began a brief correspondence with Wood in which he proposed a German translation. Wood agreed, but urged Michaelis not to share this hastily printed first edition with anyone and to await the final version before proceeding with the translation. Michaelis replied that he had only showed it to two people. One of these was Heyne, who, upon reading it, was seized with wonder, exclaiming that all that he had felt about Homer was suddenly clear to him.[71] Despite Wood's pleas for discretion, an eager Michaelis went ahead with an anonymous German translation in 1773, published at Frankfurt two years after Wood's unexpected death in 1771. The ardent hope of Michaelis and Heyne for a German translation was fulfilled. An anonymous reviewer deduced that these two had been responsible for the translation, and Michaelis was forced to disclose the identity of the translator: his son, Christian Friedrich Michaelis.[72]

These examples show that for more than two decades after his English sojourn Michaelis continued to be actively engaged with English scholarship. They represent only a fraction of Michaelis's continuous, lifelong contact with British thinkers. Far from being a pedantic Orientalist insensitive to "all that was new" in English scholarship, Michaelis possessed a clear understanding of the most important developments. Michaelis could boast broad and deep familiarity with several aspects of English literature—biblical paraphrases, political dramas, and sentimental novels. Through contact with scholars like Percy and Wood, Michaelis built a reputation as a scholar very much on the cutting edge of developments in preromantic poetics and criticism. The gradual abandonment of neoclassical canons opened new possibilities in biblical interpretation for Michaelis. Lowth had begun admirably, steering conceptions of biblical poetry away from the ideals associated with the stilted, passionless formalism of the earlier part of the century. However, it was one thing to escape Greece and Rome, but quite another to arrive fully in the ancient Near East.

Michaelis, Lowth, and the *Praelectiones*

Between 1753 and 1761, Michaelis was actively engaged with the *Praelectiones*. He published two reviews (1753 and 1754)[73] and then, as we have seen, the lectures themselves in two volumes that appeared in 1758 and 1761. Not everything in Lowth's work pleased Michaelis. The reviews and editorial notes show that Michaelis had misgivings. The first criticism concerns Lowth's ignorance of cognate languages, especially Syriac and Arabic. Michaelis found Lowth's contrasts between Greco-Roman literature and Hebrew poetry helpful, but he believed that expertise in Near Eastern languages was necessary to a full and accurate understanding of the Hebrew language and the many obscure words that are found in poetry.[74] Second, he found Lowth's position on meter puzzling. Why does Lowth affirm its existence when he admits that it cannot be identified? Given the uncertainty of Hebrew vocalization, Michaelis pointed out in a note to Lecture 3 that anyone looking for a system of meter was bound to invent—not discover—one. He made it clear that Lowth's real contribution lay in his identification of parallelism.[75] Third, Michaelis worried about exceptionalism, the view that Hebrew poetry was not an ordinary human language but, as Lowth put it in Lecture 2, an "emanation from heaven . . . from its birth possessing a certain maturity both of beauty and of strength."[76] To offset this, Michaelis used the editorial notes to reinforce and elaborate on attempts by Lowth to signal the historical development, cultural particularity, or ancient Near Eastern context of Hebrew poetry. Fourth, Michaelis deepened the separation between literary and theological modes of interpretation. Lowth, as we have seen, tended in this direction, but Michaelis differentiated them more sharply and pushed the literary into the foreground. Theologians, Michaelis claimed in the editorial preface, are actually at a disadvantage in interpreting the poetic sections of the Bible:

> Theologians tend to [judge the Bible incorrectly] and badly, though this is not the fault of their knowledge. It is rather because few among mortals and thus among theologians happen to be born with poetic genius. All may feel poetic beauty who are versed in poetic language, but few judge keenly and correctly, and for the most part only those can who are poets by nature: not critics, not grammarians.[77]

In notes to Lecture 11, Michaelis denies the operation of a "mystical sense" in Hebrew poetry, claiming that it is fully intelligible according to "laws and principles" discovered by Lowth, rules to which the Holy Spirit, moreover, has confined Himself.[78]

Despite differences on these important issues, Michaelis did not write a refutation of Lowth or create an alternative to it. Rather, he saw fit to *join* his ideas to Lowth's lectures. Michaelis drew attention to differences, but he did not regard these, in any strong sense, as true disagreements. Lowth had discovered something valuable, parallelism, but he seemed to Michaelis to grope after its true significance. Michaelis believed that Lowth's analysis was the key to understanding Israelite poetic genius. He thus used the editorial notes to shape Lowth's uneven understanding of this task into a coherent academic enterprise that was nontheological, philological, and classically Near Eastern. The Göttingen edition of the lectures reads not like a single work but rather like the parallel works of two authors in search of Israelite genius. In this it resembled the reader editions and commentaries of Gesner and Heyne, which analyzed language rigorously in order to encounter the genius or *Geist* animating a text. In the case of the *Praelectiones*, though, the neohumanistic ideal of a philology that serves aesthetics was realized by two scholars, not one. The merger of philology and aesthetics was essential to Michaelis's vision. Lowth's poetics allowed, for the first time, a compelling classicization of Hebrew poetry that respected its special characteristics and did not force the Bible into a Ciceronian form. It also thrust Israelite poetic genius into the classical foreground, alongside refined Latinity and Greek sophistication. With appropriate help, it could become a genuine classical contender.

By annotating the lectures, Michaelis aimed to keep Lowth's analysis from slipping back into theological or neoclassical categories. Michaelis had the utmost respect for Lowth's poetic abilities. As Lowth's biographer has put it, Michaelis did not see him as a "churchman *or* even as a professor, but as a poet speaking about poetry."[79] Michaelis praised Lowth's poetic abilities and Latin style wherever and whenever he could. He asked, "Who can compare to Lowth in the discussion of Hebrew poetry?"[80] He declared in a review that only a boor or ignoramus could fail to appreciate Lowth's poetic translations of the Bible.[81] And in the editorial preface, Michaelis likened Lowth to an "Oriental Orpheus" initiating the unfamiliar into the beauties of Hebrew poetry.[82] This was high praise coming from a man who considered lack of poetic taste a grave deficiency for a biblical interpreter.

At the same time, Michaelis believed that poetic taste was not enough. He pointed out that Lowth might be an excellent guide to Hebrew poetics, but he lacked an understanding of history and a knowledge of Arabic and Syriac.[83] This prevented him from understanding Hebrew poetry in a fully authentic way. In the extensive editorial preface to the *Praelectiones*, Michaelis used 1 Cor 1–2 to argue for a non-neoclassical approach to the Old Testament. In this passage, St. Paul explains that the Christian gospel is "foolishness" and a "stumbling block" to those outside the church. By making Christ triumph through the cross, God chose what was foolish in order to confound the wise, what was weak in order to overthrow the mighty. Like Christ's humble life and shameful death, the literature of the Old Testament is unappealing, even repugnant. To know the Israelites authentically was to perceive their lowliness, their modesty, their lack of culture. As we have seen, Michaelis believed that Israelite exceptionalism was a serious problem. Whether in the English or German context, the majority of biblical interpreters in the mid-eighteenth century subscribed, in one form or another, to the idea that Israel's status as the chosen people translated into some form of historical or intellectual advantage. They were considered, for example, to be bearers of the *Ursprache*, guardians of esoteric truths, and the oldest and wisest among all civilizations. At the core of Michaelis's scholarly enterprise was the belief that exceptionalism was not only untrue, it was also counterproductive. The modern study of the Bible depended upon the cultural appropriation of the Israelites as a veritable, if venerable, flesh-and-blood society. St. Paul's image of a lowly divine wisdom that overthrows the sophisticated wisdom of the world suited Michaelis's understanding of Israelite literature perfectly. As a historian and Hebrew philologist, he knew the Israelites were lowly. He needed Lowth, however, to explain why Israelite literature was, at the same time, divine. This is why he refrained from criticizing Lowth too severely for neglecting historical backgrounds and, instead, cast himself in such an eager, supporting role.

Michaelis emphasized Israel's lowliness by contrasting its poetry with classical eloquence. Classical oratory, he argued, has no analogue in biblical literature. Poetry and oratory are fundamentally different. Poetry is innovative, concise, and elevated, while oratory is perspicuous, prolix, and common.[84] Moreover, they arise in totally different circumstances:

> Eloquence, as I will show, is the daughter of free cities, which tends to be born late, in nations which are trained in all sciences, where skillful men, well versed in literary eloquence, plead copiously and hold forth on political matters, not with short propositions but in long orations, whether in the Senate or among the crowd; [eloquence] flourished at Athens and Rome, where it is now extinct . . .[85]

The Hebrews never had leisure enough to develop elegance. They lacked a republic, a forum, and, to a great degree, political autonomy.[86] Their public figures, instead of providing "rhetorical meditations," used "grave words." The result was a terse and forceful manner of speech that exhibits "a clear and doleful command of the language which pleases more than the more ornate eloquence of the Greeks."[87] Michaelis found it necessary to correct Lowth on this matter twice (Lectures 1 and 10) and to emphasize that it was wrongheaded to expect eloquence from the Hebrews.

In this way, Michaelis kept Lowth's analysis true to the Hebrews of history. Sometimes his contributions were broad and thematic (for example, poetry versus oratory). At other times, his contributions introduced or clarified details that allowed him to evoke and elaborate a proper Near Eastern background. In reference to Lowth's translation of Ps 42 in Lecture 23, for example, Michaelis adds helpfully that "whoever composed this Psalm was expelled from the sacred city, and wandered as an exile in the regions of Hermon, and the heights of Lebanon, whence Jordan is fed by the melting of perpetual snow."[88] This setting, he shows, uniquely accounts for topographical and zoological allusions within the psalm. Elsewhere, Michaelis corrects observations on Hebrew style, noting, for example, that Lowth read too much into the syntax and abrupt shifts in verbal tense found in the famous lament of Job (Job 3).[89] On a few occasions, Michaelis takes the opportunity to refine Lowth's presentation by clarifying differences and similarities between the biblical and classical traditions, for example, in Greek and Hebrew concepts of the afterlife.[90] In an extensive *epimetron* after Lecture 11, Michaelis argues further that poetic images in Greco-Roman and Israelite literatures share a common Egyptian origin: the sun retiring into the sea to spend the night indulging its passions (Psalms 19 and 139; the myth of Aurora), the deity riding in a thunderous chariot (Yahweh on the cherubim; the chariot of Jupiter), a paradise beyond the sea (Ps 90:10 and Deut 30:11–13; Elysium).[91] Editorial contributions like these are spread throughout the lectures. They were designed principally to push Lowth "eastward" and keep his enthusiasm from sliding back into exceptionalism. This does not mean that Michaelis was insensitive to Lowth's project. Rather, he wanted to preserve the value of Lowth's work by keeping it from excess and focusing it on the Near Eastern particularity of the Hebrews.

The linguistic, historical, and civilizational background of Hebrew poetry, though, was not Michaelis's only contribution to the lectures. According to Michaelis, Lowth's greatest discovery was the existence of Hebrew parallelism. In his second review (1754) of the lectures, Michaelis praised Lowth for having extended "a light for sacred interpretation."[92] Michaelis drew out its implications for exegesis in an *epimetron* placed after Lecture 19, the lecture in which Lowth offered his fullest discussion of parallelism. In the *epimetron*, Michaelis provides additional examples of how the recognition of parallelism, specifically of *parallelismus membrorum* (in which specific words in one line correspond to counterparts in the parallel line), solves interpretive problems. Thus, when a Hebrew word or expression is awkward or unclear, one need only consult the meaning of its counterpart in the parallel line to see how the word should be understood. The results can include minor modifications or large interpretive leaps. For example, Michaelis proposes a modest change in Ps 147:9, in which the literal translation of two parallel lines ("who giveth to the beast his food / and to the young ravens which cry") is adjusted so that "food" from the first line has a proper counterpart in the second line. The revised translation is clearer: "who giveth to the beast his food / and to the young ravens *that for which* they cry."[93] A more significant change is in view in Ps 25:13. The first line, literally translated, is imprecise: "his soul shall rest in good." Nevertheless, a more precise meaning of "good" can be deduced with the aid of parallelism. By examining the counterpart in the parallel line, which reads, "and his seed shall inherit the land," one arrives at a clear understanding. A blessing on the descendants of the righteous man ("his seed" inherits the land) is meant in the second line; this refers to a blessing on the righteous man *after* he himself has died. "Good" in the first line must likewise refer to a blessing *after* death. It may thus be interpreted as "his soul shall rest in happiness after the grave."[94] In addition to having exegetical value, parallelism played an important role in Michaelis's defense of the Bible against its classical despisers:

> How I wish they had followed sufficiently [Lowth's] easy way! Interpreters would have reached with ease true explanations of more difficult utterances freely, pleasantly, and without labor. Instead, ignorant and unskilled men fuss over these texts and maliciously condemn them as tautologies.[95]

Parallelism saves Hebrew poetry from accusations of the cardinal neoclassical sin of tautology and shows that its genius lay not with metrical composition or witty circumlocution but in vivid conceptual correspondences. With Lowth's identification of parallelism, Michaelis had acquired the key necessary to unlock Israelite poetic genius and defend the sacred character of the Bible. As he recognized, respect for the Bible rose and fell with verdicts on its literary merit. Many polite readers became "ashamed to hold it as divine." This was not a trivial development:

> You ask, therefore: of what concern is it for sacred things such as Hebrew songs whether they are beautiful—compared to which no zealous human mind has produced anything better or more perfect—or misshapen, pompous, laughable, and vulgar? Of great concern indeed![96]

Unlike Lowth, Michaelis did not turn explicitly to the category of the sublime to mount a defense of the Bible's literary qualities. Michaelis was not afraid to use the word, and he certainly seems to have welcomed Lowth's characterization of Hebrew poetry as sublime. Yet his project was rooted in the historical and linguistic contextualization of Hebrew literature. According to Michaelis, the historian (and not simply the literary critic) can discern what is truly admirable in Hebrew literature, namely ancient poetic genius. To be sure, there is some overlap between poetic genius and the sublime. Poetic genius may be equated, in a certain sense, with sublime style or a brilliant reflection of the sublime itself. Yet Michaelis understood the sublime not so much as Lowth did—as the subject of literary and psychological analysis—but rather as the historical manifestation of poetic genius. Comparative history sorts out the classical past. In rhetoric and philosophy, the Israelites cannot compare to the Romans and Greeks. But in poetry, the Israelites excel them both. Their genius compares favorably to the sophistication of classical antiquity:

> The graces of language elevate genius, whereas it is cramped by dryness; and most discoveries are rather the fruits of genius than the result of forced meditations or logical demonstration ... Genius, I say, is rendered

more lively and active by pleasure and beauty, whereas it is benumbed by abstractions and profundity.[97]

Thus, the Hebrew Bible has come down to us from a time and place when humans not yet "benumbed by abstractions" enjoyed a more vivid and more direct relationship with the natural world. Michaelis complained that cultured critics miss the mark when they use "interpretive laws" better suited to "the explication of the work of some bloodless metaphysician" than to "poems of beauty."[98] Like Wood, who attributed Homer's genius to his primitive environment and his ability to imitate nature creatively, Michaelis attributed the genius of the Hebrews to their ancient and simple society, their freedom from bloodless abstraction, and their closeness to nature.

In this way, Lowth's notion of the sublime received, at Michaelis's hands, a clearer historical dimension. Lowth analyzed the mechanics of sublimity, and Michaelis set them in ancient context. In doing so, though, Michaelis did not attempt a historical relativization of the sublime itself. He rather believed in the "great similarity in the human mind throughout all the countries of the globe" and across the millennia, a similarity which included universal aesthetic standards.[99] The concept of the beautiful is one, but its cultural expressions are many. To interpret Hebrew poetry correctly is to use historical and linguistic expertise to clarify obscure words, explain strange customs, and explicate background so that its beauty shines forth. Even Longinus, no mean critic in his own right, was forced to confess that Moses, despite the rough character of the Hebrew language, "yet produced much that could please Greek ears."[100]

Conclusion

"Biblical poetry" was a successful eighteenth-century invention. Though there is no word for "poetry" in biblical Hebrew, as Kugel points out, the identification of biblical literature with poetry has always been "seductive."[101] Before the age of Lowth, prophecy was not a subcategory of sacred "poetry" but rather, according to Christian tradition, a complex mosaic of images and foretellings that ultimately pictured Christ. The psalms, though lyrical, were principally liturgical. They gave voice to the experience of the chosen people enduring the vicissitudes of a troubled but triumphant salvation history. To recast all of this material as "poetry," however, was to offer a radically new frame of reference. As one scholar astutely observes, the idea of biblical poetry emerged precisely when theological definitions were receding to the margins of exegetical discourse. The concept allowed interpreters direct access to the Bible, independent of the "grand narratives" of the "canonical tradition."[102]

As a result, the point of contact between "biblical poetry" and the individual was not identity in a community of faith united by canon but rather faculties of aesthetic judgment. To Lowth and Michaelis, this only supplemented and reinforced the sacredness of the Bible. Yet their efforts show that the notion of canon was not actually necessary to a defense of the Bible or a belief in its divine character. For poetry, as a category, cuts across the canon, turning Moses, David, Solomon, and Isaiah from prophets and kings (or perhaps saints and sinners) into classical artists of the imagination. It is not difficult to understand how and why the concept of biblical poetry aided influential and far-reaching attempts to appropriate the Bible as an aesthetic resource.[103] As the first to offer a compelling explanation of what made biblical poetry distinctive, Lowth stood at the source and center of a new approach to the Bible as literature. Seeing a valuable opportunity in the promotion of Lowth's work, Michaelis introduced him to the German scholarly world, where figures like Herder, Mendelssohn, and Eichhorn, it seemed, were waiting to exploit Lowth's discovery. Michaelis's goal had been to commend Israel as a classical civilization with a unique and important cultural contribution. With the publication and smashing success of the *Praelectiones*, he seemed to have done precisely this. The prophets, once bearers of the sacred word, became ancient Israel's poetic geniuses, figures represented in a literary corpus regarded increasingly as sublime. In the middle of the eighteenth century, they emerged, naked and full-grown, not from the head of Zeus but rather from the ruins of a dismantled canon shrouded in the mist of a venerable Hebraic past.

6

Michaelis, Moses, and the Recovery of the Bible

Where tradition rationalizes itself, it has already ceased.
—Max Horkheimer[1]

It is a little-known fact that Michaelis, who denied ever feeling the inner witness of the Holy Spirit, received occasional visits from the Muse. When she appeared, he obeyed. In fact, he wrote, "it is a dangerous thing" to attempt to write poetry without being so "compelled."[2] In 1762, Michaelis appended an original poetic composition to the second edition of his 1751 work on Ecclesiastes, *Poetischer Entwurf der Gedanken des Prediger-Buch Salomons*.[3] The subject of the poem, however, was not Solomon. Entitled "Moses, der Anfang eines Gedichtes" ("Moses, the beginning of a poem"), it was supposed to have been the first part of a longer "heroic poem" (*Heldengedicht*) about the great Israelite leader.[4] The poem begins with an invocation of the Muse, also identified as the "friend" of Moses. As the scene opens, Moses is standing on the banks of the Nile moments before an encounter with Pharaoh. In an extended soliloquy, he reflects on his Egyptian upbringing and the fearsome nature of his task before finally getting up his courage. When he confronts Pharaoh, he does so not as an obsequious courtier but rather as a sturdy shepherd, staff in hand, who draws near with "unbowed back" to warn Pharaoh against obstinacy. After disparaging Yahweh as a new and obscure deity with no prestigious temple and no place on the hallowed, secret walls of Egypt, Pharaoh contemptuously refuses to pay him heed. Unimpressed, Moses displays his own knowledge of Egyptian religion and shows that it is confused, superstitious, and sclerotic. He then begins a passionate defense of Yahweh, in which he declares that his God is known simply from the natural order (*Ihn predigt die Natur*) and that the justice he demands in this case is merely a requirement of the universal morality imprinted on Pharaoh's own soul. "Justice," Moses explains, can never be silenced: it rules the world, grows angry over the chains of the oppressed, and "menaces you from within." Moses promises a bloodbath if Pharaoh denies the Israelites justice, but he does not cherish the thought, adding "only let me not see it!" An old but vigorous man, Moses defies Pharaoh to kill him then and there if he will not grant the request. Pharaoh simply departs confused and agitated, exclaiming that Moses' blood is too poor for his hands.

This poem presents a clear image of Michaelis's Moses, one which bears a resemblance to the Moses immortalized in film by Charlton Heston and Cecil B. DeMille.[5] In Michaelis's poem, Moses is the champion of a just and rational monotheism. Having absorbed Egyptian learning, he is a "classically" trained but progressive leader. Though well versed in the ways of the Egyptians, he has long since exchanged the mysteries of their ancient wisdom for the rugged goodness and egalitarianism of the simple shepherd. Above all, he is characterized by conviction and compassion. Though a man of action, he is unequalled as an orator and an apologist. Though bold, he is sensitive and humane, even melancholy. This poem, which Michaelis offered to the reading public in an uncharacteristically tentative way, reveals much about the appeal that Moses held for Michaelis.[6] It illustrates something that is not immediately obvious in Michaelis's conventional, scholarly treatments of Moses. In these works, Moses figures importantly in discussions of law, wisdom literature, and poetry. Yet nowhere does Michaelis offer a single, comprehensive discussion of Moses' significance. Instead, one gathers from scattered discussions that Moses was, for Michaelis, the embodiment of classical Israel and of what it had to offer. The "heroic poem" provides insight, ascribing aesthetic sensitivity, political conviction, and philosophical acumen to Moses. For Michaelis, these traits cohered in Moses in a way that made him a paragon. Moses opened the possibility of a civilizational recovery of Israel much as Homer, Solon, Virgil, and Cicero did for Greece and Rome. In Michaelis's scholarly corpus Moses appears as the supreme Israelite poet, the wise founding father of the Israelite state, and the sublime moralist behind the book of Job. In recovering Moses, Michaelis hoped to gain access to the cultural treasury of the biblical world.

To analyze this recovery, it is necessary to look at a range of materials. First, I will examine Michaelis's magnum opus, his six-volume *Mosaisches Recht* (1770–1775), which was a massive discussion of the political and philosophical dimensions of Pentateuchal laws. Moses figures centrally in this work as a legislator and state builder, and Michaelis's exploration of law in the Hebrew Bible is organized around the character and historical context of Moses. In looking at Mosaic law, as he does, with the "eye of a Montesquieu," Michaelis sought to glean political wisdom from it.[7] I will also examine Michaelis's efforts to interpret the book of Job as a sublime moralistic fable. In his 1787 *Einleitung in die göttlichen Schriften des Alten Bundes* (Introduction to the divine scriptures of the Old Testament), Michaelis argues that Moses was the author of Job, thus making Moses an ingenious moral philosopher as well as an exceptional statesman. This analysis, along with Michaelis's 1760 translation of Job, provides valuable insight into Moses' significance as a paragon of moral wisdom from classical Israel. To place these efforts in context, I will begin with a brief look at selected aspects of the Moses discourse in the sixteenth, seventeenth, and eighteenth centuries.

Moses in Early Modern Thought: A Brief Overview

When Michaelis turned his attention to the manifold legacy of Moses, he stood within a long and distinguished tradition of humanist attempts to come to terms with the cultural and, more commonly, political significance of the Hebrew Bible. Moses in particular was revered as a paragon of the biblical tradition, inspiring artists, reformers, and leaders. One need only think of Michelangelo's monumental sculpture for Pope Julius II or Savonarola's prophetic pretensions to appreciate the powerful appeal of Moses. As one scholar has said of the Italian Renaissance: "Moses was part of a fabric of general understanding that bordered on the obvious . . . [he] was part of the mind-set, a polyvalent—and one is tempted to say, omnipresent—cultural icon." He was a "magician, mystic, warrior, lawyer, saint, liberator, theologian, artist, philosopher, and symbol" as well as "the inventor of confession, of poetry, of history, and of law."[8] In the early modern period, many began to explore Moses' identity not as the founder of a special *nation* but as a particular nation's special *founder*. The Pentateuch became a resource for the study of leadership, political change, and statecraft. Biblical narrative was often stripped of its specific theological content and generalized to apply to contemporary political situations. Egypt stood for any national, oppressive circumstance and Canaan for its desirable opposite. Moses the prophet of Yahweh was identified with any visionary able to bring his followers from one state to the other.[9]

The most influential political interpreter of Moses in the sixteenth century was Machiavelli. Though he did not devote any specific works to Moses himself, his writings, especially the *Discourses on Livy*, contain numerous references to him. Machiavelli appears to have been a sensitive and informed reader of the Bible, with a deep affinity for Moses' own political sensibilities. For example, the man who forsook wealth and privilege to deliver his people, who boldly defended his countryman (Ex 2:11–12), and who refused to let his people be destroyed (Ex 32:9–14) is a man that Machiavelli could understand. Moses, in light of these three episodes, might be seen as one who, like Machiavelli, exemplified devotion to the nation, one who "loved his *patria* more than his own soul."[10] More importantly for Machiavelli, though, Moses succeeded in reinforcing decisive political action with a robust and worldly religion oriented toward the success of the state. In an apparent reference to the episode of the Golden Calf (Ex 32), Machiavelli describes the political calculation behind Moses' violent purging of the idolaters: "Anyone who reads the Bible intelligently will see that, in order to advance his laws and his institutions, Moses was forced to kill countless men, who were moved to oppose his plans by nothing more than envy."[11] Machiavelli's Moses also secured military advantages by teaching the Israelites that defeat was not an option and that Yahweh is a warrior that fights for Israel (Deut 3:21–22).[12] In this way, the religion of Moses was well suited to forceful military action, bold foreign policy, and practical and decisive leadership.

Moses also played an important role in the work of Spinoza. Spinoza is perhaps best remembered for his attack on the traditional belief in Mosaic authorship of the Pentateuch. He wrote in the *Theological-Political Treatise* (*TTP*) that "it is clear beyond a shadow of a doubt" that it was not written by Moses and that it is "contrary to reason" to think that it was.[13] Spinoza built a case against Mosaic authorship by looking carefully and critically at the original Hebrew text and discerning a number of passages that reflected a perspective that was non-Mosaic.[14] Though Moses had no significance for Spinoza as an author or literary figure, Spinoza held that Moses was a true prophet, the only one, in fact, who communicated directly with God. This was a mark not only of Moses' special significance but also of his extraordinary powers of cognition.[15] On the whole, biblical prophecy for Spinoza was an imaginative faculty characterized by dreams, visions, and likenesses. It was therefore of a lower order than the intuitive apprehension of true principles one finds in Moses. This is how Spinoza understands biblical verses that single out Moses and describe him as the only prophet who heard God's voice directly (Ex 33:11). By this token Moses was, for Spinoza, something more than the shrewd, patriotic Moses of Machiavelli.

In chapter 17 of the *TTP* Moses' full significance comes into view. In this section, Spinoza sketches a theory of the state based on the idea that successful governments depend on the voluntary relinquishment and wise management of natural freedoms that individuals surrender to their civic leaders. Without the surrender of these freedoms by the people, states cannot maintain control; without a government that rules justly, though, individuals cannot flourish. This understanding of government allows Spinoza to analyze the early history of the Hebrew nation in a way that, interestingly, vindicates Moses at the expense of the biblical God.

According to Spinoza, the Hebrews who escaped from Egypt organized themselves into a pure theocracy: all agreed to live under God's direct rule. Yet upon hearing the terrible words of God at Sinai, the Israelites cried out. They begged to have Moses mediate God's rule to them, because they could not bear God's voice (Ex 20:18). At this point, Spinoza explains, they "abrogated the first covenant, making an absolute transfer to Moses of their right to consult God and to interpret his decrees."[16] Moses then became an absolute ruler. He proved extraordinarily wise, creating a republic that preserved the democratic ethos of the original theocracy. Moses ordered the creation of a tabernacle, a dwelling place for God, that would be funded and built by the tribes and belong to all. He took away that time-honored tool of statist oppression, the standing army, and set up a militia, again drawn from all the tribes. Finally, he effected a separation of powers. The priests had access to divine counsel in the sacred tent, but military power belonged to "secular" leaders like Joshua. The people, for their part, were unified admirably under this theocracy. Moses cultivated forms of piety that predisposed the people to accept the claims of the government upon their freedoms and loyalties. They were taught that foreign nations were enemies of God, and the arbitrary but powerful requirements of the ceremonial law bred in them strong habits of obedience.[17] Laws prescribing love of neighbor and economic restraint (e.g., Jubilee years, prohibitions of usury) encouraged harmony, solidarity, and charity within Israelite society. Spinoza regarded this arrangement, in which religion functioned to unify and strengthen an egalitarian society, as ideal. Moses was its architect.

The theocratic Israelite republic did not endure.[18] On the basis of a willful misreading of the Golden Calf incident (Ex 32), Spinoza attributes the decline of Israel to the vengeful, capricious character of the biblical god. Prior to the incident, he explains, Moses had entrusted religious leadership to firstborn sons throughout the tribes (Num 8:17). But after witnessing the idolatrous behavior of the Israelites, the biblical god lashed out against the people with the aid of sword-bearing Levites. He then stripped the firstborn of their ministry and made the Levites the priests of Israel, requiring that the people support them with gifts and offerings associated with the "redemption" of the firstborn. The installation of a priestly class had disastrous results. The Levites became living reminders to the Israelites of their "defilement" and "rejection" by the biblical god. Spinoza characterizes the Levites as faultfinding nuisances and self-righteous, censorious "would-be theologians." The people, for their part, resented and rebelled against the priests, throwing the whole society into chaos and disorder. When a monarchy was introduced to stabilize the state, power struggles only took new forms: between king and Levite, for example, and between king and prophet. Though it was Moses and not God in Ex 32 who rallied the Levites and executed idolaters without explicit instructions to do so, Spinoza attributes the rise of the Levites and the concomitant decline of Israel to the vengefulness of the biblical god. In this way, he makes the biblical god the author of priestcraft and political disorder while saving the reputation of Moses as a philosopher attuned to the wisdom of the true God. Spinoza's Moses harnessed powerful religious impulses and kept dangerous social forces in check by creating a free and equal society held together by piety and common morality. He demonstrated how religion could serve noble political ends.

In the eighteenth century, the "Moses discourse" took an important turn. Commentators remained focused, like Machiavelli and Spinoza, on the politics and statecraft of Moses, but they turned increasingly toward Egypt to explain the origins, character, and ethos of his innovations. Jan Assmann's excellent account of this period moves across a range of English and German figures fascinated with Moses' shadowy Egyptian background.[19] John Toland, for example, seized upon this background in an attempt to offer a radical reconstruction of the Mosaic revelation. Relying heavily on what extrabiblical sources he could find, Toland followed Strabo, the Greek historian and geographer, in making Moses an actual Egyptian priest.[20] Yet, to Toland, Moses was also an iconoclast who invented a nonceremonial, pantheistic natural theology, a pure religion of nature. To this religious innovation, Moses added another: the name of a God who "necessarily exists" (Toland's understanding of the name "Yahweh") and whom Moses could invoke to sanction and enforce his own law code.[21] Another English figure, William Warburton (1698–1779), the idiosyncratic bishop of Gloucester, created a Moses controversy in the middle of the century with his *Divine Legation of Moses Demonstrated* (1738–1741).[22] Warburton sought to defend the "divine origin of the Jewish religion" by meeting an objection that critics used to denigrate the Bible. If successful governments in the ancient world depended on a doctrine of rewards and punishments in the afterlife to promote moral and lawful behavior in this life, how can the Mosaic law (of all laws!) be taken seriously when it makes no mention of the afterlife? Warburton believed that the Egyptians had perfected a religious conception of the afterlife divided into esoteric knowledge available only to political and religious leaders at the highest levels and an exoteric teaching on future rewards and punishments conducive to public morality. The "double doctrine" allowed leaders to reinforce their authority by cloaking themselves in awe and mystery. As a man close to the source of this wisdom, Moses created a public, exoteric legislation that associated lawfulness and lawlessness with rewards and punishments. Yet, as a prophet, he received esoteric knowledge of an "extraordinary providence" by which God would reward and punish the Israelites *in this life* in order to reinforce and validate the Mosaic legislation. Warburton defended Mosaic law, and thus the credibility of the Bible, in terms of the philosophical validity and Egyptian background of Moses' approach to governance. Toland and Warburton, figures on different sides of eighteenth-century debates concerning the role of the

Bible in contemporary society, nevertheless believed that the relevance of Moses could not be properly evaluated without due attention to his philosophical outlook and Egyptian identity.

The Egyptological inquiries of English critics stimulated German thinkers also interested in Moses' religious innovations. For many of them, the key point of connection between Egyptian religion and Mosaic monotheism was a secret pantheism like the one identified by Toland. Beneath the surface of a public and popular Egyptian religion, then, lay an esoteric belief in the divine "One-and-All." Karl Reinhold, for example, suggested that Moses' "new" religion was merely the attempt to declare the esoteric Egyptian belief publicly and to initiate all Israel into its mysteries at Sinai. Similarly, Friedrich Schiller asserted that Moses, discovering that the god of reason and enlightenment lay at the heart of Egyptian religion, dared to proclaim a sublime and abstract god to the Israelites. This contributed, as Assmann shows, to the revival of "cosmotheism" in the mid to late eighteenth century. Lessing used the cosmotheist slogan, *hen kai pan* (One-and-All), to represent the ideas that God is essentially anonymous and that all religions are ultimately translatable because they all testify in their core convictions to the superiority of a single divine essence.[23] Goethe also understood the Mosaic law as an elaborate fiction—but as one created by Moses to foist a violent, revolutionary, and nationalistic agenda on the Israelites. Goethe surmised, based on his critical reading of the Pentateuch, that instead of dying peacefully on Mt. Nebo, Moses was assassinated by Joshua and Caleb in the wilderness for his efforts.[24]

Michaelis was not as enthusiastic as his German contemporaries about the esoteric or fictive character of Mosaic religion. He was a more conventional Lutheran on this score: what secret religious insights Moses may have afforded were ultimately fulfilled and superseded by the New Testament.[25] Michaelis's work on Moses rather recalls the earlier, more political studies of Machiavelli and Warburton. The point here is that the early modern "Moses discourse" among humanists, critics, and philosophers was already deep and vigorous by the time of Michaelis. Michaelis's contribution was to bring this *type* of discourse on Moses—philosophical, political, cultural, Egyptological—into a philological framework, to carry on this kind of conversation within the framework of biblical scholarship. Michaelis complained that philologists had only been occupied in a narrow way with the language of Mosaic law "as a branch of Hebrew antiquities" and that non-philologists (e.g., lawyers and philosophers) did not discuss Moses learnedly.[26] The key, then, was to establish philologically who Moses was and what he wrote and then to proceed, from this basis, to a broader consideration of his contemporary significance.

This effort was complicated by the 1753 anonymous publication of a French treatise that gathered numerous arguments against simple Mosaic authorship of

Genesis and proposed instead that Moses composed this book from older written sources. The full title of the work was *Conjectures sur les mémoires originaux dont il paroit que Moyse s'est servi pour composer le Livre de la Genèse*. Its author was later revealed to be Jean Astruc (1684–1766), personal physician to Louis XV.[27] Astruc published his work reluctantly and anonymously, fearing it would be used by others to diminish the authority of the Pentateuch. A loyal Catholic, Astruc did not want to encourage "false and dangerous" errors at odds with the "love of Truth and Religion."[28] Nevertheless, Astruc was convinced that a cogent analysis of Moses' sources would be neither novel nor subversive. After all, such an analysis would only bring clarity to the traditional opinion that Moses was responsible for the creation of Genesis and the Pentateuch as a whole. Astruc was "inspired by the completely *conservative* desire to make intelligible what he regarded as firmly established fact," namely that Moses wrote from sources.[29] In the preceding century, Richard Simon had used a theory of sources to neutralize Spinoza's literary-critical denigration of the Bible. Like Simon, Astruc stripped Moses of a meaningful authorial role precisely in order to defend him. Both severed the gangrenous limb of Mosaic authorship in order to save the whole body of biblical authority.

To Astruc, Moses was the keeper of earlier documents, the *mémoires*. Moses had at his disposal twelve written documents, two major and ten minor ones, which he organized into four distinct columns. His two main sources, A and B, maintained an unvarying preference for a particular divine name: *Elohim* in the A source and *Jéhovah* in the B source. The use of divine names as a source-critical criterion was the cornerstone of his theory, an innovation that would become, through the work of Eichhorn, the basis for modern Pentateuchal criticism.[30] The bulk of the *Conjectures* is simply a division of Genesis (and Exodus 1–2) into the four putative columns. Astruc aimed to reproduce, line by line, the very documents that at one time lay before Moses. To this synopsis he added several *remarques* describing the advantages of his system. It explained away many infelicities: the puzzling alternation in the use of divine names, troubling repetitions in the narrative, and discrepancies in the chronological perspectives of the narrator (*antichronismes*). The sources that Moses inherited not only used different names for God, they also originated in different time periods. The source divisions thus saved Moses from charges of negligence and stupidity. Can it be imagined, Astruc asked, that Moses is responsible for faults, repetitions, and bizarre variations which are better and more naturally explained by the existence of multiple underlying sources?[31] Astruc's *Conjectures* was an apologetic work. It was not simply a vague, skeptical discussion of Mosaic authorship. Rather, it was a clear, constructive, and highly detailed presentation of Pentateuchal sources calculated to deflect criticism of the Bible. It was intended to acquit the biblical *text* of anachronisms and irregularities by showing that the reader of Genesis is actually dealing with disparate *texts*. How these came together to form Genesis—when Moses did not intend to join them in this way—is not entirely certain. Clearly aware that he had come to a weakness in his theory, Astruc guessed that some kind of scribal negligence or mistake was to blame for the disordered appearance of Genesis.[32] The blame, then, lay with unnamed copyists. Moses remained, for Astruc, the revered *Auteur* whose unique wisdom, education, and political experience demanded the highest respect.[33]

Michaelis and Mosaic Authorship

If Astruc's reassignment of blame was a victory for Moses, it was almost surely a Pyrrhic one. By conceding the "disorder" (*désordre*) of Genesis, he assured that the authorial activity of Moses, even if affirmed, was no longer manifest in the biblical text. Screened from readers by centuries of editorial activity, Moses was no longer accessible. The source-critical theories of Simon and Astruc amounted, then, to a functional denial of Mosaic genius. More than anything else, it was this functional denial that determined Michaelis's rejection of Astruc's literary criticism. Where earlier thinkers like Machiavelli remained confident that the Pentateuch was a literary reflection of Moses, the questions raised by Simon and Astruc effectively headed off, or at least complicated to a high degree, any attempt to recover Moses' literary persona, his voice, his mentality, his genius.

Michaelis, then, called the alleged "disorder" of Genesis into question. In his *Einleitung*, Michaelis called Astruc's negative characterization of Genesis "exaggerated" and "conjectural" before beginning an extended, cumulative argument for the literary merit and coherence of the Pentateuch.[34] He dampened critical zeal by showing that the supposed footprints of multiple sources and later editors were, for the most part, thoroughly ordinary features of any text and entirely to be expected from an ancient literary work. The alternation of divine names, then, is arbitrary and stylistic, compatible with a writerly interest in elegant variation.[35] Repetitions must not be treated as "offensive" or contemptible in such an old book, since they are a product of a more primitive time (*die Kindheit der Welt*) when repetition was thought to be useful, necessary, and pleasant. Homer, that great imitator of nature, made frequent use of repetition, and Virgil, in his own artful imitation of antiquity, did the same.[36] Similarly, the anachronisms that Astruc discovered are simply a result of Astruc's own failure to recognize that ancient storytellers organized their material topically and not chronologically, according to *Sachordnung* and not *Zeitordnung*.[37] However, it is important to point out that, for Michaelis, Moses was not the author of the entire Pentateuch. He acknowledged, for instance, that Joshua's editorial hand is occasionally evident (as presumably in the account of Moses' death). He also recognized a variety of older sources at Moses' disposal: ancient fragmentary reports (e.g., the battle of the kings in Gen 14), folktales (e.g., the etymology of Eve's name in Gen 3:20), and national songs (e.g., Num 21:27–30).[38] Unlike the extensive *mémoires* used by Astruc's Moses, these sources do not amount to a very high percentage of the Pentateuch.

Michaelis went on to describe how Moses used earlier materials. He denied emphatically that Moses was simply the "poor antiquarian" (*ärmlicher Brockensammler*) that Astruc made him out to be. Moses was not compelled to incorporate every fragment and include in his work everything that he knew. Rather, he was a wise and discriminating author who wrote with a view merely to what suited his purpose.[39] Moses, in other words, gave every evidence of being a true historian. Though he knew a great deal about the Moabites and Ammonites, for example, he left out irrelevant data and offered only pertinent information (Deut 2:10–11, 19–21). When he included an older document, he glossed unfamiliar place names, as when he pointed out that Kiriath-Arba and the cave of Machpelah are both in Hebron (Gen 23:2, 19). And when he incorporated an older story, he did so because the vocabulary rang true. Like a good historian, though, he diligently explained unfamiliar words (e.g. glossing *raham* with *hamon* in Gen 17:5). Yet, in most cases, the Pentateuch evinced a unique stylistic coherence that showed that Moses did not slavishly copy old documents but rather wrote as a historian would, drawing on source material in an orderly, intelligent, and purposeful way.

Michaelis's real case for Mosaic authorship, though, went beyond philological arguments or historiographical analysis. It stemmed from a fundamental commitment to the utility of the Bible. Mosaic authorship was ultimately to be vindicated by Michaelis's own successful attempts to encounter classical Israel paradigmatically in the person and writings of Moses. Michaelis's case rested on what he believed to be an overwhelming impression of historiographic intent, individual genius, and literary unity that reached across the Pentateuch and included Psalm 90:

> The books do not at all seem to me [to have come from secondary writers] but rather to be the work of one and the same man whom we know from these books and Psalm 90 to be a sublime poet, and, at the same time, whom we know from Deuteronomy to be a good orator for his time: why shouldn't the man also have written the historical and prosaic parts of his books?

Michaelis went on to include the book of Job among Moses' compositions, rounding out an expansive understanding of Moses' intellectual and literary character:

> If the book of Job is also from him, as seems to me for the above reasons to be most probable, then he was not merely the best writer we have

among all the Hebrews but also a scholar of very wide learning: would such a one have needed or even thought it necessary to enlist the help of another writer?[40]

Moses, then, embodies everything one might expect from classical literature: sublime poetry, good oratory, scholarly expertise, individuality.

The encounter with Astruc is instructive. Michaelis resisted Astruc's source criticism not because he denied that older sources were used in the composition of Genesis. Michaelis was sensitive to diachronic distinctions within the biblical corpus, especially as revealed in the use of archaic language and rare morphology. He departed from traditional, dogmatic defenses of Mosaic authorship and disdained dictational theories of inspiration. Rather, Michaelis's defense of Mosaic authorship was staked on the exemplarity of Moses. Without a real, full-bodied paragon like Moses, the project to create a classical Israel fails—much as classical Greece would be diminished by the denial of Homeric genius. Richard Popkin has pointed out that, in the early modern period, Mosaic authorship was important because it guaranteed the truth of the text.[41] If this statement is true in Michaelis's case, it does not simply mean that, for him, the Pentateuch is factual and trustworthy because it was written by or dictated to a great prophet of God. Rather, it means that a deeper confrontation with the "truth" of human creativity is facilitated by an identification of the Pentateuch with a single individual. By attributing the Pentateuch, Job, and Psalm 90 to a single person, Michaelis made it possible to understand this literature in a coherent way and to recognize the potential for poetic genius, political skill, and scientific expertise, both in *the* human individual (via a classical paragon) and in *a* human individual (the historical founder of Israel). Historical and humanistic inquiry converged powerfully in Michaelis's recovery of Moses.

Authorship and authority were linked for Michaelis. He connected the denial of Mosaic authorship to an undesirable denigration of the Bible's cultural and intellectual authority. Without a clear sponsor, the Pentateuch, the foundation of the Bible, threatened to come undone, to show itself a poorly edited collection of literary-historical accidents. Thus Michaelis did not join contemporaries in questioning the legitimacy of the traditional concept of authorship, which, according to Harold Love, assumed "a unitary historical author with total responsibility for the inherited text."[42] In defending the traditional conception, though, Michaelis was not actually defending tradition. His interest was in the practical value of having a renowned, ingenious author at the center of his classicizing project. He understood that it would be impossible to maintain that a "coherent, elaborately integrated work of art" like the Pentateuch could have "arisen from a prolonged process of collective composition."[43] An artful and coherent Pentateuch was more attractive to him than a critically dissected one. In the eighteenth century, scholars of classical and biblical literature experienced a tension between the critical impulse to analyze ancient literature, to break it apart in an attempt to set forth its textual history, and the interpretive impulse to articulate its cultural significance as a coherent and credible corpus. Love associates the two impulses with the time-honored categories of "splitters" and "lumpers." His description of "lumpers" is also an apt characterization of Michaelis's approach to the Pentateuch:

> Lumpers like to make connections and to compose wholes. Characteristically, they will be alert for evidence that allows new work to be added to an authorial corpus and less concerned with anomalies that challenge the additions—indeed, they may argue, like the critics of ancient Pergamon, that anomaly and a certain level of inconsistency are the natural condition of an author's lifework ... The lumper will look for features that characterise the work of 'Homer' and will try to gather as much material as possible under that broad umbrella while the splitter searches for inconsistencies within the work as evidence for collaborative composition.[44]

This distinction, as Love shows, helps avoid a teleological presentation of scholarly types (e.g., a story of the inevitable triumph of splitters over lumpers) and clarifies their potential for conflict and cooperation. It also helps explain why Michaelis, who was intent on recovering a useful and coherent portrait of Moses, could not be moved to credit the conjectures of Astruc.

The following sections examine Michaelis's portraits of Moses as a lawgiver and as a moralist. With the aid of comparative Semitic philology, Near Eastern history, and ethnography, Michaelis developed parallel understandings of Moses as a political and philosophical paragon. He believed that Moses absorbed Egyptian learning in his youth but reached a nadir in midlife when he was forced to flee Egypt. In his Midianite exile, Moses became a kind of moral philosopher, eventually clothing his reflections in the sublime poetry of the book of Job. Still vigorous in old age, Moses once again became a man of affairs, this time the founder of a nation. Though one finds in his scholarship on Moses no explicit reference to Plato's *Republic*, the notion of a philosopher-king was, perhaps, not very far from Michaelis's mind.

Moses the Lawgiver

In his massive six-volume *Mosaisches Recht*, Michaelis treats an astonishing variety of ancient Israelite legal topics, including constitutional law, property rights, criminal law, divorce, public festivals, judicial procedure, and a theory of punishments.

When Alexander Smith translated the work into English in 1814, he had difficulty deciding upon a suitable translation for the title. In the end, he decided, appropriately, to avoid a literal translation like *Mosaic Law* or *Mosaic Jurisprudence* and to follow the advice of Herbert Marsh in calling it *Commentaries on the Laws of Moses*.[45] This title captures well the character of a work organized around topical discussions of Pentateuchal laws. Michaelis's interpretive procedure in this work is always the same: to use his erudition to make the underlying logic of the law intelligible and appealing to modern readers. The work reads like the notes from a private tutorial on statecraft and jurisprudence conducted in Moses' own study for the benefit of modern students. Michaelis did not venture an explicit, comprehensive analysis of Moses as a lawgiver or political philosopher, for he discerned no overarching system in the Pentateuch.[46] Rather, he emulated Montesquieu and his 1748 *The Spirit of the Laws* by providing philosophical commentary on the laws themselves.[47] In doing so, he deliberately avoided theology. The foundational principle of the *Mosaisches Recht* is that Old Testament law has no claims to moral or religious normativity. It is to be understood as a legal code designed for a particular people in a particular time and place: "God never meant [the Mosaic law] to bind any other nation but the Israelites."[48] Once critically evaluated, it had value as a historic and philosophical resource, but it was not to be incorporated directly into modern legal systems. Many European nations continued to treat the Mosaic law as a relevant authority for civil law well into the eighteenth century (for example Sweden).[49] Michaelis's analysis, though, was based on the idea that the Mosaic law is only intelligible in the ancient Israelite context, apart from which it simply makes no sense. Once this context is understood, a clear picture of Moses emerges from the context. Michaelis underscores five points. He insists that Moses be understood 1) in terms of his Egyptian background; 2) as guided by an essential conservatism; 3) as oriented toward pragmatism; 4) as eudaimonistic with respect to political and ethical questions; and 5) as inclined toward a basically irenic social agenda. Michaelis's Moses, in short, resembles precisely the kind of leader that Georgia Augusta, in a context far removed from ancient Israel, aimed to produce.

Though the book of Exodus does not give any explicit indication that Moses received an Egyptian education, it was common, as we have seen, for early modern interpreters to assume that he was "ethnically Hebrew and culturally Egyptian."[50] In this, Michaelis was no different. Christian interpreters throughout the ages were encouraged in this view by the statement of St. Stephen in the New Testament that "Moses was instructed in all the wisdom of the Egyptians" (Acts 7:22). Michaelis went out of his way to explain that this verse had no role in compelling his interest in Moses' Egyptian background. Rather, it was the consensus of ancient sources that Moses was a kind of natural philosopher (*Naturkenner*)—a consensus, moreover, confirmed by Michaelis's own reading of the Bible.[51] The verse from Acts, then, was unnecessary: the Pentateuch was replete with evidence of Egyptian learning. This would seem to be a strange claim, though, given that the nature of "Egyptian learning" was not adequately understood before Champollion's decipherment of hieroglyphics in the 1820s. Furthermore, the Pentateuch and the book of Job manifest few explicit references to Egyptian history and culture.[52] And unlike many of his contemporaries, Michaelis did not posit an esoteric Egyptian monotheism. Why, then, did Egypt matter to a correct understanding of Moses? In Michaelis's view, Egypt was identified with three things: a successful geopolitical state, deep knowledge of the natural world, and aesthetic insight. The Egyptians had risen above their barbaric neighbors to produce a stable, powerful, and self-sufficient state organized around agriculture and the wise use of its own resources. Thus the Egyptians, according to Michaelis, did not practice nomadism or depend on foreign trade for their survival.[53] Michaelis's Moses, similarly, strove to help Israel civilize its nomadic ethos and become a stable, self-sufficient nation. Hess has shown persuasively that Michaelis's admiration for Egypt was influenced by his disdain for colonies, empire-building, and an excessive reliance on foreign trade.[54] A contemporary interest is clearly evident in this heartfelt wish to know more about Egypt:

> If we but knew more of the comprehensive, and far-extended legislative knowledge of this people ... our own political system, so far at least as connected with agriculture, and as directed to the peaceful increase of our internal strength as a nation, might receive material improvement.[55]

Michaelis regarded Moses, whom he describes as having been "raised at court," as one who knew how to create a successful state. Thus the Pentateuch may be read as a charter for a new nation, conceived by Moses in Israel's founding period and reflective of Egyptian political expertise.

Michaelis's Moses was too wise to think that a simple borrowing of actual Egyptian laws would serve the Israelites well. The two societies were fundamentally different, and the Israelites still followed "an ancient traditionary law" that was "principally nomadic" in character.[56] It fell to Moses to modify and incorporate existing customs into a framework more conducive to the just, stable, and rational society that Israel was supposed to become. A prudent recognition of the power and force of custom (*jus consuetudinarium*), then, compelled Moses to legislate *conservatively*, that is, with due respect for Israel's deep-seated nomadic ethos. Michaelis traces this ethos back to Abraham, Isaac, and Jacob; he does not, however, explain how this ethos remained strong through four hundred years of settled and enslaved life in Egypt. This oversight may be explained, in part, by Michaelis's enthusiasm for ethnography, by the fact that Michaelis, as we saw in chapter 4, regarded the wandering Arabs of his day to be the true heirs of the ancient

Israelites. He believed that parallels between the two provided the best hope of understanding ancient Israelite society. The *Mosaisches Recht* is characterized, then, by a distinct dialectic that Michaelis set up between the wisdom of the civilized and centralized Egyptians and the vibrant social traditions of the hot-blooded, rootless Hebrews.

An interesting example comes from Michaelis's discussion of the "avenger of blood" (Heb. *gô'ēl haddam*) in Articles 131 to 137. Michaelis begins with Hebrew philology. Ignoring the Masoretic vowel points, he cites an alternative (passive) pointing of this phrase in the Samaritan Pentateuch (גאול; Num 35:21) as evidence for the conjecture that the verb *gā'al* originally meant "to pollute" or "to stain." Thus the *gô'ēl* ("redeemer") was really the *gā'ûl* ("the stained"), and the *gā'ûl haddām* was really "the blood-stained one." The relative of a murder victim was thus understood to be "stained with blood" until he had avenged the death of his relation.[57] Only secondarily did the verb *gā'al* come to have a more general meaning "to redeem" which was then extended to other matters such as the redemption of land (e.g., Lev 25:25–28) and a widowed relative (as of Ruth and Naomi in the book of Ruth).

According to Michaelis, the Hebrew blood avenger, the one "stained with blood," has an exact parallel in the *thā'ir*, the Arab blood avenger. Drawing on Arabic literature, the Quran, and travel accounts, Michaelis described in detail how in Arab culture the relative of a murder victim is under a solemn obligation to avenge the death of a kinsman, that he risks being shamed and despised in the highest degree if he does not, and that he gains the highest praise and honor if he does. Though necessary and reasonable in a state of nature, Michaelis argues, the practice of blood vengeance is intolerable in civilized society, because it contains no protection for those falsely accused and often sets off murderous feuds between families in cases when the culpability of one killed by a *thā'ir* was not acknowledged by his own kin. At the time that Moses set forth his law, the *gô'el haddām* was already a settled institution. This is evident, Michaelis proposes, because Moses nowhere defines or introduces the idea; he simply takes its meaning for granted. Though blood vengeance is uncivilized, Moses could not have outlawed it entirely, since it was deeply ingrained in Israelite life and society. Thus Moses appointed six cities of refuge (Num 35:9–35; Deut 19:1–10) to which murderers could flee. This brilliant, nonrevolutionary maneuver was intended to civilize blood vengeance. By designating a safe place for an accused murderer, it allowed time for a proper investigation to take place, with the result that the *gô'ēl* would be less likely to kill an innocent man, the accused would enjoy a kind of due process, and feuds would be headed off by a public declaration of guilt or innocence.[58] In this way, Michaelis's Moses showed a conservative attitude toward the *jus consuetudinarium*, one balanced by prudent efforts to encourage a just, rational, and lawful society.

In addition to being respectful of tradition, the Moses of the *Mosaisches Recht* was fundamentally pragmatic. Moses set forth laws that were best for Israelites in their place and time. To assume that the authority of the laws extended beyond that place and time was fundamentally mistaken. Much like Montesquieu, Michaelis examined laws in terms of culture, climate, and geography. A study of the relation between the Mosaic laws and environmental factors shows that Moses gave laws that were pragmatic and well suited to the circumstances of the Israelites. The temperate climate of the eastern Mediterranean, for example, allowed Moses to prescribe a Sabbath law that prohibited the kindling of fire and the harvesting of grain and was yet humane. What effect would such a law have in Norway, Michaelis asks, with its long, harsh winters and its short, rainy harvest seasons? The law against usury was also pragmatic. Canaan is well situated for international trade, but Moses severely limited commercial activity by outlawing usury. The Israelites were forced instead to rely on agriculture, which made them self-sufficient like the Egyptians and allowed them to profit from having trading nations nearby (e.g., the Phoenicians) that needed their grain and wine.[59] Other laws that appear to be purely religious were actually given by Moses for practical ends. This is the case with laws concerning unclean animals. Some societies, for example, will eat horsemeat while others will not; the horse is "clean" in one culture and "unclean" in another. Moses used existing notions of clean and unclean animals to his own purposes. Because it is important for a fledgling nation to cultivate unity, it is also important that it protect its identity and integrity—especially when surrounded by hostile neighbors. In light of this circumstance, Moses converted customs into "immutable laws." By restricting certain foods, Moses made it difficult for Israelites to socialize with non-Israelites, thus preventing the Israelites from interacting too closely with their neighbors and being infected either by their idolatry or by their vices.[60]

Other laws aimed to promote human happiness. Michaelis took on his theological critics when he claimed that Mosaic law was based on a eudaimonistic "universal principle" of political and moral governance:

> If to any of my readers the principles already laid down should appear offensive and repugnant to the idea of a law given by God, the cause is to be sought in their not duly attending to the connection and limits of morals and politics. It is the business of both to promote human happiness, and both alike admit this universal principle, from which all their particular precepts flow—*Endeavor to extend happiness as far as possible*.[61]

Michaelis is not on particularly solid ground in stating that a universal notion of human happiness is the telos of biblical law. He offers no direct evidence for this, textual or otherwise. His argument depends on the cumulative effect of his eudaimonistic interpretations of laws, which characterize Moses as a lawgiver fundamentally interested in human happiness. For example, Michaelis explains the three great annual feasts prescribed by the Pentateuch (Passover, Pentecost, Tabernacles) primarily as occasions for recreation, fellowship, and the refreshment of laborers. "Every individual," he explains, should "taste also the pleasures of life," with even the slaves and poorest people included in the prescribed festivals.[62] A more sophisticated example comes from Michaelis's exposition of the biblical injunction against boiling a kid in its mother's milk (Ex 23:19, 34:26; Deut 14:21), a law which he says has suffered more at the hands of commentators than any other law. Even the most acceptable of the traditional explanations (that such an act would be cruel and abusive) still seems implausible to Michaelis. For, he asks, "how came the Israelites to hit upon the strange whim of boiling a kid in milk, and just in the milk of its own mother?" Michaelis's interpretation begins with a geographical consideration. Palestine is the best country for the cultivation of the olive tree. Egypt, however, does not have olive trees, and Egyptians must therefore use butter in their cooking. In order to encourage the Israelites to stay in Palestine and be content there, Moses forbid them from preparing their meat in Egyptian fashion. Michaelis interpreted "milk" in this law as butter. He disliked buttery dishes and complained of their constant use in German cooking. He saw in the biblical law, then, an attempt on Moses' part to wean the Israelites from food prepared in this way and to help them appreciate their homegrown products.[63] These brief examples show that Michaelis's Moses was not only conservative and practical; he was also interested in the Israelites' happiness and enjoyment.

The apparent humaneness of Mosaic legislation is evident, finally, in its foundational commitment to a philosophical monotheism. Michaelis regarded monotheism as a basic principle of the Mosaic legislation and the new Israelite state. In imposing monotheism on the Israelites, Moses required them to resist and contravene the conventional wisdom (*sensus communis*) of the ancient world. Polytheism was self-evident to Greeks, Romans, Egyptians, and Canaanites; alternative belief systems were more or less inconceivable.[64] The allegiance to Yahweh that Moses required set the Israelites apart and served two additional purposes. First, theirs was a *civic* monotheism: allegiance to Yahweh was the source of Israelite identity and the logical response to Israel's emergence from slavery in Egypt as a people under Yahweh's leadership. It was a national identity marker derived from a shared historical reality. This particular understanding is evident in Michaelis's paraphrase of the first commandment:

> In case you stupidly believe that there are several gods who can hear prayers and reward sacrifices: I alone am the one who freed you from slavery in Egypt, who made a people out of poor slaves, who am the founder of your state. In this state, no other god besides me should be worshipped.[65]

Second, monotheism was, in Michaelis's view, the most rational belief system. A monotheistic cult—indeed *any* monotheistic cult—functions pedagogically to encourage human flourishing. One need not have faith in revealed religion to see that the institution of a state-sponsored monotheism is a boon for any people; one need only be an enemy of superstition and fraud.[66] In this way, Michaelis's Moses was less a convinced Yahwist than a philosophical monotheist.

Michaelis, however, was careful to point out that Moses did not actually legislate *belief*. He did not require the Israelites to espouse any particular theological doctrines, such as a belief in a future Messiah. Instead, he instituted a monotheistic cult and made claims only on the kind of formal worship that the state would recognize. He understood monotheism as a philosophical doctrine and not as a religious identity. Thus he distinguished sharply between a reasonable, state-sponsored monotheism and the different, altogether unwise attempt to compel belief in religious particulars—as when European rulers foolishly made it "the goal of the state to uphold many doctrines, true or false, of the Reformed, Lutheran, and Catholic."[67] In a display of religious restraint, Michaelis's Moses also refrained from invoking a metaphysical basis for any of his prescriptions. Echoing Warburton, Michaelis noted that Moses connected lawlessness only to punishments in this world and not in an afterlife. He also departed from Egyptian practice in refusing to spiritualize civic laws.

In these ways, Moses pursued an irenic social agenda. Like Münchhausen, the founder of Georgia Augusta, who feared sectarianism and deemphasized theological particulars, the Moses of the *Mosaisches Recht* was too wise to believe that strict ideological purity was necessary, achievable, or desirable. Both Münchhausen and Michaelis's Moses also agreed that whatever common belief was prescribed had to be basic, general, and intelligible to reason. Its primary benefit was social cohesiveness. According to Michaelis, Moses the lawgiver worked in a pragmatic, conservative way to make ancient Israel a rational, tolerant, and happy society. To readers of the *Mosaisches Recht* this program would have seemed familiar. The goals of statesmen and reformers in the age of *Aufklärung* were to subordinate churchly interests to civic ones and to use the university to produce "educated servants of the state," "tolerant churchmen," and men "able to meet the high demands of rationality."[68] To a philological philosophizer like Michaelis, these were educational goals, as it were, straight out of the Bible.

Moses the Moralist

Faced with the task of producing a new German translation of the Bible, Michaelis chose to begin not with Genesis but with the book of Job. The translation of this book, along with accompanying "notes for the layperson," appeared in the first of thirteen volumes. In the 1769 preface to the translation project, Michaelis explained that Job was the oldest of all the biblical books.[69] This was a common and relatively unproblematic scholarly opinion at the time, and Michaelis neither explained nor defended it. The second reason for beginning with Job was that the book, taken as a whole, contains two doctrines that form the basis for any religion: the immortality of the soul and the existence of an afterlife containing rewards and punishments for one's conduct in this life. According to Michaelis, other parts of the Hebrew Bible only hint at answers to these questions. What few references to them can be found in the Psalms, Pentateuch, and prophets would not be sufficient by themselves to answer these central religious questions. It would be far better to address them early in the canonical ordering, and to do so explicitly. For Michaelis, Job was not simply the oldest book in the Bible. By virtue of its teaching on the soul and the afterlife, it was also the foundational one.

An earnest belief in the importance of the book of Job would have been entirely unremarkable in the eighteenth century. In the middle of the century, England played host to a "Job controversy" that placed the interpretation of the book at the center of a heated and intricate debate between Whigs and Tories, philosophers and literary men.[70] Jonathan Lamb, in his insightful study of this period, locates Job in a larger discourse about an aesthetic and political representation, where the biblical figure functioned as a trope signifying the "disturbance of representational technique," "the agitated and complaining voice" of the individual, and the "power of this complaint, unabated by orthodox interpretation and unocculted as delinquent nicety."[71] By interpreting the book as national allegory composed after the Exile, Bishop Warburton turned the book of Job into dramatization of Jewish national redemption. His great opponent in this debate, Bishop Lowth, insisted on the historicity and individuality of Job's suffering. For Lowth, parallelism bore additional witness to the raw, undigestible emotional force of the book. Lowth and other opponents of Warburton read the book as an "interruptive and excessive narrative of personal affliction" that shows how the integrity of the individual can "achieve sublimity in the vacuum of all regulatory systems."[72] German thinkers also wrestled with the normativity of Job.[73] If it were merely an ancient tale, it would simply be one of many. If it were merely a sympathetic exploration of human suffering, it might well be superseded. Herder's response was to attend both to the historical situation and to the section of universal, psychological terrain illuminated by Hebrew literature. Herder presented the Old Testament as a coherent body of literature that expressed the particular genius of the Israelite *Volk*. For Herder, the normativity of the Hebrew Bible, its value as a guide to modern life, lay not in its doctrines but rather in a Hebraic model for developing an authentic literary culture: through "differentiation and emulation, Hebrew poetry would be transfigured into an exemplar of German national literature."[74] The book of Job was ground zero for this attempt. Unlike Herder and Warburton, Michaelis did not see the value of Job in its status as a piece of national literature. Instead, it was the foundation for his philosophy of religion. What distinguished Michaelis from other philosophically minded interpreters, though, was his commitment to philology. Hebrew language and antiquities were a natural point of departure for him, and they brought Michaelis once again to the figure of Moses.

Michaelis believed that Moses was the author of the book of Job. His reasons for believing this fell into two categories. The first concerns Moses' unique history and cultural background. Michaelis argued that several details in the book of Job require deep familiarity with Egyptian culture and natural history. The book mentions African animals such as the elephant (40:15–24) and the crocodile (40:25–41:26). It also describes commercial activities for which Egypt was known: papyrus-making (8:11–12) and gold-mining (22:24–25; 28:1–28). There are allusions to practices that began in Egypt and only spread to west Asia centuries after (Michaelis believed) the book of Job was written. These include the use of horses in battle (39:19–25) and the creation of sacred burial complexes (Michaelis translates *khoravot* in 3:14 as "mortuary shrines" not "ruins").[75] The book also shows familiarity with the geography of greater Arabia. Since the book was certainly composed in Hebrew, only an Israelite who was raised in Egypt and who lived in Egypt's eastern desert could have written the book. Also noteworthy is the fact that the book shows no real familiarity with Palestine. For Michaelis, these circumstances point clearly to Moses.

A second category concerns literary evidence. Michaelis identified many concepts, poetic images, and vocabulary common only to Job, the Pentateuch, and Psalm 90. Since he believed that Moses was the author of the Pentateuch and Psalm 90, then special vocabulary also found in Job would naturally signal Mosaic authorship of Job. Michaelis's list of parallels is very extensive, but a few examples will suffice here. Common poetic images include a description of very ancient times as the time "before the hills or mountains were born" (Job 15:7 and Ps 90:2), of the abode of the dead as an island beyond the sea (Ps 90:10; Deut 30:13; Job 26:5), and of human vitality as coming from the breath of God (Job 27:3 and Gen 2:7). Rare vocabulary common to Job and other Mosaic writings include *shekhin* "boils" (Job 2:7; Ex 9:10–11; Deut 28:27, 35; Lev 13:18–20), *'akhu* "reed grass" (Job 2:7; Gen 41:2, 18), *'alumim* in the sense of "hidden sins" (Job 20:11; Ps 90:8), and *qadim* in the sense of "eastern storm wind" (Job 27:21 and Ex 14:21). Because Michaelis believed that Moses wrote the book of Job at midlife, years before he returned to Egypt and brought the Israelites to Sinai, it did not trouble him that there are no references to the Mosaic law in the book of Job. Michaelis nevertheless discerned interesting parallels between the Mosaic law and the morality of the book of Job. He saw a connection between an implicit condemnation of those who strip their debtors by taking clothing in repayment (Job 22:6; 24:3, 7–9) and laws against taking a neighbor's cloak as surety for a loan (Deut 24:10–13 and Ex 22:26–27). Michaelis also related an unfavorable description of those who abuse servants by withholding food (Job 24:10–11) and the law against muzzling the ox while it treads out the grain (Deut 25:4).[76] Finally, for good measure, Michaelis mentioned that he had the support of tradition.[77]

Mosaic authorship was crucial to Michaelis's interpretation of Job. Equally important was his understanding of the book's genre. As the Warburton controversy indicates, there were two main options. Either the book was seen as a true story of a historical figure, or it was a moralistic fable. It pained Michaelis a little to break ranks with his colleagues and teachers—Albert Schultens, Robert Lowth, and his own father—but he was convinced that the book could not be read profitably as a true story.[78] If it were a transcript of actual conversations, how could one decide with certainty what the central idea (*Meinung*) of the book was? How could one distinguish the true ideas from the false ones? When classical writers like Cicero create fictional conversations, one is able to extract from them the author's opinion.[79] Michaelis thus assumed that fictionalized dialogues manifest the *Tendenz* of the author in a more or less straightforward way. A transcript of actual dialogues, though, does not allow the reader to draw out a single, coherent meaning. It is a literary orphan. By making the book of Job a moralistic fable, Michaelis treated it as a unified literary creation with a particular message. Just as Michaelis could not see the value of an authorless, fragmented Pentateuch, he was not willing to sacrifice Job's philosophical contribution on the altar of literary criticism.

According to Michaelis, Moses wrote the book of Job when he was a stateless exile in the land of Midian. At that point, he had fallen far, from prestige and power at the Egyptian court to a liminal existence in the desert. The vicissitudes of his life to that point presumably prompted reflection on the meaning and consequences of piety, for Moses' good deeds to that point had apparently not gone unpunished. He thus wrote the book of Job as a moralistic fable reflecting on the problematic relation between piety and prosperity, wickedness and misfortune. Michaelis's concise summary of the book's moral philosophy is worth quoting at length:

> Fortune and misfortune, even those that are most intense and last one's whole life, are not apportioned in this life according to what one deserves. Often one sees that the virtuous prosper and the wicked suffer misfortune, but often one sees the exact opposite: the virtuous suffer external misfortune until the end of life as the most wicked live the happiest possible lives, peaceful and respectable until the end. The stage of divine justice is not in this world; we believe in it but see it not: there

is a life after death, full of rewards and punishments and including a bodily resurrection, and in this future world the virtuous will prosper and the evil suffer.[80]

In Job's world (and in our own), fortune and misfortune are not apportioned justly. According to Michaelis, Moses responded to this state of affairs by affirming that the "stage of divine justice" is not in this world but in the next. In doing so, he safeguarded both justice and morality. The conduct of the individual, however unfairly repaid in this world, is nevertheless warranted by future, justly distributed rewards and punishments. The doctrine of future punishments and rewards in the book of Job serves as a counterpoint to Michaelis's portrait of Moses as an irenic legislator. The Mosaic law was wise, Michaelis argued, because it did not overreach religious boundaries and compel belief in any doctrine. Recognizing that belief in divine judgment was nevertheless essential to morality and civic order, Michaelis attributed this belief to Moses by virtue of his philosophical insight as the author of Job. He was, in short, the consummate leader.

But does the book of Job, in fact, teach that the soul is immortal and that it will stand on the "stage of divine justice" in the next life? Though Michaelis insisted that it did, he was forced to resort to inventive translation to make his case. By his reading, Job stood against his friends in maintaining that justice is only meted out in the next world. Eliphaz, Bildad, and Zophar all tried in different ways to convince Job that God's governance of *this* world includes just deserts and that Job's suffering must therefore correspond to some sin on his part. Job, though, refused to allow that there was a necessary connection between one's moral state and his lot in this life. The linchpin to Michaelis's argument is Job's famous statement in chapter 19. Michaelis called this verse "the golden confession of [Job's] certain hope in a resurrection and in an effusive blessedness in a future life."[81] Michaelis translates verses 25 through 27 as follows:

> I know that my savior lives! Someday, another "I" will arise from the dust,
> My skin, this food for boils, will be different; And I will see God out of my own body,
> I will see him for myself, My eyes, and not a stranger will see him.[82]

The key verse is 19:25b: "Someday, another 'I' will arise from the dust."[83] In Michaelis's translation, it reads like a clear declaration from Job that, because of a living savior (19:25a), he will rise (*aufstehen*) from the dead in his own physical body in order to face God's judgment. 19:25b presents problems to any translator, but Michaelis, in fashioning a "golden confession" from this verse, was unusually tendentious. The verb in 19:25b (יָקוּם) is third person singular (lit. "he/she/it will arise"). Yet Michaelis makes this verb correspond to the subject of the first-person verb (יָדַעְתִּי) in 19:25a (lit. "I know"), with the result that Job awkwardly refers to himself in the third person. A second problem is the word אַחֲרוֹן (lit. "latter" or "last"). Michaelis appears to have translated it twice: adjectivally in the sense of a related but different word אַחֵר (lit. "another") and adverbially as *dereinst* ("someday"). He then supplies a subject not found anywhere in the verse (*Ich*) and creates the clause: "Someday another 'I' will arise." Finally, Michaelis translates the fairly unproblematic עַל־עָפָר (lit. "upon the dust" or "upon the earth") as "*from* the dust" (*aus dem Staube*). By making a series of questionable maneuvers, Michaelis placed in Job's mouth a bold confession of faith in a future bodily resurrection.

Unfortunately for Michaelis, this confusing verse is the clearest reference in the book to any expectation of resurrection and vindication after death. The other verses that he adduced rely on readings that are even more speculative than the one underlying his translation of 19:25b.[84] If Michaelis seems cavalier, it is partly because he regarded the willingness to take certain exegetical liberties as a mark of intellectual freedom. In this, Luther was his model. Perhaps Michaelis drew inspiration from the fact that Luther's own translation of Job 19:25 ("I know that my savior lives and that he will awaken me from the earth in the hereafter") was a nonliteral, clearly Christianized rendering of the Hebrew. In his preface to the *Deutsche Übersetzung*, Michaelis praised the Reformer, above all, for exercising natural powers of judgment and a certain "freedom of thought" that allowed him to escape the taint of two particular "Jewish prejudices": that the consonantal text is perfect and that the Masoretic pointings are correct.[85] Luther was able to produce an intelligent, authentic German translation precisely because he rejected these two beliefs. Instead of offering a literal translation that was slavishly true to defective texts, Luther produced a Bible that was instead the work of a "free spirit" alive to the *meaning* of the biblical text.[86] Ranging across the linguistic ruins of an old philosophical fable, Michaelis's own free spirit found the true faith of Moses and the key to a rational and morally satisfying religion.

Conclusion

In his effort to provide a paragon of classical Israel, Michaelis delivered a Moses who was no longer recognizably Israelite. In one sense, this was an ironic result. As we have seen, Michaelis constantly insisted on the need for erudition and knowledge of the geographically, historically, and linguistically particular. His treatments of Moses bristle with philological detail; they are strewn with ancient Near Eastern antiquities. This learning, however, never coalesced into a clear image of a distinct *Israelite* leader. Rather, Michaelis used his scholarship to make Moses into an abstraction, a vessel for philosophical doctrines, whose identity and significance transcended Israel altogether. Thus, Moses' worship of Yahweh became a sane, rational, and irenic monotheism. Cultic laws became examples of a universal eudaimonism. The book of Job, revered by Lowth and the English preromantics for its tenacious particularity, became, in Michaelis's hands, a philosophical fable teaching general religious truths like the doctrine of future rewards and punishments. It is tempting to characterize Michaelis, who seemed to have one foot in the "philosophical" eighteenth century and the other in the "historical" nineteenth century, as a transitional figure.

The temptation should be resisted. It is clear that Michaelis projected Enlightenment values onto his reading of the Bible. Yet he was not groping after irreducible historical particulars by employing philosophical frameworks, as the characterization above suggests. The reception of Homer provides a useful parallel. In her valuable study of Homer in the eighteenth century, Kirsti Simonsuuri chronicles the development of notions of Homeric genius. She observes a shift from neoclassical admiration of Homer as the "traditionally eminent poet" to a dominant form of Homeric criticism, at the end of the eighteenth century, based on the notion that "Homer" was the "collective voice of a tribal society."[87] As Homer's traditional authority declined in this period, his identities as a primitive bard, an ingenious poet close to nature, and an organ of an ancient *vox populi* came into clearer focus. It was a shift from universal to particular. Michaelis's younger contemporaries, Herder and Schiller for example, staked a great deal on particularity. They made it the basis for a new kind of cultural authority. Moderns ought to imitate the ancients, they believed, but they should do so formally and not materially, respecting them as authentic embodiments of specific cultures rather than as trustworthy bearers of timeless truth. On this view, the Germans must imitate the Greeks in order to become better Germans.

As we saw in chapter 3, Göttingen neohumanists did not share these anxieties about cultural self-possession. A greater degree of confidence in the stability of their own cultural identity and in the value of their religious inheritance yielded a different environment for the study of the past. Michaelis understood the allure of particularity but saw it, ultimately, as a component of a rooted cosmopolitanism. He could embrace and advance new research on the ancient context of the Bible without feeling compelled to surrender to its vision of life. At the same time, it seemed obvious to him as a Western intellectual that the Bible had enduring value. By recovering Moses as a classical figure, Michaelis balanced the demands of *Wissenschaft* for a critical, historical engagement with his subject against the deep commitment to theological irenicism and social utility required by his university context. That his Moses was no longer recognizably Israelite does not mean that Michaelis backslid unwittingly (as many eighteenth-century polymaths are said to have done) from history into philosophy, from particularity back into universality. The question for Michaelis was not an idle inquiry into who Moses *was* as a historical individual. His question was larger and more interesting. He wanted to know whether Moses and the Bible as a whole were capable of bearing the full weight of Western culture. Michaelis sensed that for a historical figure, even one as great as Moses, to bear such a burden, it was not enough to be strong and wise. He also needed deep roots in a classical past.

Conclusion

Can one know the past if one does not even understand the present?—
And who will take the right concepts from the present, without knowing
the future?

—Johann Georg Hamann, *Kleeblatt
Hellenistischer Briefe* (1762)

Few things about Michaelis's scholarly project are more interesting than
this: its methods lived on well into the modern era even as its principal
ideal, the recovery of a classical Israel, did not. As a German university
professor, an expert on the ancient Near East, and a lifelong Lutheran,
Michaelis balanced a variety of interests and loyalties: some complementary, many conflicting. Taken together, they lend vitality to a complex
image of a scholar of the Bible forging a new path at the postconfessional
Enlightenment university. Refracted one way, it is the image simply of
another half-forgotten figure in an eighteenth-century landscape already
crowded with brilliant minds. Seen another way, though, it is a reflection
of a brief but consequential moment in which Western biblical interpretation suddenly seemed to lurch back to life and, unexpectedly, regain its
feet. How and why it did so is an important question, one that, as we
have seen, has a good deal to do with Michaelis and the University of
Göttingen. Much of what Michaelis tried to do came to naught. Other
aspects of his legacy proved durable and decisive. Nevertheless, when
seen in its broadest outlines from our twenty-first-century vantage

point, Michaelis's project must be judged a clear (but qualified) success. In what follows, I will explain these judgments.

The fading discipline of "classics" still belongs to Greece and Rome. One reason that Michaelis failed to make Israel a classical civilization on a par with Greece and Rome is that his reconstruction of ancient Israel did not, even in his lifetime, stand up to the demands of the newer critical science. The most eloquent witness to this fact is Michaelis's own student and successor at Göttingen, J. G. Eichhorn. To Eichhorn, Michaelis was a father of German biblical criticism and a pioneer in the use of "ancillary" disciplines like ethnography, geography, and comparative Semitic philology to interpret the Bible. With the publication of Michaelis's annotated translation of the Old Testament, Eichhorn believed, "a new period of biblical exegesis began."[1] After training scores of scholars in the art of research and teaching to full lecture halls year after year, Michaelis became, according to Eichhorn, "a true teacher of Europe."[2] Yet Eichhorn also notes in his retrospective on Michaelis's life that he outlived his influence, lingering on while his research, contributions, and even his assumptions became passé. The chief reason for this, according to Eichhorn, was that Michaelis's Israel, in the end, was only a figment of historical imagination. Michaelis's commitment to the classical venerability of Israel hindered his project. His work was characterized by contradictory impulses to recover the historically primitive and to revere it, at the same time, as wise. The evidence, for example, did not support Michaelis's vision of Moses as a "poet-philosopher" with "comprehensive knowledge of the natural world" and a "wealth of additional learning." Eichhorn, who seized enthusiastically upon Astruc's source-critical approach, denied that the historical Moses was accessible to the biblical reader in any straightforward way. Moreover, proper historical understanding required the recognition of a more fundamental disjunction between the intellectual world of the primitive, Oriental past and modern sensibilities of truth, science, and knowledge. Without clear evidence for the reconstruction of Israelite natural and political philosophy, Eichhorn favored a presumption of difference, not similarity. Attempts to connect ancient Israelite thought with developments in modern philosophy, for example, were bound to involve anachronism and distortion.

Eichhorn was not the only member of his generation to find Michaelis's historical sense lacking. J. G. Herder complained that Michaelis, the learned Orientalist, did not really understand Oriental culture: he did not grasp its spirit. Michaelis's numerous researches merely amounted, in Herder's judgment, to a lifeless and incoherent collection of information. In the end, Michaelis manufactured a senseless "Near Eastern mythology" comprised of amusing images and catalogs of parallel passages from ancient sources. He offered mere "notions" that failed to convey the "context, value, sense, and understanding" of the Israelites. Michaelis, for all his learning, simply did not possess what Herder called the "feel of the Orient."[3] To

Herder, the Mosaic law expressed a form, an ideal of national life connected to an irreducible cultural whole. For Herder, the specific laws "embrace the whole character and mode of thinking of the nation" and "all the peculiar qualities of the country." History, geography, language, and especially poetry formed a seamless national culture. To understand the Israelites one must recognize that everything connects to everything else: "their law, every season of the year, every fertile spot and watered glen, but still more their religious worship, with its festivals and ceremonies." From this, Herder maintains, flows "the genuine national spirit of the Psalms and Prophets."[4] The laws of Moses cannot be isolated from one another, analyzed in terms of modern philosophy, and reconstructed simply as "good European common sense."[5] The touchstone of Herder's understanding of Israel was its poetry, which expressed a deep connection to the land and a rugged, natural, and unaffected faith in Yahweh. Though it was Michaelis's scholarship that first allowed Herder and his generation to see ancient Israel in this light, Herder believed that Michaelis had not gone far enough. Michaelis's knowledge of the ancient world allowed him, perhaps, to see something of the ancient *Moses*, but it did not illuminate the Israelite *people*. Michaelis thus created an enlightened Moses at the expense of a benighted Israel. To Herder, Moses' greatness lay precisely in his ability to create laws that expressed the genius of the *Volk*, the theocratic ideal at the heart of ancient Israelite cultural identity. Michaelis's erudite rationalizations of Mosaic laws did not penetrate this ethos. Divorced from a nationalistic conception of poetry, Michaelis's explanations, in Herder's judgment, failed to yield a convincing picture of the "Oriental who feels the veins of his tribe." Instead, they "loaned" to Moses mere "commonplaces" that were "alien to that people, that time, that lawgiver."[6]

Herder's own work on language, philosophy, and history show that in the last quarter of the eighteenth century, the atmosphere was changing. In the German lands, the enthusiasm for *Orientalistik* generated by Michaelis proved to be the undoing, ironically, of his classical project. The movement toward distinctness and cultural incommensurability that was exemplified by Herder emerged from the edifice of biblically oriented ancient Near Eastern scholarship that Michaelis built at the university. At the center of Michaelis's work was a denial of the theological exceptionalism that tended to characterize earlier, confessional interpretation of the Old Testament. Michaelis's Israelites became flesh-and-blood denizens of antiquity just as European intellectuals were turning to the ancient world to recover cultural resources outside the Christian tradition. It was precisely because Michaelis and others succeeded in embedding the Bible in this antiquity that their successors, the vaunted generation of Goethe and Herder, possessed the confidence and critical tools to leave the Christian tradition behind and fan out into the wider Mediterranean—especially Greece and Egypt—and points east, notably Persia,

Babylon, and India. Within decades of Michaelis's greatest achievements, a new Orientalism inclined toward "cultural radicalism," the destruction of "Western self-satisfaction," and the diminishment of Christianity began to take shape.[7] The study of Arabic, for example, had long been regarded principally as a help to Hebrew philology. Yet figures like Johann Jakob Reiske, who grew up at Halle but later gave up on the Bible, showed that "ancillary" disciplines no longer needed theological justification. Toward the end of his life in 1774 he declared that, as a "martyr" of Arabic literature, the "so-called holy philology" associated with the Old Testament was entirely a matter of indifference to him.[8] The shift is also apparent in the career of Friedrich Schlegel, who studied with Michaelis at Göttingen in the heyday of Hebrew Orientalism. After his studies, Schlegel left for Jena and immersed himself in Greek literature in the 1790s. Early in the nineteenth century, though, he played an important role in the rise of Sanskrit studies, which by that time had begun to eclipse Hebrew as the oldest and most venerable Eastern language. As his scholarship matured, he struggled to locate ancient Israel in the history of world literature; he tried vainly to support a vestigial attachment to the sacredness of Hebrew. Yet even Schlegel's modest efforts in this regard exceeded those made by his contemporaries who, after 1800, gave up on Hebrew altogether.[9] The frontier of Orientalism moved east, stranding ancient Israel and its small linguistic corpus in a disciplinary no-man's-land.

Classical Israel also faced competition on its western front. As we have seen, German philhellenism became a powerful movement in the final quarter of the eighteenth century. Unlike the pacific neohumanism of Gesner and Heyne, the fervid idealism of Goethe's circle propelled its members outward into new institutions and endeavors designed to overcome traditional Christian culture. Fichte and Schelling, in particular, argued that the content of the theological tradition had to be reanalyzed in historical and philosophical terms in order to be readmitted to the university.[10] Wilhelm von Humboldt, perhaps the most ardent of the philhellenists, was tasked with organizing the new university at Berlin in 1809. He decided ultimately to keep theology and the other humanistic disciplines housed in separate faculties. In this arrangement, history, philosophy, and classics became the center of gravity for Humboldtian *Wissenschaft*, leaving a (Michaelian) scientific study of Israel on the margins. Moreover, the classical image that Israel briefly enjoyed gave way, in the early nineteenth century, to its older, more familiar Judaic one. Largely because of Schleiermacher's influential reformulation of Protestant faith, the study of the Bible retained a place in academic theology—yet Schleiermacher's religion, with its negative attitudes toward Judaism, assigned no value to an ancient Israel understood on its own terms. The German reinvention of a non-Judaic Christianity on the one hand and the philhellenism of Berlin luminaries like Humboldt and Wolf on the other left little room for a classical Israel. These two movements also coincided, as Sheehan has shown, with a resurgence of anti-Jewish cultural prejudice: "If Christianity was an expression of German culture, Judaism expressed the culture of the Jews."[11] Michaelis's classical Israel was an academic casualty of these developments. In the end, though, even Greece and Rome ceased to be classical. The scientific, highly specialized study of antiquity that developed at German universities in the nineteenth century gradually undermined belief in the normativity of classical aesthetics and moral philosophy.[12] As Grafton puts it, classical philology "tended inevitably to fall apart into an increasing number of sub-disciplines," and as the century wore on, professors "tended to lecture more and more about less and less."[13]

As the foundation for Jewish and Christian scriptural canons, the Old Testament held sway over vast cultures and territories for millennia. But as the remnant of a classic Eastern civilization, it held the interest of scholars for only a few decades. Michaelis's Israel was an unstable scholarly creation. It was old and exotic enough to stimulate a kind of romantic primitivism, but too traditional to sustain European tastes for the Oriental. It was familiar enough to warrant the close scrutiny of a classical civilization, but on this score too distant from the springs of modern cultural identity; Greece and Rome proved closer. It was venerable enough to be a plausible part of religious scholarship, but too impoverished theologically to sustain an actual community of faith. In what sense, then, did Michaelis's project endure? For a variety of reasons, the Israelite classical project did not succeed in exactly the aesthetic, philological, and historical form that Michaelis gave to it. It nevertheless paved the way for three ways of understanding and appropriating the Old Testament: as part of a cultural Bible, a scriptural Bible, and, finally, the academic Bible. Michaelis's legacy includes vital contributions to the first of these, the cultural Bible. But his true significance lies with the other two. It was Michaelis who made the academic Bible a viable alternative to the scriptural Bible in the context of the university.

Jonathan Sheehan has shown what, precisely, was involved in the cultural transformation of biblical authority in the second half of the eighteenth century. According to Sheehan, the various "Enlightenment Bibles" were drawn from fields to which Michaelis made important contributions—history, poetry, pedagogy, and moral philosophy. These coalesced in the nineteenth century into a "cultural Bible" that may, with justice, be called a modern European "classic."[14] The surprising durability of the modern cultural Bible is an interesting and important story. Yet, from a late or postmodern perspective, it is a story that seems less relevant than it once did. On the one hand, the powerful resurgence of religious traditionalism in contemporary life has strengthened devotional and churchly reading, which is oriented toward the Bible as scripture and not merely as cultural material. On the other hand, the alienation of the Bible from public life and the rise of ideological multiculturalism call the viability of the Bible as a western "classic" into question.[15] Northrop Frye compared the Bible to the "great Boyg" of Ibsen's *Peer Gynt*, likening it to a massive sphinx that dominates our cultural heritage. The comparison was already less apt in 1982 when *The Great Code* was published than in the 1940s when Frye first confronted the Bible's hold over the imagination of William Blake.[16] And though the image surely captures the experience of a scholar trying to uncover the architecture of the Western literary tradition, encountering the cultural Bible in recent times has been less like coming up against a great Boyg, inscrutable and inevitable, and more like a chance meeting with a distant relative whom one may or may not see again.

In light of this, it is appropriate to examine whether the critically reconstructed Bible of Michaelis and others retains significance, more specifically, on *religious* grounds. The most fundamental question that one can address to Michaelis's biblical project is whether the Bible—given its particular shape, contents, and afterlife—can be fully comprehended in cultural categories. This question occupied one of Michaelis's earliest and strongest critics, Königsberg thinker Johann Georg Hamann (1730–1788), the enigmatic "Magus of the North" and father of *Sturm und Drang*. Though Hamann moved in avant-garde literary circles as a young man, he underwent a religious conversion and subsequently became a critic (though also a friend) of Kant, eventually earning a place among the well-known opponents of Enlightenment. He mentored Herder and inspired the generation of Goethe, but—and I take this to be a significant fact—he never held a university post. In Hamann's view, Michaelis embodied a mode of criticism that was predicated on a fundamental misunderstanding of what the Bible is. For Hamann, biblical interpretation derived its importance from the divine origin of the Bible. Hamann was shattered by the idea of divine authorship. He opened his essay on biblical interpretation with the exclamation, "God, a writer!" (*Gott ein Schriftsteller!*).[17] He held this belief while fully aware of developments in biblical criticism. Hamann read Hebrew and Arabic, and his Latin and Greek were better still. His personal library was stocked with classical philology and Near Eastern reference works, including those of Michaelis. He possessed a sophisticated understanding of the historical and linguistic rootedness of the Bible, its characteristics as an artifact of human culture. Yet all of this erudition, Hamann believed, did not create bridges of understanding between the Bible and the modern Christian as Michaelis believed they did. On the contrary, erudition threw them down. Ancient Israel, illuminated by modern scholarship, did not swell in dignity and classical grandeur; it rather shrank into an alien, linguistically saturated paradox. Its stories do not exemplify accepted principles of human life. Instead, the Bible delves into the strange and irrational, consistently confounding the senses and drawing the reader into a "nature in reverse."[18]

The cultural overlay of the Bible, when scrutinized by scholarship, shows the human character of the scriptures to be deliberately low and base. It is like the dirty rags used to pull Jeremiah from the well (Jer 38:11–13), the spittle formed by Jesus to heal the blind man (John 9:6), and David's pretended insanity in Gath (1 Sam 21:13–15).[19] The fact that these things served useful purposes, rather than transforming their lowliness, only highlights the extraordinary nature of the uses to which they were put. So it is with the Bible. One must not attend to historical and linguistic minutiae in these passages but rather cultivate perception of the divine truths to which they paradoxically point. The low, strange character of the biblical materials cannot be understood, let alone commended, apart from a belief in their use in a divine economy of meaning. Michaelis' philology, in Hamann's view, ultimately amounts to a theologically impotent preoccupation with the debased, external forms of scriptural realities.

In 1762, Hamann published a collection of ironic, allusive essays. In one of them, "Aesthetica in nuce" (Aesthetics in a nutshell), Hamann attacked the futility of Michaelis's interpretive method from several angles. Hamann's overarching strategy was to question the internal coherence of a method that contextualized the Bible purely in human terms. An important impulse in contextualization is the softening of difference. Israelites, once contextualized, become, in effect, a subset of the Canaanites, one of many ancient Near Eastern societies. Yet, in the Bible, Israelites and Canaanites were mortal enemies who clashed violently. Hamann uses this dichotomy to suggest a distinction between philological contextualizers, the pro-Canaanite party, and spiritual readers, true Israelites. Hamann sets the scene this way:

> Not a lyre! Nor a painter's brush! A winnowing-fan for my Muse, to clear the threshing-floor of holy literature! Praise to the Archangel on the remains of Canaan's tongue!—on white asses he is victorious in the contest, but the wise idiot of Greece [i.e., Hamann himself] borrows Euthyphro's proud stallions for the philological dispute.[20]

He casts Michaelis ("the Archangel" is a reference to St. Michael) as a Canaanite champion who rides into battle to cheers spoken in the "remains of Canaan's tongue." Hamann goes out to meet him, but not with "lyre" or "painter's brush"; instead, he bears a "winnowing fan" to "clear the threshing-floor of holy literature." That is, he will not vindicate the Bible by resorting to a demonstration of its aesthetic superiority (via the "lyre" or "painter's brush"). Rather, he will appear like John the Baptist who announced that the one to come was about to clear the threshing floor by winnowing the chaff (Matt 3:12). As a more specific frame of reference for this confrontation between Canaanites and Israelites, Hamann draws attention to Judges 5, the Song of Deborah that celebrates a miraculous Israelite victory over the Canaanites. He places Michaelis on the "white asses" mentioned in Jud 5:10, and he takes the opening epigraph (Jud 5:30) of the essay from this biblical poem. Hamann quotes the last part of Jud 5:30 in untranslated, unpointed Hebrew; in English it reads as follows: "*spoil* of dyed stuffs embroidered, two pieces of dyed work embroidered for my neck as *spoil*" (NRSV; italics added). In this part of the song, the mother of the Canaanite general Sisera waits for the return of the victorious army, staring out her window and imagining the spoil that her son will bring her. The spoil she imagines will be beautiful fabric, both dyed and embroidered. It is a poignant scene because, as the biblical reader knows, Sisera and the Canaanites, defeated and killed by the Israelites in Judges 4, will never return. The epigraph, then, subtly compares philologists like Michaelis to Canaanite despoilers in search of beauty. The Bible, though, does not reward those who come to it in search of aesthetic satisfaction. It cuts against the grain of the ancient world, defeating the "Canaanites" who try to colonize it and make it part of a generic Levant.

Playing on the title of Michaelis's 1757 treatise on the "dead" Hebrew language and his sponsorship of the Niebuhr expedition to Arabia, Hamann asks whether philology and ethnography can really deliver an adequate understanding of the Bible:

> Nature and Scripture then are the materials of the beautiful spirit which creates and imitates . . . But how are we to raise the defunct language of Nature from the dead? By making pilgrimages to the fortunate lands of Arabia, and by going on crusades to the East, and by restoring their magic art. To steal it, we must employ old women's cunning, for that is the best sort. Cast your eyes down, ye idle bellies, and read what Bacon has to say about the magic art. Silken feet in dancing shoes will not bear you on such a weary journey, so be ready to accept guidance from this hyperbole.[21]

Though Michaelis planned and conceived the dangerous and ultimately disastrous expedition to Arabia, he never left the comfort and safety of Göttingen. Here Hamann points out the hypocrisy: the scholar's "silken feet" are more used to dancing in polite society than to rough journeying. The deeper problem, though, is with the very idea that ethnography and comparative philology can replenish biblical language. In Hamman's view, Michaelis's Arabian expedition is a "pilgrimage" or "crusade" to the East that relies on "cunning" to extract bits of linguistic knowledge. Though conceived as a scientific expedition, the trip, for Hamann, was a quasi-religious, even magical attempt to find the key to biblical language. Can the name of a biblical plant here and a bit of biblical geography there make the word of God accessible to humankind? Hamann points to Bacon to correct this way of thinking. In a footnote, Hamann cites Bacon's definition of magic as the exploitation of correspondences between the "architectures and fabrics of things natural and things civil."²² For Hamann the natural and civil orders stem from a single divine source. The failure of philologists and ethnographers even to see the truth in the "magic" to which they aspire makes them superstitious thieves.

In yet another passage, Hamann addresses Michaelis as a "Master in Israel," a "Most Worthy and Learned Rabbi."²³ This is an allusion to John 3:10, where Jesus converses with Nicodemus, a respected Jewish teacher and leader. As their conversation progresses, Jesus chides Nicodemus for being a "teacher of Israel" who does not possess even a basic understanding of spiritual realities. In the Nicodemus passage of the "Aesthetica," Hamann argues that language operates both in a natural sense and in a spiritual one.

> Do the elements of the ABC lose their natural meaning, if in their infinite combinations into arbitrary signs they remind us of ideas which dwell, if not in heaven, then in our brains? But if we raise up the whole deserving righteousness of a scribe upon the dead body of the letter, what sayeth the spirit to that? Shall he be but a groom of the chamber to the dead letter, or perhaps a mere esquire to the deadening letter? God forbid!²⁴

If words signify intellectual or divine realities that extend metaphorically beyond their "normal" range, no one doubts that they can retain a natural meaning as well. Similarly, if biblical language can be shown to have a "natural" referent, then it is also capable of retaining a spiritual meaning at the same time. Interpreters who discover the natural dimension of biblical language are not thereby warranted in denying that it also operates spiritually. To abandon or subordinate the spiritual would be to place the whole value of the Bible on what Hamann believes is its least deserving part: "the dead body of the letter."²⁵ Like Nicodemus, Michaelis ought to understand this but does not. As Hamann points out, Michaelis has "copious insight into physical things" like climate, weather, and geography. Yet he fails to realize that the "wind" blows where it wants.²⁶ In saying this, Hamann quotes from John 3:8, where Jesus tells Nicodemus that the wind, like the spirit, is unpredictable. The word for "wind" and "spirit" is the same in Greek; this allows Hamann to play on the fact that Michaelis knows about *pneuma* ("wind") but remains ignorant of *pneuma* ("spirit").

Hamann saw many things clearly and accurately. With mordant wit, he showed that Michaelis's approach to the Bible was not consistent with a scriptural hermeneutic based, above all, on the authorial role of God. What he perhaps did not see was that this inconsistency was intentional. There is too much arrogance, too much condescension in Hamann's sarcasm to permit the conclusion that Hamann understood Michaelis's interpretive mode to be the serious, clear-eyed, and deliberate circumvention of confessional interpretation that it, in fact, was. For Hamann, the most troubling feature of Michaelis's project was not simply its profane, rationalistic bent but rather its growing cultural authority. Hamann recognized Michaelis as a philological champion, a respected teacher with broad influence, and a member of polite society. Michaelis was, at that time, a rising star at what was fast becoming Germany's most renowned university. Hamann, from his decidedly nonacademic vantage point, discerned that the new irenic mode of reading, despite what he thought were its foolish pretensions, was becoming a dominant one. As this brief discussion of the "Aesthetica" shows, Hamann did not believe that its conceptual frameworks—aesthetic, philological, and scientific—actually did justice to what the Bible, fundamentally, was and is. And he resented the fact that those who employed it, Michaelis above all, were in a position to shape the future.

In the future that Michaelis envisioned, it is the academic Bible, and not the scriptural one, that shapes culture. Michaelis created the academic Bible in the first place by generating new conceptual frameworks for biblical interpretation. In order to interpret the Bible, one must have a point of reference outside the passage he or she is interpreting. Biblical texts can only be interpreted in relation to *something else*: a concept, a question, a belief, a historical reality. Convinced of the fundamental unity of their canonical Bibles, rabbinic and patristic interpreters, for example, read biblical verses in light of other biblical verses in order to generate or illuminate meanings that reach across scripture as a whole. Similarly, confessional interpreters study the Bible in light of creeds, councils, and catechisms, applying theological judgments expressed there to the exegesis of specific passages. When they read the Bible as scripture, they draw interpretive contexts from traditions, rules, or concerns that flow from their specific religious identities. To men and women of the Enlightenment, though, it was precisely the particularity and incommensurability of these religious identities that had led to war, fraud, and superstition in modern life. As impediments to the kind of moral, irenic, and happy society that Enlightenment figures hoped to create, they had to be disallowed. To cameralists like Münchhausen and loyal professors like Michaelis, the goal was social transformation, and the university was the engine of that transformation.

Michaelis succeeded, then, in creating frames of reference that allowed professors and students to engage the Bible and employ interesting frameworks not dependent on religious identity. To name these frameworks is to mark how decisive his work was in this regard. Though archaeology had not yet come into its own as a scientific discipline, Michaelis and Heyne had begun to show that a full understanding of ancient literature could have as much to do with geography, climate, numismatics, and sculpture as with explicitly theological resources. Michaelis was the first biblical scholar in Germany to make extensive use of travel literature and contemporary ethnography, unraveling linguistic questions, investigating biblical botany and zoology, and integrating knowledge of Near Eastern customs and societies into biblical interpretation. Though not a pioneer in the use of Hebrew's cognate languages (what Schlözer would later call "Semitic" languages), Michaelis, through his widely used grammars and innumerable specialized studies, did more to carry the field forward in the middle decades of the eighteenth century than any other German scholar. Some, like Reiske and, before him, Albert Schultens, were better Arabists. Many were better, certainly, in Talmud and Rabbinic Hebrew, though in knowledge of Syriac and Ethiopic Michaelis perhaps stood out. Yet it was his mastery of *all* these languages, his successful efforts to clarify their relations to one another, and his clear demonstration of how to use them in biblical exegesis that put the modern discipline of comparative Semitic philology in his debt. From the English Michaelis absorbed new approaches to critical philology and poetics, which he subsequently introduced into German scholarship. Benjamin Kennicott stimulated his interest in textual criticism, modeling new methods for the collection and comparison of variants across a wide array of ancient versions. Under this influence Michaelis became an enthusiastic and undisciplined textual emender. Ultimately it fell to Michaelis's student Eichhorn to bring German textual criticism under control, but Michaelis's mediating role in this case should not be diminished. Finally, Michaelis deserves credit for putting Lowthian poetics on the European critical agenda. Because Michaelis showed that Lowth's insights could successfully withstand and, indeed, assimilate Near Eastern erudition, the category of "biblical poetry" gained a currency that it retains to the present day. The growth and unification of these disciplines—ethnography, history, comparative Semitics, textual science, and biblical poetics—constitute the durable legacy of Michaelis. Anyone who has studied the Bible at a modern university will recognize the success of Michaelis's methodological achievement. In his lifetime, the study of the Bible found a new home in the philosophical faculty. *Theologia exegetica* became "biblical studies." Under Michaelis's leadership, the university became the host of a new interpretive mode that at the time seemed as rigorous, coherent, and totalizing as traditional and confessional modes had been for centuries. The scattered researches of earlier skeptics and freethinkers, though every bit as critical, did not coalesce into a compelling interpretive program until unified at the university. Guided by methods and assumptions that reinforced the statism and irenicism of the Enlightenment cameralists, the new discipline of biblical studies allowed practitioners to create a *post*-confessional Bible by reconstructing a *pre*-confessional Israel.

Yet it would be a mistake to think of these methodological innovations collectively as "historical criticism" of the Bible or, worse, as the "historical-critical method" of biblical study. These remain the most common ways of referring to the tradition of modern biblical criticism now established at universities and seminaries.

The fact that these labels are prevalent shows that contemporary ways of thinking about the modern study of the Bible have been shaped to a great degree by questions that only really gained urgency and paradigmatic proportions in the nineteenth century. These came to the fore in debates concerning the historical Jesus, the reliability of biblical prehistory vis-à-vis geology and biology, the implications of Wellhausian source criticism, the Lagardean quest for the *Urtext*, the researches of the *religionsgeschichtliche Schule* (History of Religions School), the challenges of pan-Babylonianism, the results of "biblical archaeology," and so on. It is important to remember that modern biblical criticism had already taken definitive shape long before questions of history, historicity, and historicization came to occupy, indeed dominate, the attention of critical interpreters and their churchly interlocutors. This is not to say, of course, that historical questions were unimportant in the eighteenth-century Enlightenment context. As we have seen, and as intellectual historians like Peter Hanns Reill and, more recently, Michael Carhart have shown, the historical reflexes of the *Aufklärer* were strong and well exercised. In Michaelis's time, the ancient context of biblical language and literature was already a natural place to work out the significance of the moribund scriptural Bible for modern society. Yet, as this study and Jonathan Sheehan's before it have shown, history was only one dimension of a broader cultural recovery that included aesthetics, moral philosophy, and political theory as well. This indicates, at the very least, that "historical criticism" and modern criticism are not coterminous.

Historical questions, then, do not bring us to the core of the modern critical project. Historical critics once believed that unfettered inquiry would produce compelling truths about the history of the Bible that would ultimately guide theology and religion away from tradition and toward reconciliation with science and philosophy. To a great degree, then, debates between modern biblical critics and traditional readers have been staged in the courtroom of history. They begin, typically, with the historical veracity of the Bible and then radiate outward. Consider the following progression. What does modern historical science, informed by epigraphy, comparative philology, paleontology, and archaeology, reveal about the truth of the Bible and the people and events behind it? How, if at all, can the results of modern scholarship, once established, be coordinated with traditional beliefs about the Bible? What becomes of the doctrine of inspiration if the two are not compatible? What are the implications of these questions for larger notions concerning God and humankind, faith and reason, and science and religion? How do they bear on the choice among religious options oriented toward liberalism, conservatism, traditionalism, and fundamentalism? And so on. The point here is that, despite the fact that modern biblical criticism seems fundamentally concerned with history, historical inquiry has served as a way to engage larger moral and religious questions.

Now that historical criticism proper has succumbed to a form of late modern fatigue, we see with new clarity that historical questions have always been epiphenomenal. As I indicated in chapter 1, biblical studies have entered a period of crisis having to do, among other things, with methodological disarray, lack of consensus on key questions, the triviality of a great deal of historical scholarship, and a problematic relation to the Bible's religious readership.[27] It is not surprising that prominent scholars seeking to clarify the nature and purpose of the discipline have begun to jettison historical criticism. John Barton, for example, has proposed that modern criticism be divorced from historical criticism and understood in terms of its Renaissance humanist roots.[28] Barton argues that the discipline ought to be called simply "biblical criticism" in order to reflect its essential nature as a first-order *literary* operation aimed at making sense of the biblical text, whether this sense-making involves the familiar historical contextualizations or not. Barton believers, furthermore, that the literary operations of biblical criticism are simply expressions of intellectual attentiveness necessary to the reading of any text and that they are, therefore, religiously neutral or, more accurately, that they are readerly operations that logically precede religious judgments. By conceding the failures of historical criticism, Barton offers a way forward. Despite the fresh and incisive quality of many of his observations, though, his larger thesis is not persuasive. It is one thing to shed the historicism of modern criticism, but quite another to shed its modernity. Barton wants to avoid responsibility for modernist epistemologies by identifying the discipline with a "biblical criticism" that he discerns in ancient, medieval, and Renaissance interpretation.[29] Whatever is gained by reducing biblical criticism to a timeless intellectual procedure, though, is offset by a significant loss of historical perspective. The similarities that are uncovered across periods are real but trivial. To argue for a timeless biblical criticism is to suggest that vast changes in the assumptions, social contexts, and institutional realities of biblical interpretation are ultimately superficial. Julius Africanus, Richard Simon, and Robert Lowth may share certain readerly impulses, but more is lost than gained in designating them all simply as "biblical critics." Finally, Barton is conscious of the work of Brevard Childs. Childs argued that modern criticism, preoccupied with the speculative prehistory of biblical texts, fails to account for the aspects of the Bible about which we actually know the most: the religious afterlife of texts and their assimilation into the canons of communities of faith. Barton believes that critical attention to the literary contours of the text itself, though, must operate prior to and independently of the Bible's religious *Nachleben*.[30] In maintaining this, Barton simply reaffirms commitment to the modern textual hermeneutic that grew out of the Reformation controversies (see chapter 1). He does not overturn Childs's point that the "text" which Barton hopes to honor is not a text at all, but rather, on historical grounds, a canon of *scripture* formed and transmitted by communal, traditional reading practices at odds with Barton's methodological individualism.

Another prominent biblical scholar, John Collins, has also abandoned historical criticism, though he has not admitted to doing so.[31] In a 2005 volume containing lectures from the previous year, Collins's purpose was to assess the relation of postmodern biblical criticism (including deconstructionist, feminist, liberationist, and postcolonial interpretation) to historical criticism. By arguing that postmodern interpretive strategies can be fully assimilated into modern biblical criticism (which Collins calls "historical criticism"), Collins aims to redeem the discipline from irrelevance and defend it from methodological supersessionism. In his judgment, postmodern interpretation is only an extension of historical criticism, despite the fact that postmodernists programmatically deny the objectivity, knowability, and truthfulness of history. Postmodern criticism and historical criticism are ultimately compatible, in Collins's view, because the real value of historical criticism is its usefulness in structuring a nonconfessional mode of discourse. As Collins says, the "historical focus has been a way of getting distance from a text, of respecting its otherness"; it allows "participants" to structure a "conversation" about the Bible according to academic rules.[32] Postmodern methods may ignore, deny, or even demonize historical research, but they are just as useful in structuring academic conversations. As a result, Collins concludes, they are an asset to "historical criticism." What is left of Collins's method after this engagement with postmodernism is not historical criticism but rather academic criticism. The point here is not to denigrate Collins's maneuver but rather to benefit from the astute observations behind it. After all, the realizations that questions of social location and of the politics of inquiry are actually the most urgent ones in contemporary "historical criticism" and that these comport nicely with postmodern critiques of conventional scholarship constitute a genuine and important insight.[33]

With the recent pronouncements of Barton and Collins, we have moved beyond the "historical" nineteenth century and returned, I believe, to the eighteenth. Biblical scholars at the Enlightenment university were employees of the state charged with creating a way of studying the Bible that would allow it to nourish a common life on new principles. They set aside the scriptural Bible, bound as it was to the confessional identities that had torn Europe apart. In a decisive moment, Michaelis lent his talents and energies to the creation of a new academic Bible keyed to the unifying power of the postconfessional state. In doing so, he showed that academic criticism could not only generate new interpretive frameworks, it could also provide the study of a textualized Bible with a hospitable *place*—the philosophical faculty of the university—and a useful social *purpose*—the reinforcement of religious irenicism. Michaelis revivified the Bible in order to enrich and shore up a social and cultural order based on a generic, progressive Protestantism. Like Michaelis's,

Collins's principal academic interest is ultimately a moral one. He wants to protect a version of academic freedom and to fight fundamentalism by using scholarship to defeat religious certitude.[34] Michaelis and Collins both have serious moral projects, and both believe that these are integral to scholarship itself. It is not surprising that Collins sees himself as an heir, most of all, of the Enlightenment.[35] That he does so as a biblical scholar fully committed to history and philology while disdainful of confessional interpretation is a testimony to the durability of Michaelis's legacy.

What, finally, of the scriptural Bible? In this story, it has been the shadowy counterpart to the academic Bible forged during the Enlightenment. Though perhaps only a shade, it has lived on in religious communities as long as men and women have revered its authority. A full account of the relationship between the scriptural Bible and its counterparts is beyond the scope of this work. In concluding this study, though, I would like to offer a brief reflection. I believe that the scriptural Bible and the academic Bible are fundamentally different creations oriented toward rival interpretive communities. Though in some ways homologous, they can and should function independently if each is to retain its integrity. While it is true that the scriptural reader and the academic interpreter can offer information and insights that the other finds useful or interesting, they remain, in the end, loyal to separate authorities. I grant the moral seriousness of the modern critical project and, to a modest degree, the social and political utility of the academic Bible. I also grant the intellectual value of academic criticism. A rational, irenic study of the Bible supported by state resources and disciplined by academic standards cultivated across a range of fields has produced, in a relatively short time, an astonishing amount of useful information. It has become clear, though, that academic criticism in its contemporary form cannot offer a coherent, intellectually compelling account of what this information is actually *for*. What critics like Collins have done as a result is to shift the rationale for modern criticism away from the intellectual and back toward the social and moral. There is value in the social and moral by-products of academic criticism, in things like tolerance, reasonableness, and self-awareness. The problem is that these rather thin, pale virtues seem only thinner and paler when compared to the classic virtues associated with the scriptural Bible: instead of bland tolerance, *love* that sacrifices self; instead of an agreeable reasonability, *hope* that opens the mind to goodness and greatness that it has not yet fully imagined; and instead of critical self-awareness, *faith* that inspires and animates the human heart. Academic criticism tempers belief, while scriptural reading edifies and directs it. In this sense, they work at cross-purposes. Yet each mode presumes the value of knowledge. Perhaps the two are closest, then, when in that brief moment before thought recognizes itself, the mind wavers between words that have suddenly become strange, and knowledge is a choice between knowing what the text said and knowing what the words might be saying. It is a choice, at such a moment, between the letter that has been revived and the letter that never died.

Notes

CHAPTER 1

1. Robert Morgan and John Barton, *Biblical Interpretation* (New York: Oxford University Press, 1988), 7.

2. Scholarly literature on "scripture" is voluminous. I have drawn from a variety of sources in formulating this definition. For a general orientation to the special issues raised by religious use of texts, see Paul J. Griffiths, *Religious Reading: The Place of Reading in the Practice of Religion* (New York: Oxford University Press, 1999) and Wilfred Cantwell Smith, *What Is Scripture? A Comparative Approach* (Minneapolis: Fortress, 1993). On "transparency," or the use of scripture to see and order the world, see Smith, *What is Scripture?*, ch. 2 and George Lindbeck, *The Nature of Doctrine: Religion and Theology in a Post-Liberal Age* (Philadelphia: Westminster, 1984). On the oral, supertextual quality of scripture, see William A. Graham, *Beyond the Written Word: Oral Aspects of Scripture in the History of Religion* (Cambridge: Cambridge University Press, 1987) and Miriam Levering, ed., *Rethinking Scripture* (Albany: SUNY Press, 1989). On the relation of a divine economy of meaning to the concept of scripture, see John Webster, "Biblical Reasoning," *Anglican Theological Review* 90, no. 4 (2008): 733–51; John Webster, *Holy Scripture: A Dogmatic Sketch* (Cambridge: Cambridge University Press, 2003).

3. Northrop Frye, *The Great Code: The Bible and Literature* (New York: Harvest/HBJ, 1982).

4. Richard Popkin, *The History of Skepticism: From Savonarola to Bayle*, rev. ed. (New York: Oxford University Press, 2003).

5. Brevard Childs, "Foreword," in *Renewing Biblical Interpretation*, ed. Craig Bartholomew, Collin Greene, and Karl Möller (Grand Rapids, MI.: Zondervan, 2000), xv.

6. On the "unfortunate" vestiges of theology in modern scholarship, see Robert Oden, *The Bible without Theology* (San Francisco: Harper & Row, 1987). On the irreconcilability of modern biblical scholarship with traditional reading practices, see James L. Kugel, *How to Read the Bible: A Guide to Scripture Then and Now* (New York: Free Press, 2007).

7. Griffiths, *Religious Reading*, 182.

8. Jon D. Levenson, *The Hebrew Bible, the Old Testament, and Historical Criticism* (Louisville, KY: Westminster John Knox, 1993), 118.

9. Paul Hazard, *The European Mind: 1680–1715*, trans. J. Lewis May (Cleveland and New York: Meridian, 1964).

10. Robert Leventhal, *The Disciplines of Interpretation: Lessing, Herder, Schlegel, and Hermeneutics in Germany 1750–1800* (Berlin: Walter de Gruyter, 1994), 32.

11. Peter Hanns Reill, *The German Enlightenment and the Rise of Historicism* (Berkeley: University of California Press, 1975), 42–45.

12. Jonathan Sheehan, *The Enlightenment Bible: Translation, Scholarship, Culture* (Princeton: Princeton University Press, 2005), xi.

13. Carl L. Becker, *The Heavenly City of the Eighteenth-Century Philosophers* (New Haven: Yale University Press, 1932).

14. Jacob Burckhardt, *The Civilization of the Renaissance in Italy*, trans. S. G. C. Middlemore (New York: Macmillan, 1904), 203.

15. See Charles G. Nauert, *Humanism and the Culture of Renaissance Europe*, 2nd ed. (Cambridge: Cambridge University Press, 2006), 1–7, for a concise review.

16. Alister McGrath, *The Intellectual Origins of the European Reformation* (Oxford: Basil Blackwell, 1987), 40.

17. Euan Cameron, *The European Reformation* (Oxford: Clarendon, 1991), 418.

18. Cameron, *European Reformation*, 136, 144.

19. See Erika Rummel, *The Humanist-Scholastic Debate in the Renaissance & Reformation* (Cambridge: Harvard University Press, 1995). Rummel points out that Luther received a great deal of support from northern humanists early on. Aspects of Luther's program were very congenial to humanism: he endorsed an *ad fontes* program, supported language study, and denounced scholasticism (129). Yet, as the reformation wore on, it ultimately swallowed up the humanist-scholastic debate, scattering the humanist forces (40). In the nice formulation of McGrath, "the essential *continuity* between humanist and Reformer in relation to Scripture concerns the fields of textual and philological inquiry, with a potential *discontinuity* in relation to . . . hermeneutical principles" (68). See McGrath, *Intellectual Origins*, 32–68.

20. As quoted in Cornelis Augustijn, *Erasmus: His Life, Works, and Influence*, trans. J. C. Grayson (Toronto: University of Toronto Press, 1991), 89.

21. Allan K. Jenkins and Patrick Preston, *Biblical Scholarship and the Church: A Sixteenth-Century Crisis of Authority* (Hampshire: Ashgate, 2007), 79–80.

22. Jenkins and Preston, *Biblical Scholarship and the Church*, 80.

23. Quoted in Erika Rummel, *Erasmus and His Catholic Critics* (Nieuwkoop: De Graaf, 1989), 64.

24. Ep. 980, Erasmus to Luther; Louvain, May 30, 1519. As quoted in Erika Rummel, ed., *The Erasmus Reader* (Toronto: University of Toronto Press, 1990), 197.

25. Popkin, *History of Skepticism*, 8.

26. Quoted in Cornelis Augustijn, "The Ecclesiology of Erasmus," in *Scrinium Erasmianum*, ed. Joseph Coppens (Leiden: Brill, 1969), 153.

27. Quoted in J. K. McConica, "Erasmus and the Grammar of Consent," in *Scrimium Erasmianum*, ed. Coppens, 94.

28. Erika Rummel, *Erasmus* (London: Continuum, 2004), 96.

29. Jacques Le Brun, "Das Entstehen der historischen Kritik im Bereich der religiösen Wissenschaften im 17. Jahrhundert," *Trierer Theologische Zeitschrift* 89, no. 2 (1980): 102.

30. Ephraim Radner, *The End of the Church: A Pneumatology of Christian Division in the West* (Grand Rapids, MI: Eerdmans, 1998), 15.

31. R. R. Reno, "Theology in the Ruins of the Church," *Pro Ecclesia* XII, no. 1 (2003): 20.

32. Reno, "In the Ruins," 29.

33. Cameron, *European Reformation*, 416, 418.

34. David W. Kling, *The Bible in History: How the Texts Have Shaped the Times* (New York: Oxford University Press, 2004), 77–78.

35. Jean Morin, *Exercitationes biblicae* (Paris, 1633), 198.

36. Anthony Grafton, *Defenders of the Text: The Traditions of Scholarship in an Age of Science, 1450–1800* (Cambridge: Harvard University Press, 1991), 73.

37. "Utinam essem bonus grammaticus. Non aliunde discordiae in religione pendent quam ab ignoratione grammaticae." Quoted in Herbert Jaumann, "Bibelkritik und Literaturkritik in der frühen Neuzeit," *Zeitschrift für Religions- und Geistesgeschichte* 49, no. 2 (1997): 129.

38. Peter N. Miller, "The 'Antiquarianization' of Biblical Scholarship and the London Polyglot Bible (1653–57)," *Journal of the History of Ideas* 62, no. 3 (July 2001): 463–82.

39. Miller, "Antiquarianization," 470–71.

40. Miller, "Antiquarianization," 474.

41. Baruch Spinoza, *Theological-Political Treatise*, trans. Samuel Shirley (Indianapolis: Hackett, 2001), 158.

42. Spinoza, *TTP*, 87.

43. Jonathan Israel, *Enlightenment Contested: Philosophy, Modernity, and the Emancipation of Man 1670–1752* (Oxford: Oxford University Press, 2006), 411.

44. Kugel, *How to Read the Bible*, 681.

CHAPTER 2

1. Johann David Michaelis, *Raisonnement über die protestantischen Universitäten in Deutschland* (Frankfurt and Leipzig, 1768–76), vol. 1, 130.

2. Thus August Tholuck, quoted in Götz von Selle, *Die Georg-August-Universität zu Göttingen 1737–1937* (Göttingen: Vandenhoeck & Ruprecht, 1937), 84.

3. The theologian Christoph August Heumann also complained that Michaelis, too much influenced by English thought, held "unfounded" religious opinions. See Jörg Baur, "Die Anfänge der Theologie an der 'wohl angeordneten evangelischen Universität' Göttingen," in *Zur geistigen Situation der Zeit der Göttinger Universitätsgründung 1737,*

ed. Jürgen von Stackelberg (Göttingen: Vandenhoeck & Ruprecht, 1988), 39. Michaelis was also suspected of crypto-Calvinism, a charge which was false. See von Selle, *Georg-August*, 85.

4. Rudolf Smend, "Johann David Michaelis und Johann Gottfried Eichhorn—Zwei Orientalisten am Rande der Theologie," in *Theologie in Göttingen. Eine Vorlesungsreihe*, ed. Bernd Moeller (Göttingen: Vandenhoeck & Ruprecht, 1987), 60.

5. See, for example, Carl Diehl, *Americans and German Scholarship 1770–1870* (New Haven: Yale University Press, 1978).

6. Thomas Albert Howard, *Protestant Theology and the Making of the Modern German University* (New York: Oxford University Press, 2006), 6.

7. Howard, *Theology and the University*, 11, 14.

8. Howard, *Theology and the University*, 402–18.

9. Gerhard Ebeling, "The Significance of the Critical Historical Method for Church and Theology in Protestantism," in *Word and Faith* (London: SCM Press, 1963), 17–61.

10. Ebeling, "Critical Historical Method," 38–39.

11. Max Weber, "Wissenschaft als Beruf," in *Gesammelte Aufsätze zur Wissenschaftslehre* (Tübingen: J. C. B. Mohr, 1922), 524–55.

12. Frederic W. Farrar, *History of Interpretation* (London: Macmillan, 1886), 16.

13. Jonathan Sheehan, *The Enlightenment Bible: Translation, Scholarship, Culture* (Princeton: Princeton University Press, 2005), xi.

14. Sheehan, *Enlightenment Bible*, 27–30.

15. Sheehan, *Enlightenment Bible*, xi.

16. Sheehan, *Enlightenment Bible*, 54–57.

17. See chapter 3.

18. Michael Legaspi, "What Ever Happened to Historical Criticism?" *Journal of Religion and Society* 9 (2007).

19. Charles E. McClelland, *State, Society, and University in Germany 1700–1914* (Cambridge: Cambridge University Press, 1980), 71.

20. Michaelis, *Raisonnement*, vol. 4, 248. Quoted in Howard, *Theology and the University*, 82.

21. Michaelis, *Raisonnement*, vol. 1, 2.

22. Michaelis, *Raisonnement*, vol. 1, 92, 89.

23. Michaelis, *Raisonnement*, vol. 1, 35–36.

24. Michael J. Hofstetter, *The Romantic Idea of a University: England and Germany, 1770–1850* (New York: Palgrave, 2001), 7.

25. Michaelis, *Raisonnement*, vol. 1, 113.

26. McClelland, *State, Society, and University*, 95.

27. Michaelis, *Raisonnement*, vol. 3, 187. Quoted in Anthony J. La Vopa, *Grace, Talent, and Merit: Poor Students, Clerical Careers, and Professional Ideology in Eighteenth-Century Germany* (Cambridge: Cambridge University Press, 1988), 203.

28. Michaelis, *Raisonnement*, vol. 1, 72–73.

29. See Conclusion.

30. William Clark, *Academic Charisma and the Origins of the Research University* (Chicago: University of Chicago Press, 2006), *passim*.

31. Friedrich Paulsen, *Geschichte des gelehrten Unterrichts auf den deutschen Schulen und Universitäten vom Ausgang des Mittelalters bis zur Gegenwart*, vol. 2, 3rd ed. (Berlin: Walter de Gruyter, 1921), 127.

32. Notker Hammerstein, "Die Universitätsgründungen im Zeichen der Aufklärung," in *Beiträge zu Problemen deutscher Universitätsgründungen der frühen Neuzeit*, ed. Peter Baumgart and Notker Hammerstein (Nendeln: KTO Press, 1978), 291.

33. Clark, *Academic Charisma*, 7, 13.

34. Quoted in Wilhelm Ebel, *Memorabilia Gottingensia. Elf Studien zur Sozialgeschichte der Universität* (Göttingen: Vandenhoeck & Ruprecht, 1969), 27.

35. Hermann Wellenreuther, "Von der Manufakturstadt zum 'Leine-Athen.' Göttingen, 1714–1837," in *"Eine Welt allein ist nicht genug" Großbritannien, Hannover und Göttingen 1714–1837*, ed. Elmar Mittler (Göttingen: Niedersächsische Staats- und Universitätsbibliothek Göttingen, 2005), 11–28.

36. Wilhelm Ebel, *Memorabilia Gottingensia*, 24.

37. See chapter 3.

38. See Michael Legaspi, Review of William Clark, *Academic Charisma and the Origins of the Modern University*, *Journal of Early Modern History* 11, no. 4/5 (2009): 389–91.

39. Clark, *Academic Charisma*, 377–81. The quotation about Gedike is on p. 381.

40. Quoted in Clark, *Academic Charisma*, 377.

41. Clark, *Academic Charisma*, 379, 381.

42. See McClelland, *State, Society, and University*, 58–60. Like many historians, McClelland sees Halle and Göttingen as part of a single "university reform tradition" that marks the beginning of the modern university era. While it is true that the founders of Göttingen patterned the university after Halle (see below), they strove just as hard to differentiate themselves from it. When it came to the role of theology, Göttingen broke decisively from the Halle model in diminishing theology's status; this is important to any claim for Göttingen's "modernity." To say this, however, is not to claim that the diminishment of theology is somehow intrinsically "modern." Rather, it is to point out that Göttingen scholars undertook a more profound reevaluation of the role of the Bible in public life, one that ultimately did prove decisive for subsequent scholarly traditions. In this sense, its claim to at least a Whiggish kind of modernity is stronger.

43. Ian Hunter, "Multiple Enlightenments: Rival *Aufklärer* at the University of Halle, 1690–1730," in *The Enlightenment World*, ed. Martin Fitzpatrick et al. (London: Routledge, 2007), 576–95.

44. Wilhelm Schrader, *Geschichte der Friedrichs-Universität zu Halle* (Berlin: Ferd. Dümmler, 1894), 19.

45. Richard L. Gawthrop, *Pietism and the Making of Eighteenth-Century Prussia* (Cambridge: Cambridge University Press, 1993), 63.

46. Howard, *Theology and the University*, 89.

47. Hammerstein, "Universitätsgründungen," 269–74.

48. Hunter, "Multiple Enlightenments," 579.

49. McClelland, *State, Society, and University*, 36.

50. The full text of this document, "Erster Entwurf des Hofraths J. D. Gruber" (August 30, 1732), can be found in Emil Rössler, *Die Gründung der Universität Göttingen:*

Entwürfe, Berichte und Briefe der Zeitgenossen (Göttingen: Vandenhoeck & Ruprecht, 1855), 3f.

51. Rössler, *Gründung*, 3.
52. See Paulsen, *Geschichte des gelehrten Unterrichts*, 9, and von Selle, *Georg-August*, 14.
53. Rössler, *Gründung*, 4.
54. Rössler, *Gründung*, 8.
55. See "Joh. Lor. von Mosheims Denkschrift über die Einrichtung einer Academie mit den Bemerkungen Just. Hennig Böhmers" in Rössler, *Gründung*, 20–27. The quote is from p. 21.
56. See the "Nachträgliches Votum Münchhausens über die Einrichtung der Universität in der Sitzung des Geheimen Raths-Collegium" in Rössler, *Gründung*, 34.
57. von Selle, *Georg-August*, 24.
58. von Selle, *Georg-August*, 29.
59. Wilhelm Ebel, ed., *Die Privilegien and ältesten Statuten der Georg-August-Universität zu Göttingen* (Göttingen: Vandenhoeck & Ruprecht, 1961), 90.
60. von Selle, *Georg-August*, 40.
61. Paulsen, *Geschichte des gelehrten Unterrichts*, 12.
62. Werner Schneider, "Thomasius, Christian," in *Deutsche Biographische Enzyklopädie*, ed. Walther Killy and Rudolf Vierhaus (München: K.G. Saur, 1999), 10:20. In 1688, Thomasius founded a journal which he used to criticize the pedantry (*Pedanterey*) of the academic establishment in Leipzig. As a jurist, he is well remembered for his opposition to torture and witch trials.
63. von Selle, *Georg-August*, 11.
64. von Selle, *Georg-August*, 43.
65. von Selle, *Georg-August*, 21–23.
66. McClelland, *State, Society, and University*, 49–52. See also Christopher C. W. Bauermeister, "Hanover: *Milde Regierung* or *Ancien Régime?*" *German History* 20, no. 3 (2002): 287–308.
67. Paulsen, *Geschichte des gelehrten Unterrichts*, 11. Paulsen also cites J. S. Pütter, who carefully noted that "11 Prinzen, 148 Grafen, und 14828 andere Personen" visited the university in 1788.
68. McClelland, *State, Society, and University*, 56.
69. Bauermeister, "Hanover," 295.
70. McClelland, *State, Society, and University*, 45.
71. Paulsen, *Geschichte des gelehrten Unterrichts*, 137.
72. Hammerstein, "Universitätsgründungen," 278.
73. Ulrich Hunger, "Die Georg-August-Universität als landesherrliche Gründung. Ein Bericht über ihre Genese," in *"Eine Welt allein ist nicht genug" Großbritannien, Hannover und Göttingen 1714–1837*, ed. Elmar Mittler (Göttingen: Niedersächsische Staats- und Universitätsbibliothek Göttingen, 2005), 104.
74. Wilhelm Ebel, *Privilegien und Statuten*, 61.
75. Wilhelm Ebel, *Privilegien und Statuten*, 57.
76. Wilhelm Ebel, *Privilegien und Statuten*, 59.

77. For this see Luigi Marino, *Praeceptores Germaniae: Göttingen 1770–1820* (Göttingen: Vandenhoeck & Ruprecht, 1995).

78. Bernd Moeller, "Johann Lorenz von Mosheim und die Gründung der Göttinger Universität," in *Theologie in Göttingen. Eine Vorlesungsreihe*, ed. Bernd Moeller (Göttingen: Vandenhoeck & Ruprecht, 1987), 11–12.

79. Inge Mager, "Zu Johann Lorenz von Mosheims theologischer Biographie," in *Johann Lorenz Mosheim (1693–1755). Theologie im Spannungsfeld von Philosophie, Philologie und Geschichte*, ed. Martin Mulsow et al. (Wiesbaden: Harrassowitz, 1997), 279.

80. See Moeller, "Mosheim," 19, and Florian Neumann, "Mosheim und die westeuropäische Kirchengeschichtsschreibung," in *Johann Lorenz Mosheim (1693–1755). Theologie im Spannungsfeld von Philosophie, Philologie und Geschichte*, ed. Martin Mulsow et al. (Wiesbaden: Harrassowitz, 1997), 111–46.

81. Johann Gottfried Eichhorn, "Bemerkungen über J. D. Michaelis litterarischen Character," in *Lebensbeschreibung von ihm selbst abgefasst*, by Johann David Michaelis (Leipzig, 1793), 156. In his review of Michaelis's life and work, Eichhorn points to three Göttingen professors who influenced the young Michaelis: Mosheim, professor of medicine Albrecht von Haller (1708–1777), and classicist Johann Matthias Gesner (1691–1761). More on Gesner in chapter 3.

82. Moeller, "Mosheim," 15.

83. *Kurze Anweisung, die Gottesgelahrtheit vernünftig zu erlernen, un academischen Vorlesungen vorgetragen*, ed. C. E. von Windheim (1756), p. 170. Quoted in Moeller, "Mosheim," 15.

84. Henning Graf Reventlow, "Johen Lorenz Mosheims Auseinandersetzung mit John Toland," in *Johann Lorenz Mosheim (1693–1755). Theologie im Spannungsfeld von Philosophie, Philologie und Geschichte*, ed. Martin Mulsow et al. (Wiesbaden: Harrassowitz, 1997), 93–110. As Reventlow shows, Mosheim engages the substance of Toland's argument and argues against it largely on scholarly grounds (see p. 99).

85. For the discussion of Mosheim's 1723 (*De theologo non contentioso*) and 1747 (*De odio theologico*) speeches, I am indebted to Mager, "Mosheims theologischer Biographie."

86. Mager, "Mosheims theologischer Biographie," 291.

87. Mosheim's ideal was a broad-based Protestantism bounded on two sides by Roman Catholicism and Socinianism. E. P. Meijering, "Mosheim und die Orthodoxie," in *Johann Lorenz Mosheim (1693–1755). Theologie im Spannungsfeld von Philosophie, Philologie und Geschichte*, ed. Martin Mulsow et al. (Wiesbaden: Harrassowitz, 1997), 273.

88. *Anderweitiger Versuch einer vollständigen und unpartheyischen Ketzergeschichte* (1748), Vorrede, p. 28. Quoted in Moeller, "Mosheim," 22.

89. I am indebted here to the discussion of Neumann, "Kirchengeschichtsschreibung."

90. Baur, "Die Anfänge," 26–33.

91. Baur, "Die Anfänge," 35.

92. Joachim Ringleben, "Göttinger Aufklärungstheologie—von Königsberg her gesehen," in *Theologie in Göttingen. Eine Vorlesungsreihe*, ed. Bernd Moeller (Göttingen: Vandenhoeck & Ruprecht, 1987), 104–10.

93. Walter Sparn, "Auf dem Wege zur theologischen Aufklärung in Halle: Von Johann Franz Budde zu Siegmund Jakob Baumgarten," in *Halle, Aufklärung und Pietismus*, ed. Norbert Hinske (Heidelberg: Lambert Schneider, 1989), 78.

94. I borrow the phrase from Charles Taylor, *A Secular Age* (Cambridge: Belknap, 2007).

95. Johann David Michaelis, *Erklärung der Begräbnis- und Auferstehungsgeschichte Christi nach den vier Evangelisten, mit Rücksicht auf die in den Fragmenten gemachte Einwürfe und deren Beantwortung* (Halle, 1783). The work was later translated into English: Johann David Michaelis, *The Burial and Resurrection of Jesus Christ: According to the Four Evangelists* (London: J. Hatchard, 1827).

96. John W. Rogerson, "Michaelis, Johann David," in *Dictionary of Major Biblical Interpreters*, ed. Donald K. McKim (Downers Grove, Illinois: Intervarsity Press, 2007), 738.

97. Johann David Michaelis, *Entwurf einer typischen Gottesgelahrtheit* (Göttingen: G. L. Förster, 1763) and Johann David Michaelis, *Gedanken über die Lehre der Heiligen Schrift von Sünde und Genugthuung, als eine der Vernunft gemässe Lehre* (Göttingen and Bremen: Johann Heinrich Cramer, 1779).

98. See, for example, Hans-Joachim Kraus, *Geschichte der historisch-kritischen Erforschung des Alten Testaments* (Neukirchen-Vluyn: Neukirchener Verlag, 1982), 97–103.

99. Michael C. Carhart, *The Science of Culture in Enlightenment Germany*, Harvard Historical Series (Cambridge: Harvard University Press, 2007). On the study of history during the Enlightenment, see also Peter Hanns Reill, *The German Enlightenment and the Rise of Historicism* (Berkeley: University of California Press, 1975) and Hans Erich Bödeker et al., *Aufklärung und Geschichte. Studien zur deutschen Geschichtswissenschaft im 18. Jahrhundert* (Göttingen: Vandenhoeck & Ruprecht, 1986).

100. Carhart, *Science of Culture*, 22.

101. Carhart, *Science of Culture*, 26.

102. Carhart, *Science of Culture*, 52.

103. See Bauermeister, "Hanover," 289. Bauermeister argues that "in order to be properly understood, the ideas and actions of the Hanoverian governing elite must be examined within the context of the *Aufklärung* notions of moderate Enlightenment, gradual change, and state involvement predominant within late-eighteenth-century German political theory and practice."

CHAPTER 3

1. Johann Wolfgang Goethe, *Maxims and Reflections*, ed. Peter Hutchinson, trans. Elisabeth Stopp (New York: Penguin, 1998), 35.

2. See Richard L. Gawthrop, *Pietism and the Making of Eighteenth-Century Prussia* (Cambridge: Cambridge University Press, 1993) and Carl Hinrichs, *Preußentum und Pietismus. Der Pietismus in Brandenburg-Preußen als religiös-soziale Reformbewegung* (Göttingen: Vandenhoeck & Ruprecht, 1971).

3. Eliza Marian Butler, *The Tyranny of Greece over Germany* (Cambridge: Cambridge University Press, 1935).

4. Johann Wolfgang Goethe, "Winckelmann und sein Jahrhundert (1805)," in *Goethe Werke. Band XII*, ed. Herbert von Einem and Hans Joachim Schrimpf (Hamburg: Christian Wegner, 1967), 98–99.

5. Walter Rehm, *Griechentum und Goethezeit: Geschichte eines Glaubens*, 4th ed. (Bern and Munich: Francke Verlag, 1969).

6. Johann Joachim Winckelmann, *Reflections on the Imitation of Greek Works in Painting and Sculpture*, trans. Elfriede Heyer and Roger C. Norton (La Salle, IL: Open Court, 1987), 5.

7. Goethe dismissed Winckelmann's conversion to Roman Catholicism as a prudential move to fit in among the Romans, a "disguise" (*Maskenkleid*) to be worn. To Goethe, Winckelmann was a "natural-born heathen" (*ein gründlich gebornen Heiden*). Goethe, "Winckelmann," 105–06.

8. Charles A. Grair, "Antiquity and Weimar Classicism," in *The Literature of Weimar Classicism*, ed. Simon Richter (Rochester, NY: Camden House, 2005), 69.

9. Sixth letter, section 2. Friedrich Schiller, *On the Aesthetic Education of Man, in a Series of Letters*, trans. and ed. Elizabeth M. Wilkinson and L. A. Willoughby (Oxford: Clarendon, 1967), 31.

10. Friedrich Schlegel, "Athenaeum Fragments," in *Classical and Romantic German Aesthetics*, ed. J. M. Bernstein (Cambridge: Cambridge University Press, 2003), 249.

11. *Ideas* (1800), no. 95; quoted in *Classical and Romantic German Aesthetics*, ed. J. M. Bernstein (Cambridge: Cambridge University Press, 2003), 265.

12. From the *Allgemeinen Brouillon* (1798–1799), section 67. Friedrich Leopold von Hardenberg, *Novalis Werke*, ed. Gerhard Schulz (Munich: Beck, 1969), 468.

13. Anthony Grafton, "Prolegomena to Friedrich August Wolf," in *Defenders of the Text: The Traditions of Scholarship in an Age of Science, 1450–1800* (Cambridge: Harvard University Press, 1991), 223.

14. Ulrich von Wilamowitz-Moellendorff, *History of Classical Scholarship* (1927), ed. Hugh Lloyd-Jones, trans. Alan Harris (London: Duckworth, 1982), 105–08.

15. Hermann Funke, "F. A. Wolf," in *Classical Scholarship: A Biographical Encyclopedia*, ed. Ward W. Briggs and William M. Calder (New York: Garland, 1990), 526.

16. Wilhelm Humboldt, "Ueber den Charakter der Griechen, die idealische und historische Ansicht desselben," in *Schriften zur Altertumskunde und Ästhetik. Die Vasken*, ed. Andreas Flitner and Klaus Giel (Stuttgart: J.G. Cotta'sche Buchhandlung, 1961), 65.

17. Suzanne L. Marchand, *Down from Olympus: Archaeology and Philhellenism in Germany, 1750–1970* (Princeton: Princeton University Press, 1996), 28.

18. Quoted in Heinrich Graffmann, *Die Stellung der Religion im Neuhumanismus* (Göttingen, 1929), 52.

19. Marchand, *Down from Olympus*, xvii–xviii.

20. Grair, "Antiquity," 85–86.

21. R. Steven Turner, "Historicism, *Kritik*, and the Prussian Professoriate, 1790 to 1840," in *Philologie und Hermeneutik im 19. Jahrhundert*, ed. Martin Bollack, Heinz Wismann, and Theodor Lindken (Göttingen: Vandenhoeck & Ruprecht, 1983), 260.

22. In a June 18, 1797, letter to Wolf, for example, Humboldt compares a scholar he met in Berlin (Caillard) to Heyne. Though he has some positive things to say, he puzzles

over much of Caillard's work: "He seems to set a lot of store by Heynian manners, arguments, aesthetic commentary, and all such trash. It is horrible that poor Germany has to be known in France by such men [as Heyne]!" Wilhelm Humboldt, *Briefe an Friedrich August Wolf* (Berlin: Walter de Gruyter, 1990), 185.

23. Clemens Menze, *Wilhelm von Humboldt und Christian Gottlob Heyne* (Ratingen: A. Henn, 1966), 36–42.

24. On Schlegel and Heyne, see Werner Mettler, *Der junge Friedrich Schlegel und die griechische Literatur. Ein Beitrag zum Problem der Historie* (Zurich: Atlantis, 1955).

25. Quoted in Graffmann, *Neuhumanismus*, 31.

26. Graffmann, *Neuhumanismus*, 32–34.

27. Graffmann, *Neuhumanismus*, 42.

28. Reinhold Friedrich, *Johann Matthias Gesner: Sein Leben und sein Werk* (Roth: Genniges, 1991), 23.

29. Reinhold Friedrich, *Gesner*, 21.

30. Graffmann, *Neuhumanismus*, 25.

31. See Werner Deetjen, "Johann Matthias Gesner und die Weimarer Bibliothek," in *Festschrift Armin Tille zum 60. Geburtstag* (Weimar: Hermann Böhlaus Nachfolger, 1930).

32. Reinhold Friedrich, *Gesner*, 33.

33. The motive was apparently envy of Gesner's success. Reinhold Friedrich, *Gesner*, 39.

34. Thomas Haye, "Göttingens Ruhm in der Dichtung des Johann Matthias Gesner (1691–1761)," in *1050 Jahre Göttingen. Streitflichter auf die Göttinger Stadtgeschichte*, ed. Klaus Grubmüller (Wallstein, 2004), 49.

35. Reinhold Friedrich, *Gesner*, 43.

36. Ulrich Muhlack, "Klassische Philologie zwischen Humanismus und Neuhumanismus," in *Wissenschaften im Zeitalter der Aufklärung*, ed. Rudolf Vierhaus (Göttingen: Vandenhoeck & Ruprecht, 1985), 108.

37. See the fine articles of Ulrich Schindel: "Johann Matthias Gesner, Professor der Poesie und Beredsamkeit 1734–1761," in *Die Klassische Altertumswissenschaft an der Georg-August-Universität Göttingen. Eine Ringvorlesung zu ihrer Geschichte*, ed. Carl Joachim Classen (Göttingen: Vandenhoeck & Ruprecht, 1989), 9–26, and "Die Anfänge der Klassischen Philologie in Göttingen," in *Philologie in Göttingen: Sprach- und Literaturwissenschaft an der Georgia Augusta im 18. und beginnenden 19. Jahrhundert*, ed. Reinhard Lauer (Göttingen: Vandenhoeck & Ruprecht, 2001), 9–24.

38. Quoted in Theodor Gericke, *Joh. Matth. Gesners und Joh. Gottfr. Herders Stellung in der Geschichte der Gymnasialpädogogik* (Borna-Leipzig: PhD diss., University of Erlangen, 1911), 25.

39. Schindel, "Gesner," 20.

40. Johann Matthias Gesner, *Enchiridion sive prudentia privata ac civilis* (Göttingen, 1745), Praefatio III–IV, quoted in Schindel, "Gesner," 20.

41. Johann Matthias Gesner, *Kleine deutsche Schriften* (Göttingen, 1756), 355, quoted in Friedrich Paulsen, *Geschichte des gelehrten Unterrichts auf den deutschen Schulen und Universitäten vom Ausgang des Mittelalters bis zur Gegenwart*, vol. 2, 3rd ed. (Berlin: Walter de Gruyter, 1921), 20–21.

42. Schindel, "Gesner," 19.
43. *Claudia Opera*, 1759, Prefatio xiv–xv, in Hermann Sauppe, ed., *Weimarische Schulreden* (Weimar: Böhlau, 1856), 10, n.2, quoted in Schindel, "Gesner," 19.
44. "Die Praefatio zur Liviusausgabe (1735)" quoted in Schindel, "Gesner," 19.
45. Schindel, "Gesner," 18.
46. Paulsen, *Geschichte des gelehrten Unterrichts*, 24.
47. Paulsen, *Geschichte des gelehrten Unterrichts*, 24.
48. Johann Matthias Gesner, *Schulordnung vor die Churfürstlich Braunschweigisch-Lüneburgischen Lande* (Göttingen: Vandenhoeck, 1738), sections 97, 95–96.
49. Ch. XXVII of the *Schulordnung* contains an extensive description of the Philological Seminar; see §186–199, 209–222.
50. Gesner, *Schulordnung*, §190.
51. Schindel, "Anfänge," 16.
52. Gesner, *Schulordnung*, §193.
53. Friedrich Klinger, *Christian Gottlob Heyne* (Leipzig: Poeschel & Trepte, 1937), 3.
54. Klinger, *Heyne*, 4.
55. Klinger, *Heyne*, 5.
56. A. H. L. Heeren, *Christian Gottlob Heyne. Biographisch dargestellt* (Göttingen: Johann Friedrich Röwer, 1813), 24–25.
57. Heeren, *Heyne*, 26.
58. Heeren, *Heyne*, 26.
59. Heeren, *Heyne*, 26.
60. Irene Polke, *Selbstreflexion im Spiegel des Anderen. Eine Wirkungsgeschichte Studie zum Hellenismusbild Heynes und Herders* (Königshausen: Neumann, 1999), 121.
61. Quoted in Heinz Berthold, "Bewunderung und Kritik. Zur Bedeutung der Mittlerstellung Christian Gottlob Heynes," in *Winckelmanns Wirkung auf seine Zeit. Lessing, Herder, Heyne*, ed. Johannes Irmscher (Stendal, 1988), 161.
62. Quoted in Götz von Selle, *Die Georg-August-Universität zu Göttingen 1737–1937* (Göttingen: Vandenhoeck & Ruprecht, 1937), 156.
63. Ulrich Schindel, "Historische Analyse und Prognose im 18. Jh. Christian Gottlob Heyne und die spätantike römische Historiographie," *Antike und Abendland* 50 (2004): 1.
64. Martin Vöhler, "Christian Gottlob Heyne und das Studium des Altertums in Deutschland," in *Disciplining Classics / Institutionalisierung der Antike*, ed. G. W. Most (Göttingen: Vandenhoeck & Ruprecht, 2002), 42.
65. Ulrich Schindel, "In Memoriam C. G. Heyne," *Göttingische Gelehrte Anzeigen* 232, no. 1/2 (1980): 3.
66. For a comprehensive treatment of Heyne's role in the study of ancient history, see Marianne Heidenreich, *Christian Gottlob Heyne und die Alte Geschichte* (München: K. G. Saur, 2006). Heidenreich provides a useful review of Heyne historiography over the last two hundred years that is focused on the ways that Heyne's significance within the history of scholarship has been assessed (7–23).
67. Quoted in Johann Stephen Pütter, ed., *Versuch einer academischen Gelehrten-Geschichte von der Georg-August-Universität zu Göttingen* (Göttingen: Vandenhoeck & Ruprecht, 1788), 347.

68. Heidenreich, *Heyne und Geschichte*, 14–16.

69. The "mere enthusiasm" here belongs to Winckelmann. Heyne's program drew inspiration from Winckelmann's imaginative reconstruction of the spirit of ancient Greek art. Yet Heyne thought it necessary to go beyond Winckelmann and to base the study of antiquity on more rigorous criteria. In a letter to C. L. Hagedorn (Oct. 3, 1772; quoted in Vöhler, "Heyne," 48), Heyne drew an analogy in which Winckelmann gathered scattered antiquarian studies into "regelmäßigen und übersehbaren Gebäude," while Heyne wanted to introduce more order: "alles auf gute Ordnung der Teile, auf die Auswahl des Wichtigen und Wesentlichen, und auf das Übersehbare des Ganzen ankommen." Heyne described two ways that Winckelmann's aesthetic criticism might be improved: 1) "antiquarische Kritik," by which the critic first judges the authenticity of the artifact; 2) a "wissenschaftliche Fundierung" for ancient studies, consisting of an explicit method and the use of auxiliary disciplines.

70. Mettler, *Schlegel und Literatur*, 46–97, especially 60–64, 82.

71. Humboldt, *Briefe*.

72. Humboldt, *Briefe*, Anhang 1, lines 89–98.

73. Humboldt, *Briefe*, Anhang 1, lines 114–70.

74. Humboldt, *Briefe*, Anhang 1, lines 220–28.

75. Mettler, *Schlegel und Literatur*, 12.

76. Heeren, *Heyne*, 192.

77. Hermann Sauppe, "Johann Matthias Gesner und Christian Gottlob Heyne," in *Göttinger Professoren. Ein Beitrag zur deutschen Cultur- und Literaturgeschichte in acht Vorträgen* (Gotha: Friedrich Andreas Porthes, 1872), 86–87.

78. Hermann Sauppe, "Gesner und Heyne," 89.

79. Wolf Hartmut Friedrich, "Heyne als Philologe," in *Der Vormann der Georgia Augusta: Sechs akademische Reden* (Göttingen: Vandenhoeck & Ruprecht, 1980), 30.

80. Hermann Sauppe, "Gesner und Heyne," 76–78.

81. See Sotera Fornaro, "Deutschland. III. Bis 1806," in *Der Neue Pauly. Enzyklopädie der Antike*, ed. M. Landfester (Stuttgart: J. B. Metzler, 1999), 799; Paulsen, *Geschichte des gelehrten Unterrichts*, 36; Schindel, "Anfänge," 21.

82. According to Wolf and his biographer and son-in-law, W. Körte, Wolf walked from Nordhausen to Göttingen to study philology with Heyne in 1776, only to be told that it was not possible to study only philology and that Wolf must also be a law or theology student. According to the story, a determined Wolf followed his original plan against Heyne's advice and became the university's first *studiosus philologiae*. University records, however, show that students were registering in philology as early as 1736.

83. Quoted in Pütter, *Versuch*, 273.

84. Pütter, *Versuch*, 274.

85. Christian Gottlob Heyne, *Einleitung in das Studium der Antike, oder Grundriß einer Anführung zur Kenntniß der alten Kunstwerke* (Göttingen and Gotha: Johann Christian Dieterich, 1772), 5–9. Quote is taken from p. 9.

86. Christian Gottlob Heyne, "Prüfung einiger Nachrichten und Behauptungen vom Laocoon im Belvedere," in *Sammlung Antiquarischer Aufsätze. Zweites Stück* (Leipzig: Weidmanns, Erben, und Reich, 1779), 18.

87. Bettina Preiss, *Die archäologische Beschäftigung mit der Laokoongruppe. Die Bedeutung Christian Gottlob Heynes für die Archäologie des 18. Jahrhunderts* (PhD diss., University of Bonn, 1992), 140–41.

88. Jacob Bernays, *Phokion und seine neueren Beurtheiler. Ein Beitrag zur Geschichte der griechischen Philosophie und Politik* (Berlin: Wilhelm Hertz, 1881), 1–7. See also Heidenreich, *Heyne und Geschichte*, 19.

89. Bernays, *Phokion*, 15.

90. The full text of this speech is reprinted in Polke, *Selbstreflexion*, 122–25.

91. § 7, 11, and 19 of *De genio saeculi Ptolemaeorum*, quoted in Polke, *Selbstreflexion*, 122–25.

92. Fornaro, "Deutschland," 799.

93. Quoted in Ulrich Schindel, "Heyne und die Historiographie," in *Memoria Rerum Veterum. Neue Beiträge zur antiken Historiographie und alten Geschichte. Festschrift für Carl Joachim Classen zum 60. Geburtstag*, ed. Wolfram Ax (Stuttgart: Franz Steiner, 1990), 205.

94. Friedrich August Wolf, *Prolegomena to Homer 1795*, ed. Anthony Grafton, Glenn W. Most, and James E. G. Zetzel (Princeton: Princeton University Press, 1985), "Introduction," 15.

95. Menze, *Humboldt und Heyne*, 34–42.

96. Heidenreich, *Heyne und Geschichte*, 22.

97. B. G. Niebuhr, *Vorträge über alte Länder- und Völkerkunde, an der Universität gehalten* (Berlin, 1851), 518. Quoted in Heidenreich, *Heyne und Geschichte*, 10 (italics added).

98. Heeren, *Heyne*, 185.

CHAPTER 4

1. Johann Gottfried Herder, *Philosophical Writings*, ed. and trans. Michael N. Forster (Cambridge: Cambridge University Press, 2002), 33.

2. Amy Newman, "The Death of Judaism in German Protestant Thought from Luther to Hegel," *Journal of the American Academy of Religion* LXI, no. 3 (1993): 455–84.

3. See chapter 5 for more on this.

4. See the Conclusion.

5. J. W. Goethe, *Dichtung und Wahrheit* 1.14, 265 in Goethe, *Sämtliche Werke* II, 6 (Frankfurt am Main: Deutscher Klassiker Verlag, 1985).

6. Rudolf Smend, "Johann David Michaelis und Johann Gottfried Eichhorn—Zwei Orientalisten am Rande der Theologie," in *Theologie in Göttingen. Eine Vorlesungsreihe.*, ed. Bernd Moeller (Göttingen: Vandenhoeck & Ruprecht, 1987), 61.

7. On rationalism, see, for example, John W. Rogerson, "Michaelis, Johann David," in *Dictionary of Major Biblical Interpreters*, ed. Donald K. McKim (Downers Grove, IL: Intervarsity Press, 2007), 736–39. On "critical method," see, for example, Hans-Joachim Kraus, *Geschichte der historisch-kritischen Erforschung des Alten Testaments* (Neukirchen-Vluyn: Neukirchener Verlag, 1982), 97–103.

8. Johann David Michaelis, *Lebensbeschreibung von ihm selbst abgefaßt, mit Anmerkungen von Hassencamp. Nebst Bemerkungen über dessen litterarischen Character von Eichhorn, Schulz—und dem Elogium von Heyne* (Rinteln and Leipzig, 1793), 43.

9. "Memoria auf Johann Matthias Gesner," reprinted in Wilhelm Ebel, ed., *Göttinger Universitätsreden aus zwei Jahrhunderten (1737–1934)* (Göttingen: Vandenhoeck & Ruprecht, 1978), 64–80.

10. Johann David Michaelis, *Lebensbeschreibung*, 87, 94–95.

11. Heyne's house at Papendiek 16 was just around the corner from the substantial "Michaelishaus" at Prinzenstraße 21. Caroline Michaelis and Theresea Heyne, together with Dorothea Schlözer, daughter of Göttingen historian A. L. Schlözer, were part of a circle of friends and professors' daughters who feature prominently in academic literary circles in the early nineteenth century. See Ida Hakemeyer, *Kleines Universitätsmosaik* (Göttingen, 1960), 72–87.

12. Hans Hecht, *T. Percy, R. Wood und J. D. Michaelis. Ein Beitrag zur Literaturgeschichte der Genieperiode* (Stuttgart, 1933), 25–26.

13. "Memoria Viri illustris Jo. Dav. Michaelis celebrata in consessu Societatis Regiae scientarum d. xxiv Septembris MDCCXCI," reprinted in Johann David Michaelis, *Lebensbeschreibung*, 265–94. The quote is from page 274.

14. Heyne, "Memoria," 277–78.

15. Stephen Burnett, *From Christian Hebraism to Jewish Studies. Johannes Buxtorf (1564–1629) and Hebrew Learning in the Seventeenth Century* (Leiden: Brill, 1996), 241.

16. A. H. L. Heeren, *Christian Gottlob Heyne. Biographisch dargestellt* (Göttingen: Johann Friedrich Röwer, 1813), 85.

17. Johann David Michaelis, *Beurtheilung der Mittel, welche man anwendet, die ausgestorbene Hebräische Sprache zu verstehen* (Göttingen, 1757), 253.

18. Johann David Michaelis, *Lebensbeschreibung*, 13.

19. Though concerned with the accents of the Masoretic text, which represent בראשית as a temporal clause (*bereshit* "when [God] began . . ."), J. H. Michaelis, following the Septuagint and classical Christian interpretation, treats the noun ראשית as a definite noun: thus, *bareshit* "in *the* beginning."

20. Johann Heinrich Michaelis, *Gründlicher Unterricht von den Accentibus prosaicis u. metricis oder Hebräischen Distinctionibus der Heil. Schrift A.T.* (Halle: Wäysen-Hause, 1720), 34–40.

21. Wilhelm Gesenius, *Geschichte der hebräischen Sprache und Schrift. Eine philologisch-historische Einleitung in die Sprachlehren und Wörterbücher der hebräischen Sprache* (Leipzig, 1815), 130–31.

22. *Hebräische Grammatik* was published at Halle; there were three editions: 1745, 1753, and 1778. The *Beurtheilung* was published at Göttingen in 1757 and later translated into Dutch.

23. Johann David Michaelis, *Hebräische Grammatik* (Halle, 1745), 12–13.

24. Organizational changes in Michaelis's grammar include: 1) the use of fewer headings to discuss vowels, consonants, and parts of speech; 2) the decision to move the discussion of sound changes in vowels and consonants to later sections; 3) the treatment of verbs before nouns because, as Michaelis states, nouns originate from verbs in Hebrew.

25. Johann David Michaelis, *Hebräische Grammatik*, 12.

26. Johann David Michaelis, *Hebräische Grammatik*, 12. Hiller and Simonis identified a correspondence between certain vowel patterns and various semantic categories. For a

more contemporary discussion of this correspondence, see Paul Joüon, *A Grammar of Biblical Hebrew*, T. Muraoka, trans. (Rome: Pontifical Biblical Institute, 1993) § 88.

27. Johann David Michaelis, *Beurtheilung*, Vorrede (unpaginated).
28. Johann David Michaelis, *Beurtheilung*, §1, 1–2.
29. Johann David Michaelis, *Beurtheilung*, §43, 246–50.
30. Johann David Michaelis, *Beurtheilung*, §6, 28.
31. Johann David Michaelis, *Beurtheilung*, §6, 29.
32. Johann David Michaelis, *Beurtheilung*, §6, 32. Michaelis cites examples of entries in Jewish lexicons for various tree and plant species: "it is a type of tree" or simply "an herb." To the Jews, Michaelis mocks, "all trees are alike."
33. Johann David Michaelis, *Beurtheilung*, §8, 45.
34. Johann David Michaelis, *Beurtheilung*, § 8, 47–48.
35. Johann David Michaelis, *Beurtheilung*, § 9, 54.
36. Johann David Michaelis, *Beurtheilung*, § 9, 58f.
37. Johann David Michaelis, *Beurtheilung*, §10, 60–63.
38. Johann David Michaelis, *Beurtheilung*, § 21, 115.
39. Johann David Michaelis, *Beurtheilung*, § 16, 95.
40. Johann David Michaelis, *Beurtheilung*, § 21, 115. Michaelis says of Neumann, for example, that he "commonly finds in words what he already knew and had previously learned, which becomes as false as he wants it to be. As a result, whatever 'new light' arises must be illegitimate; if the hieroglyphic meaning were true, it would be a poor tool of discovery because one finds from it what one wants."
41. Johann David Michaelis, *Beurtheilung*, § 17–20, 97–114.
42. Johann David Michaelis, *Beurtheilung*, § 13, 75–76.
43. Johann David Michaelis, *Beurtheilung*, § 15, 87–88.
44. Johann David Michaelis, *Beurtheilung*, § 28, 154–55.
45. See the two articles of Robert Hetzron: "La division des langues sémitiques" in *Actes du premier congrès international de linguistique sémitique et chamito-sémitique*, ed. André Caquot and David Cohen, Paris 16–19 juillet 1969 (The Hague and Paris, 1974), 181ff; "Two Principles of Genetic Reconstruction," *Lingua* 38 (1976), 89–108. Also see Rainer M. Voigt, "The Classification of Central Semitic," *Journal of Semitic Studies* 21 (1987), 1–21, and Aaron D. Rubin, "The Subgrouping of the Semitic Languages," *Languages and Linguistics Compass* 2/1 (2008), 61–84.
46. Johann David Michaelis, *Beurtheilung*, § 28, 156–59. Michaelis argued that Arabic was closer to Hebrew than Syriac and Aramaic were. His wide-ranging arguments included appeals to the Bible and observations concerning phonology and morphology. The biblical evidence includes the account of Gideon overhearing and understanding a conversation between two Easterners (either Midianites or Amalekites; see Judges 7:9–14) and the genealogical proximity of Arabs and Hebrews (sons of brothers Ishmael and Isaac, respectively). Hebrew and Arabic both have a definite article (unlike Aramaic and Syriac), and both have a "hissing letter" and interchange *s* and *sh*. Michaelis explains apparent differences away. Arabic appears to have many more conjugations than Hebrew only because of the way Hebrew conjugations are counted (e.g., counting Pi'el and Po'el as one) and because Hebrew has many rare conjugations not counted by most grammarians.

Though Arabic has three feminine nominal endings, Michaelis argued, they were all actually identical to the Hebrew -*ah* in common speech; the difference was merely orthographic. It only appears that Arabic nouns have cases and Hebrew nouns do not because cases in Arabic, said Michaelis, were a scholarly invention. The appearance of the paragogic *nun* in Hebrew he explained by recourse to Arabic, and he pointed out that the conjugation of the verb in the Hebrew converted imperfect and the Arabic *futurum apocopatum* were identical.

47. Johann David Michaelis, *Dissertation qui a remporté le prix proposé par l'Académie Royale des Sciences et Belles Lettres de Prusse, sur l'influence réciproque de langage sur les opinions, et des opinions sur le langage* (Berlin, 1760). This edition includes Michaelis's original German essay and the French translation.

48. Johann David Michaelis, *Dissertation*, 5. Michaelis refers in this quotation to Horace: "Multa renascentur quae jam cecidere, cadentque / Quae nunc sunt in honore vocabula, si volet usus" (*Ars Poetica*, lines 70–71).

49. Johann David Michaelis, *Dissertation*, 15.

50. Johann David Michaelis, *Beurtheilung*, § 25, 139.

51. Johann David Michaelis, *Hebräische Grammatik*, Anhang, §II, 2.

52. Johann David Michaelis, *Hebräische Grammatik*, Anhang, §IV, 5–6.

53. Johann David Michaelis, *Hebräische Grammatik*, Anhang, §V, 6 (emphasis added).

54. Johann David Michaelis, *Beurtheilung*, §28, 160–61.

55. Johann David Michaelis, *Hebräische Grammatik*, Anhang, §VII, 9.

56. Johann David Michaelis, *Hebräische Grammatik*, Anhang §X, 19–20.

57. Johann David Michaelis, *Hebräische Grammatik*, Anhang §XIV, 25–27.

58. Johann David Michaelis, *Hebräische Grammatik*, Anhang §XVII, 31.

59. Johann David Michaelis, *Hebräische Grammatik*, Anhang, §XXI, 44f.

60. Johann David Michaelis, *Commentaries on the Laws of Moses*, 4 vols., trans. Alexander Smith (London, 1814), art. 3.

61. For vivid and insightful discussions of this expedition, see Michael C. Carhart, *The Science of Culture in Enlightenment Germany*, Harvard Historical Series (Cambridge: Harvard University Press, 2007), 27–44, and Jonathan Sheehan, *The Enlightenment Bible: Translation, Scholarship, Culture* (Princeton: Princeton University Press, 2005), 186–199.

62. Sheehan, *Enlightenment Bible*, 186.

63. See Frank Manuel, *The Broken Staff: Judaism through Christian Eyes* (Cambridge: Harvard University Press, 1992); Allison P. Coudert and Jeffrey S. Shoulson, eds., *Hebraica Veritas? Christian Hebraists and the Study of Judaism in Early Modern Europe* (Philadelphia: University of Pennsylvania Press, 2004); Guiseppe Veltri and Gerold Necker, eds., *Gottes Sprache in der philologischen Werkstatt. Hebräistik vom 15. bis zum 19. Jahrhundert* (Leiden: Brill, 2004).

64. Karl Heinrich Rengstorf, "Die Deutschen Pietisten und ihr Bild von Judentums," in *Begegnungen von Deutschen und Juden in der Geistesgeschichte des 18. Jahrhunderts. Wolfenbütteler Studien zur Aufklärung. Bd. 6*, ed. Jacob Katz and Karl Heinrich Rengstorf (Heidelberg: Lambert Schneider, 1994), 1–16.

65. Manuel, *Broken Staff*, 254.

66. Manuel, *Broken Staff*, 164.

67. Jonathan M. Hess, *Germans, Jews, and the Claims of Modernity* (New Haven: Yale University Press, 2002), 68.

68. Hess, *Claims*, 3–4.

69. Christian Wilhelm Dohm, *Ueber die bürgerliche Verbesserung der Juden*, reprinted from 1781 edition (Teil 1) and 1783 edition (Teil 2) (New York and Hildesheim: Georg Olms, 1973), Teil 2, 44–51, quote from 51.

70. Hess, *Claims*, 89.

71. Anna-Ruth Löwenbrück, *Judenfeindschaft im Zeitalter der Aufklärung. Eine Studie zur Vorgeschichte des modernen Antisemitismus am Beispiel des Göttinger Theologen und Orientalisten Johann David Michaelis (1717–1791)* (Frankfurt: Peter Lang, 1995).

72. Anna-Ruth Löwenbrück, "Johann David Michaelis und Moses Mendelssohn. Judenfeindschaft im Zeitalter der Aufklärung," in *Mendelssohn und die Kreise Seiner Wirksamkeit*, ed. Albrecht Michael, Eva Engel, and Norbert Hinske (Tübingen: Niemeyer, 1994), 325.

73. Dohm, *Verbesserung*, Teil 2, 32.

74. Newman, "Death of Judaism," 459.

75. Hess, *Claims*, 54–55, 57.

76. Dohm, *Verbesserung*, Teil 2, 32–33. See also Sheehan, *Enlightenment Bible*, 215.

77. Johann David Michaelis, *Fragen an eine Gesellschaft gelehrter Männer, die auf Befehl Ihro Majestät des Königes von Dännemark nach Arabien reisen* (Frankfurt, 1762), Vorrede (unpaginated).

78. Johann David Michaelis, *Uebersetzung des Alten Testaments, mit Anmerkungen für Ungelehrte* (13 vols; Göttingen and Gotha, 1769–85). The 13-volume *Uebersetzung* was reissued in a two-volume work without notes, published in Göttingen in 1789.

79. From the 1769 Preface to the *Uebersetzung*, reprinted in the 1789 edition, i. 31.

80. Johann David Michaelis, *Hebräische Grammatik*, Anhang, §XIX, 35.

81. Johann David Michaelis, *Beurtheilung*, § 43–44. Gesner was known for introducing new methods of language instruction that were modeled on the natural, experiential mode of language acquisition observed in small children. See Ulrich Schindel, "Johann Matthias Gesner, Professor der Poesie und Beredsamkeit 1734–1761," in *Die Klassische Altertumswissenschaft an der Georg-August-Universität Göttingen. Eine Ringvorlesung zu ihrer Geschichte*, ed. Carl Joachim Classen (Göttingen: Vandenhoeck & Ruprecht, 1989), 22. In a similar way, Michaelis criticized methods of instruction that were strictly grammatical. In the *Beurtheilung* (§ 19, 103), he noted that "when it comes to understanding the origin of language, children are our best teachers."

82. Johann David Michaelis, *Beurtheilung*, § 56, 353.

83. Smend, "Zwei Orientalisten," 63. Michaelis taught through the entire text of the Hebrew Bible in a mere two years.

84. Johann David Michaelis, *Beurtheilung*, § 55, 344, and §56, 364.

85. Johann David Michaelis, *Lebensbeschreibung*, 2. Michaelis complained that his father's slow, analytical method of reading made him rebellious toward grammatical study. He also noted that he eventually learned Latin grammar simply by reading Virgil and that this was a "great proof" of Gesner's theories on language instruction (9).

86. Johann David Michaelis, *Beurtheilung*, §4, 10–12.

87. "Von dem Geschmack der Morgenländischen Dichtkunst," in Johann Friedrich Löwens, *Poetische Nebenstunden* (Leipzig, 1752).

88. Johann David Michaelis, *Abhandlung von der Syrischen Sprache, und ihrem Gebrauch: Nebst dem ersten Theil einer Syrischen Chrestomathie* (Göttingen, 1786), § 15, 104–05.

89. Johann David Michaelis, *Beurtheilung*, § 25, 144.

CHAPTER 5

1. Samuel Taylor Coleridge, *The Complete Works of Samuel Taylor Coleridge*, ed. W. G. T. Shedd (New York: Harper & Brothers, 1884), vol. 1, 294–95.

2. Karl Christ, *Römische Geschichte und deutsche Geschichtswissenschaft* (Munich: C. H. Beck, 1982), 24–27.

3. Alexandre Grandazzi, *The Foundation of Rome: Myth and History*, trans. Jane Marie Todd (Ithaca: Cornell University Press, 1997), 14.

4. Walter Rehm, *Griechentum und Goethezeit: Geschichte eines Glaubens*, 4th ed. (Bern and Munich: Francke Verlag, 1969), 19–22.

5. Jürgen von Stackelberg, "Klassizismus und Aufklärung—der Blick nach Frankreich," in *Zur Geistigen Situation der Zeit der Göttinger Universitätsgründung 1737. Eine Vortragsreihe aus Anlaß des 250jährigen Bestehens der Georgia Augusta*, ed. Jürgen von Stackelberg (Göttingen: Vandenhoeck & Ruprecht, 1988), 169–72.

6. Erich Auerbach, *Mimesis: The Representation of Reality in Western Literature*, trans. Willard R. Trask (Princeton: Princeton University Press, 2003), 15.

7. My thanks to R. R. Reno for this point.

8. "Von dem Geschmack der Morgenländischen Dichtkunst," in Johann Friedrich Löwens, *Poetische Nebenstunden* (Leipzig, 1752). See also Johann David Michaelis, *Abhandlung von der Syrischen Sprache, und ihrem Gebrauch: Nebst dem ersten Theil einer Syrischen Chrestomathie* (Göttingen, 1786) and the preface to the first edition, reprinted in Johann David Michaelis, *Arabische Grammatik, Nebst einer Arabischen Chrestomathie, und Abhandlungen vom Arabischen Geschmack, sonderlich in der Poetischen und Historischen Schreibart*, 2nd rev. ed. (Göttingen: Victorinus Botziegel, 1781).

9. Johann David Michaelis, *Lebensbeschreibung von ihm selbst abgefaßt, mit Anmerkungen von Hassencamp. Nebst Bemerkungen über dessen litterarischen Character von Eichhorn, Schulz—und dem Elogium von Heyne* (Rinteln and Leipzig, 1793), 33.

10. Murray Roston, *Prophet and Poet: The Bible and the Growth of Romanticism* (London: Faber and Faber, 1965), 21.

11. Robert Lowth, *Lectures on the Sacred Poetry of the Hebrews* (1787), trans. G. Gregory (Hildesheim: Georg Olms, 1969), Lect. 1, 1–2.

12. For example, Stephen Prickett: "To Lowth we owe the rediscovery of the Bible as a work of literature within the context of ancient Hebrew life." Stephen Prickett, *Words and the Word: Language, Poetics, and Biblical Interpretation* (Cambridge: Cambridge University Press, 1986), 105.

13. I will refer to the original Latin as *Praelectiones*, citing the 1770 second edition (Göttingen). When citing Gregory's 1787 English translation, I will refer to it as *Lectures*.

Gregory did not translate Michaelis's editorial preface and he only translated some of Michaelis's editorial notes. When quoting Lowth and Michaelis, then, I use Gregory's translation. If Gregory did not translate the passage, then I offer my own translation of the Latin *Praelectiones* text.

14. Lowth, *Lectures*, Lect. 1, 35.
15. Lowth, *Lectures*, Lect. 1, 7.
16. Lowth, *Lectures*, Lect. 1, 38.
17. Lowth, *Lectures*, Lect. 1, 37.
18. Lowth, *Lectures*, Lect. 2, 44.
19. Roston, *Prophet and Poet*, 45.
20. Lowth, *Lectures*, Lect. 2, 43–44.
21. Lowth, *Lectures*, Lect. 2, 50–51.
22. Lowth, *Lectures*, Lect. 2, 53.
23. Roston, *Prophet and Poet*, 52–59.
24. Lowth, *Lectures*, Lect. 2, 48.
25. Samuel H. Monk, *The Sublime: A Study of Critical Theories in XVIII-Century England* (New York: Modern Language Association, 1935), 13–14.
26. Lowth, *Lectures*, Lect. 14, 307.
27. Monk, *The Sublime*, 4–8.
28. Roston argues persuasively that Lowth's "discovery" of parallelism allowed English literature to move beyond the formalism and artificiality of a poetics dominated both by the imitation of classical literature and by doctrinaire poetics derived from classical sources. In Monk's analysis, Lowth's concept of the sublime, at once rooted in the neoclassical and tending toward Kantian subjectivism, makes him a transitional figure; Monk, *The Sublime*, 77–83. See also Anna Cullhed, "Original Poetry: Robert Lowth and Eighteenth-Century Poetics," in *Sacred Conjectures: The Context and Legacy of Robert Lowth and Jean Astruc*, ed. John Jarick (New York: T & T Clark, 2007), 25–47; Prickett, *Words and the Word*, 105–13; Vincent Freimarck, "Introduction," in *Lectures on the Sacred Poetry of the Hebrews*, Robert Lowth (Hildesheim: Georg Olms, 1969), xi–xii; and Brian Hepworth, *Robert Lowth* (Boston: Twayne, 1978), 98.
29. Roston, *Prophet and Poet*, 70–125. See also Robert Marsch, "Neoclassical Poetics," *Encyclopedia of Poetry and Poetics*, ed. Alex Preminger (Princeton: Princeton University Press, 1965), 559–64.
30. Roston, *Prophet and Poet*, 41.
31. Cullhed, "Original Poetry," 37.
32. James Kugel, *The Idea of Biblical Poetry: Parallelism and Its History* (Baltimore: Johns Hopkins University Press, 1998), 277.
33. Lowth, *Lectures*, Lect. 3, 56.
34. Christoph Bultmann, "After Horace: Sacred Poetry at the Centre of the Hebrew Bible," in *Sacred Conjectures: The Context and Legacy of Robert Lowth and Jean Astruc*, ed. John Jarick (New York: T & T Clark, 2007), 63–64.
35. Lowth, *Lectures*, Lect. 3, 56.
36. Lowth, *Lectures*, Lect. 3, 68.
37. Lowth, *Lectures*, Lect. 3, 71.

38. Lowth, *Lectures*, Lect. 4, 101.
39. Lowth, *Lectures*, Lect. 19, 25–31.
40. Lowth, *Lectures*, Lect. 19, 34.
41. Kugel, *Idea of Biblical Poetry*, 12–15, 274–86. Kugel's *Idea of Biblical Poetry: Parallelism and Its History* remains the definitive refutation of Lowth's analysis of "biblical poetry."
42. Lowth, *Lectures*, Lect. 6, 120–21.
43. Lowth, *Lectures*, Lect. 6, 124.
44. Roston, *Prophet and Poet*, 126–42.
45. Lowth, *Lectures*, Lect. 5, 113–14.
46. John Rogerson, *Old Testament Criticism in the Nineteenth Century: England and Germany* (London: SPCK, 1984), 23.
47. After 1758, when the first volume of the German edition of the lectures was published, Michaelis learned of his mistake and made contact with Lowth.
48. Hepworth, *Lowth*, 35.
49. Rudolf Smend, "Lowth in Deutschland," in *Epochen der Bibelkritik* (Munich: Chr. Kaiser, 1991), 48.
50. Smend, "Lowth in Deutschland," 49.
51. Smend, "Lowth in Deutschland," 47, 49.
52. Jonathan Sheehan, *The Enlightenment Bible: Translation, Scholarship, Culture* (Princeton: Princeton University Press, 2005), 200–01; Johann Gottfried Eichhorn, "Bemerkungen über J. D. Michaelis litterarischen Character," in *Lebensbeschreibung von ihm selbst abgefasst*, by Johann David Michaelis (Leipzig, 1793), 206–08.
53. Lowth, *Lectures*, xxi–xxii.
54. Smend, "Lowth in Deutschland," 50.
55. Hans-Joachim Kraus, *Geschichte der historisch-kritischen Erforschung des Alten Testaments* (Neukirchen-Vluyn: Neukirchener Verlag, 1982), 97; Rudolf Smend, "Johann David Michaelis," in *Festrede im Namen der Georg-August-Universität zur Akademischen Preisvertheilung Am VIII. Juni MDCCCSCVIII* (Göttingen, 1898), 5; Rudolf Smend, "Johann David Michaelis und Johann Gottfried Eichhorn—Zwei Orientalisten am Rande der Theologie," in *Theologie in Göttingen. Eine Vorlesungsreihe*, ed. Bernd Moeller (Göttingen: Vandenhoeck & Ruprecht, 1987), 65.
56. Michaelis, *Lebensbeschreibung*, 36.
57. Smend, "Zwei Orientalisten," 70.
58. Lowth, *Lectures*, Lect. 12, 270–71. Is 55:10–11 (AV): "For as the rain cometh down, and the snow from heaven, and returneth not thither, but watereth the earth, and maketh it bring forth and bud, that it may give seed to the sower, and bread to the eater: So shall my word be that goeth forth out of my mouth: it shall not return unto me void, but it shall accomplish that which I please, and it shall prosper *in the thing* whereto I sent it."
59. Lowth, *Lectures*, Lect. 12, 270–71, n. 24.
60. Lowth, *Lectures*, Lect. 12, 270 (emphasis added).
61. Lowth, *Lectures*, Lect. 12, 270.
62. Two exceptions are Hans Hecht, *T. Percy, R. Wood und J. D. Michaelis. Ein Beitrag Zur Literaturgeschichte der Genieperiode* (Stuttgart: Kohlhammer, 1933) and Ida Hakemeyer, *Kleines Universitätsmosaik* (Göttingen, 1960).

63. Anna-Ruth Löwenbruck, "Johann David Michaelis' Verdienst um die philologisch-historische Bibelkritik," in *Historische Kritik und Biblischer Kanon in der Deutschen Aufklärung*, ed. Henning Graf Reventlow, Walter Sparn, and John Woodbridge (Wiesbaden: Otto Harrassowitz, 1988), 159.

64. Hakemeyer, *Universitätsmosaik*, 75, 82–84.

65. Hans Hecht, *T. Percy, R. Wood und J. D. Michaelis. Ein Beitrag zur Literaturgeschichte der Genieperiode* (Stuttgart, 1933).

66. Hecht, *Percy, Wood, Michaelis*, 12.

67. Robert Wood, *An Essay on the Original Genius and Writings of Homer: With a Comparative View of the Ancient and Present State of the Troade* (London: H. Hughs for T. Payne and P. Elmsly, 1775), 223.

68. Wood, *Essay on Homer*, 155–56.

69. Wood, *Essay on Homer*, 248, 280.

70. Kirsti Simonsuuri, *Homer's Original Genius: Eighteenth-Century Notions of the Early Greek Epic (1688–1798)* (Cambridge: Cambridge University Press, 1979), 142.

71. As reported by Heyne's biographer A. H. L. Heeren; see Irene Polke, *Selbstreflexion im Spiegel des Anderen. Eine wirkungsgeschichtliche Studie zum Hellenismusbild Heynes und Herders* (Königshausen: Neumann, 1999), 34.

72. Hecht, *Percy, Wood, Michaelis*, 19–31.

73. Johann David Michaelis, Review of Lowth's *Praelectiones*, *Göttingische Anzeigen von Gelehrten Sachen* (1753): 947–50; Johann David Michaelis, Review of Lowth's *Praelectiones*, *Relationes de Libris Novis* X (1754): 317–37.

74. Michaelis, Review (1753), 947.

75. Robert Lowth, *De sacra poesi Hebraeorum praelectiones*, 2nd ed. (Göttingen: Joan. Christ. Dieterich, 1770), Lect. 3, Nota editoris 5, 53.

76. Lowth, *Lectures*, Lect. 2, 46–47.

77. Lowth, *Praelectiones*, Praefatio editoris, xv.

78. Lowth, *Lectures*, Lect. 11, n. 2, 240.

79. Hepworth, *Lowth*, 39 (original emphasis).

80. Lowth, *Praelectiones*, preface to the second volume (unpaginated).

81. Michaelis, Review (1754), 321–22.

82. Lowth, *Praelectiones*, Praefatio editoris, vi.

83. Lowth, *Praelectiones*, Praefatio editoris, vii.

84. Lowth, *Praelectiones*, Lect. 1, n. 15, 33–34.

85. Lowth, *Praelectiones*, Praefatio editoris, xxiii.

86. Lowth, *Praelectiones*, Praefatio editoris, xxix–xxxiii.

87. Lowth, *Praelectiones*, Praefatio editoris, xxx–xxxviii.

88. Lowth, *Lectures*, Lect. 23, n. 7, 148.

89. Lowth, *Lectures*, Lect. 14, n. 6, 314.

90. Lowth, *Lectures*, Lect. 7, n. 16, 156–57. Against many of his contemporaries, Michaelis argued that the Israelites believed in an afterlife and in the immortality of the soul. Here he claims that the Hebrews were rather more extravagant in this belief than their classical counterparts, for the Israelites "not only suppose the human souls to descend to the infernal regions, but those of trees, and even of kingdoms, Is xiv. 9–20. Ezek xxxi. 14, 16, 17, 18. xxxii."

91. Lowth, *Lectures*, Lect. 9, 204–11.

92. Michaelis, "Review," 333.

93. Lowth, *Lectures*, Lect. 19, n. 29, 59.

94. Lowth, *Lectures*, Lect. 19, n. 29, 58.

95. Michaelis, "Review," 334.

96. Lowth, *Praelectiones*, Praefatio editoris, xiv.

97. Johann David Michaelis, *Dissertation qui a remporté le prix proposé par l'Académie Royale des Sciences et Belles Lettres de Prusse, sur l'influence réciproque de langage sur les opinions, et des opinions sur le langage* (Berlin, 1760), 90–91.

98. Lowth, *Praelectiones*, Praefatio editoris, xvii.

99. Lowth, *Lectures*, Lect. 4, n. 10, 85.

100. Lowth, *Praelectiones*, Praefatio editoris, xxxi. Michaelis refers here to the fact that Longinus in his *Peri hupsous* counted the creation account in Genesis as an example of sublime literature.

101. Kugel, *Idea of Biblical Poetry*, 69.

102. Bultmann, "After Horace," 81–82.

103. See Prickett, *Words and the Word*; Stephen Prickett, *Origins of Narrative: The Romantic Appropriation of the Bible* (Cambridge: Cambridge University Press, 1996); Sheehan, *Enlightenment Bible*, ch. 6; David Norton, *A History of the Bible as Literature. Volume Two: From 1700 to the Present Day* (Cambridge: Cambridge University Press, 1993).

CHAPTER 6

1. Quoted in Loren Graham, Wolf Lepenies, and Peter Weingart, eds., *Functions and Uses of Disciplinary Histories* (Dordrecht: D. Reidel, 1983), 281.

2. Michaelis included his own German translations of Pss 2, 8, and 42 in an appendix to the 1770 Göttingen edition of Lowth's *Praelectiones*. The quotation comes from a brief preface to the translations in the appendix.

3. This poem first appeared in *Hamburgische Beyträge zu den Werken des Witzes und der Sittenlehre* (part 1; Hamburg, 1753), 254–74.

4. Johann David Michaelis, *Poetischer Entwurf der Gedanken des Prediger-Buch Salomons* (Bremen and Leipzig: Georg Ludewig Förster, 1762), 79–88.

5. *The Ten Commandments*, directed by Cecil B. DeMille (1956).

6. In the (unpaginated) preface to the second edition of the *Poetischer Entwurf*, Michaelis explained that poetic ability diminishes with age. He apologized for his poetic effort, acknowledging that it may seem "laughable" or "pathetic" to some.

7. Johann David Michaelis, *Commentaries on the Laws of Moses*, 4 vols., trans. Alexander Smith (London, 1814), Art. 1, 1–2.

8. John H. Geerken, "Machiavelli's Moses and Renaissance Politics," *Journal of the History of Ideas* 60, no. 4 (1999): 586–87.

9. Steven Marx, "Moses and Machiavellism," *Journal of the American Academy of Religion* 65, no. 3 (1997): 553.

10. Geerken, "Machiavelli's Moses," 582.

11. Niccolò Machiavelli, *Discourses on Livy*, trans. Julia Conway Bondanella and Peter Bondanella (Oxford: Oxford University Press, 1997), III.20, p. 326.

12. Marx, "Moses and Machiavellism," 566.

13. Baruch Spinoza, *Theological-Political Treatise*, trans. Samuel Shirley (Indianapolis: Hackett, 2001), Ch. 8, 109–10.

14. These include the death narrative of Moses at the conclusion of Deuteronomy, third-person references to Moses (e.g., "Moses was the meekest of men," Num 12:3), geographically incongruous statements (e.g., a reference to the Transjordan as "beyond the Jordan," Deut 1:1), and parenthetical additions from a later time (e.g., "the Canaanites were then in the land," Gen 12:6). Spinoza allowed that a few things like the Song of Moses (Deut 32:1–43) and select portions of the Law (e.g., the Book of the Covenant in Ex 20:22–23:33) may have originated with Moses. Spinoza, *TTP*, ch. 8, 106–10.

15. Spinoza, *TTP*, ch. 1, 13–14.

16. Spinoza, *TTP*, 190.

17. Spinoza, *TTP*, 199. See also ch. 5, p. 65, where Spinoza says that the object of the ceremonial law was that "men should do nothing of their own free will, but should always act under external authority."

18. The following description is based on Spinoza, *TTP*, 200–04.

19. Jan Assmann, *Moses the Egyptian: The Memory of Egypt in Western Monotheism* (Cambridge: Harvard University Press, 1997), ch. 4, "The Moses Discourse in the Eighteenth Century."

20. The Egyptian priest Manetho, writing in the first half of the third century BCE, also identified Moses as an Egyptian priest. A portion of his writings on Moses survives in two excerpts that Josephus included in his *Contra Apionem*. See Assmann, *Moses the Egyptian*, 30–34.

21. Assmann, *Moses the Egyptian*, 91–96.

22. See the helpful discussions of Assmann, *Moses the Egyptian*, 96–102 and Jonathan Lamb, *The Rhetoric of Suffering: Reading the Book of Job in the Eighteenth Century* (Oxford: Clarendon Press, 1995), ch. 6, 110–27.

23. Assmann, *Moses the Egyptian*, 19.

24. Horst Lange, "Reconstructing a Nation's Birth: Monotheism, Nationalism, and Violence in Goethe's Reading of the Pentateuch," *Colloquia Germanica* 33, no. 2 (2000): 103–21.

25. See Johann David Michaelis, *Entwurf einer typischen Gottesgelahrtheit* (Göttingen: G. L. Förster, 1763). There Michaelis describes in detail how the religious imagery of the Hebrew Bible may be coordinated to articles of Christian faith. It is clear from this work that Michaelis was not interested in consulting the Hebrew Bible *directly* as a religious resource but rather as a text that, in its religious appropriation, had to be mediated at all times by the New Testament.

26. Michaelis, *Commentaries on the Laws of Moses*, § 1.

27. The *Conjectures* was recently published in a new edition: Jean Astruc, *Conjectures sur la Genèse*, ed. Pierre Gibert (Paris: Éditions Noêsis, 1999). Subsequent citations will refer to this edition. For a helpful discussion of Astruc's life and background, see the recent articles of Rudolf Smend: Rudolf Smend, *From Astruc to Zimmerli* (Tübingen: Mohr

Siebeck, 2007), 1–14; Rudolf Smend, "Jean Astruc: A Physician as a Biblical Scholar," in *Sacred Conjectures: The Context and Legacy of Robert Lowth and Jean Astruc*, ed. John Jarick (New York: T & T Clark, 2007), 157–73.

28. Astruc, *Conjectures sur la Genèse*, 123–24.

29. Otto Eissfeldt, *The Old Testament: An Introduction*, trans. Peter R. Ackroyd (New York: Harper and Row, 1965), 161 (emphasis added). Astruc noted in the "Avertissement" to the *Conjectures* that his thesis regarding Moses' use of documentary sources "avait été déjà avancé, quant au fond, par plusieurs auteurs dans des ouvrages très approuvés" (123).

30. In 1711, Hildesheim pastor H. B. Witter published a work entitled *Jura israelitarum in Palaestinam terram Chananaeam Commentatione in Genesin perpetua sic demonstrata ut idiomatis authentici nativus sensus fideliter detegatur, Mosis autoris primaeva intentio sollicite definiatur, adeoque corpus doctrinae et juris cum antiquissimum, tum consumatissimum tandem eruatur*. Like Astruc, he advanced a theory of sources based on divine names. Yet Witter gained no immediate following. Michaelis was largely responsible for making Astruc's work known in Germany. Despite Michaelis's rejection of Astruc's theory, his student J. G. Eichhorn built on it in developing his own approach to source criticism. For a comparison of Witter and Astruc, see Pierre Gibert, "De l'intuition a l'évidence: La multiplicité documentaire dans la Genèse chez H. B. Witter et Jean Astruc," in *Sacred Conjectures: The Context and Legacy of Robert Lowth and Jean Astruc*, ed. John Jarick (New York: T & T Clark, 2007), 174–89.

31. Astruc, *Conjectures sur la Genèse*, 140.

32. Astruc, *Conjectures sur la Genèse*, 489.

33. Astruc, *Conjectures sur la Genèse*, 513–15.

34. Johann David Michaelis, *Einleitung in die Göttlichen Schriften des Alten Bundes* (Hamburg: Bohnsche Buchhandlung, 1787), 268.

35. Michaelis, *Einleitung*, 277.

36. Michaelis, *Einleitung*, 300.

37. Michaelis, *Einleitung*, 300.

38. Michaelis, *Einleitung*, 226, 272–94.

39. Michaelis, *Einleitung*, 294.

40. Michaelis, *Einleitung*, 221–22.

41. Richard H. Popkin, "Spinoza and Bible Scholarship," in *The Cambridge Companion to Spinoza*, ed. Don Garrett (New York and Cambridge: Cambridge University Press, 1996), 388.

42. Harold Love, *Attributing Authorship: An Introduction* (Cambridge: Cambridge University Press, 2002), 25.

43. Love, *Attributing Authorship*, 26.

44. Love, *Attributing Authorship*, 219.

45. Michaelis, *Commentaries on the Laws of Moses*, xvi.

46. Michaelis, *Commentaries on the Laws of Moses*, Article 16.

47. Michaelis, *Commentaries on the Laws of Moses*, Article 1. See also Rudolf Smend, "Aufgeklärte Bemühung um das Gesetz: Johann David Michaelis," in *Epochen der Bibelkritik*, by Rudolf Smend (Munich: Chr. Kaiser, 1991), 63–73. Smend points out that no

review gave him greater joy than one that claimed Michaelis had penetrated the spirit of the Mosaic laws "with the acumen of a Montesquieu" (66).
48. Michaelis, *Commentaries on the Laws of Moses*, Article 2.
49. Jonathan M. Hess, *Germans, Jews, and the Claims of Modernity* (New Haven: Yale University Press, 2002), 60.
50. Assmann, *Moses the Egyptian*, 127.
51. Michaelis, *Einleitung*, 222.
52. The book of Exodus clearly describes and requires an Egyptian setting, but it evinces only a generically Egyptian context. While the general outlines of the Exodus story, for example the presence of Semites in the Delta and the migration of "Asiatics" to Egypt in times of famine in the Late Bronze period, are not historically implausible, the biblical text makes few references to specific places and names. The names of two "supply cities" in Ex 1:11, Pithom and Rameses, are notable exceptions.
53. Michaelis does not indicate what his sources for Egyptian history are. He may have regarded his characterization of Egypt as a commonplace. In general, knowledge of ancient Egypt before the Napoleonic mission to that country (1798) was vague and unreliable: "Europe knew the pharaonic civilization only from secondhand sources, mainly Roman works containing ill-understood Egyptian iconography." Fernand Beaucour, Yves Laissus, and Chantal Orgogozo, *The Discovery of Egypt* (Paris: Flammarion, 1990), 204.
54. Hess, *Claims*, 50–89.
55. Michaelis, *Commentaries on the Laws of Moses*, Article 4.
56. Michaelis, *Commentaries on the Laws of Moses*, Article 4.
57. Michaelis, *Commentaries on the Laws of Moses*, Article 131.
58. Michaelis, *Commentaries on the Laws of Moses*, Article 136.
59. Michaelis, *Commentaries on the Laws of Moses*, Article 8.
60. Michaelis, *Commentaries on the Laws of Moses*, Article 203.
61. Michaelis, *Commentaries on the Laws of Moses*, Article 11.
62. Michaelis, *Commentaries on the Laws of Moses*, Article 198.
63. Michaelis, *Commentaries on the Laws of Moses*, Article 205.
64. Michaelis, *Commentaries on the Laws of Moses*, Article 32.
65. Michaelis, *Commentaries on the Laws of Moses*, Article 33.
66. Michaelis, *Commentaries on the Laws of Moses*, Article 32.
67. Michaelis, *Commentaries on the Laws of Moses*, Article 32.
68. Notker Hammerstein, "Die Universitätsgründungen im Zeichen der Aufklärung," in *Beiträge zu Problemen deutscher Universitätsgründungen der frühen Neuzeit*, ed. Peter Baumgart and Notker Hammerstein (Nendeln: KTO Press, 1978), 291.
69. Johann David Michaelis, *Uebersetzung des Alten Testaments, mit Anmerkungen für Ungelehrte* (Göttingen and Gotha: Johann Christian Dieterich, 1769–85), 38.
70. Lamb, *Rhetoric of Suffering*, 110–27.
71. Lamb, *Rhetoric of Suffering*, 5.
72. Lamb, *Rhetoric of Suffering*, 114.
73. Jonathan Sheehan, *The Enlightenment Bible: Translation, Scholarship, Culture* (Princeton: Princeton University Press, 2005), 168.
74. Sheehan, *Enlightenment Bible*, 172.

75. Michaelis, *Einleitung*, § 12, 72–81.
76. These examples come from Michaelis, *Einleitung*, § 13, 81–88.
77. Michaelis, *Einleitung*, § 14, 88–90.
78. Michaelis, *Einleitung*, §1, 1–2.
79. Michaelis, *Einleitung*, § 1, 3.
80. Michaelis, *Einleitung*, § 4, 23.
81. Michaelis, *Uebersetzung*, vol. 1, 38.
82. Michaelis, *Uebersetzung*, vol. 1, 40. "Ich weiß nehmlich daß mein Erlöser lebt! Ein anderer Ich wird dereinst aus dem Staube aufstehen, Meine Haut, dieser Eiterfraß, wird eine andere seyn; Und aus meinem Leibe werde ich Gott sehen, Mir werde ich ihn sehen, Meine Augen werden ihn sehen, und kein Fremder."
83. Compare English translations of the Hebrew of Job 19:25: "For I know *that* my redeemer liveth, and *that* he shall stand at the latter *day* upon the earth" (Authorized Version); "But as for me, I know that my Vindicator lives, and that he will at last stand forth upon the dust" (New American Bible); "For I know that my Redeemer lives, and that at the last he will stand upon the earth" (New Revised Standard Version); "But I know that my Vindicator lives; In the end He will testify on earth—" (Jewish Publication Society).
84. Michaelis adduced Job 14:13; 24:18; 11:17 as evidence for belief in an afterlife. His translations, though, rely on unsupported conjectural emendations. He also interpreted the hymn to wisdom in Job 28 as an expression of the belief that humans cannot understand wisdom *in this world* but presumably will in the next. Even if Job 28 denies the possibility of a comprehensive human wisdom in this life, it does not come close to affirming a belief in future rewards and punishments.
85. Michaelis, *Uebersetzung*, vol. 1, 24–25.
86. Michaelis, *Uebersetzung*, vol. 1, 26.
87. Kirsti Simonsuuri, *Homer's Original Genius: Eighteenth-Century Notions of the Early Greek Epic (1688–1798)* (Cambridge: Cambridge University Press, 1979), 153.

CONCLUSION

1. Johann Gottfried Eichhorn, "Bemerkungen über J. D. Michaelis litterarischen Character," in *Lebensbeschreibung von ihm selbst abgefasst*, by Johann David Michaelis (Leipzig, 1793), 206.
2. Eichhorn, "Bemerkungen," 147.
3. Quoted in Christoph Bultmann, *Die biblische Urgeschichte in der Aufklärung: Johann Gottfried Herders Interpretation der Genesis als Antwort auf die Religionskritik David Humes* (Tübingen: Mohr Siebeck, 1999), 133, 139.
4. Johann Gottfried Herder, *The Spirit of Hebrew Poetry*, 2 vols, trans. James Marsh (Burlington: Edward Smith, 1833), vol. 2, 128.
5. Johann Gottfried Herder, *Sämtliche Werke*, ed. Bernhard Suphan (Hildesheim: Olms, 1967–68), 5:425.
6. Herder, *SW*, 5:425.
7. Suzanne Marchand, "German Orientalism and the Decline of the West," *Proceedings of the American Philosophical Society* 145, no. 4 (December 2001): 465, 467.

8. Quoted in Dominique Bourel, "Die deutsche Orientalistik im 18. Jahrhundert. Von der Mission zur Wissenschaft," in *Historische Kritik und biblischer Kanon in der deutschen Aufklärung*, ed. Henning Graf Reventlow, Walter Sparn, and John Woodbridge (Wiesbaden: Otto Harrassowitz, 1988), 124.

9. Anna Cullhed, "Original Poetry: Robert Lowth and Eighteenth-Century Poetics," in *Sacred Conjectures: The Context and Legacy of Robert Lowth and Jean Astruc*, ed. John Jarick (New York: T & T Clark, 2007), 46–47.

10. Thomas Albert Howard, *Protestant Theology and the Making of the Modern German University* (New York: Oxford University Press, 2006), 155–66.

11. Jonathan Sheehan, *The Enlightenment Bible: Translation, Scholarship, Culture* (Princeton: Princeton University Press, 2005), 235.

12. See Suzanne L. Marchand, *Down from Olympus: Archaeology and Philhellenism in Germany, 1750–1970* (Princeton: Princeton University Press, 1996).

13. Anthony Grafton, "Polyhistor into *Philolog*: Notes on the Transformation of German Classical Scholarship, 1780–1850," *History of Universities* 3 (1983): 183–84.

14. Sheehan, *Enlightenment Bible*, 220, 258.

15. Jon D. Levenson, *The Hebrew Bible, the Old Testament, and Historical Criticism* (Louisville, KY: Westminster John Knox, 1993), 107–08.

16. Northrop Frye, *The Great Code: The Bible and Literature* (New York: Harvest/HBJ, 1982), xviii–xix.

17. Johann Georg Hamann, *Sämtliche Werke*, ed. Josef Nadler (Wien: Thomas-Morus-Presse, 1949), vol. 1, "Über die Auslegung der Heiligen Schrift," 5.

18. Luigi Marino, *Praeceptores Germaniae: Göttingen 1770–1820* (Göttingen: Vandenhoeck & Ruprecht, 1995), 287.

19. Hamann, *SW*, vol. 1, "Über die Auslegung der Heiligen Schrift," 5.

20. Johann Georg Hamann, "Aesthetica in nuce: A Rhapsody in Cabbalistic Prose," in *Classical and Romantic German Aesthetics*, J. M. Bernstein (Cambridge: Cambridge University Press, 2003), 2.

21. Hamann, "Aesthetica in nuce," 16.

22. Hamann, "Aesthetica in nuce," 16, note yy.

23. Hamann, "Aesthetica in nuce," 7.

24. Hamann, "Aesthetica in nuce," 9.

25. Hamann, "Aesthetica in nuce," 9.

26. Hamann, "Aesthetica in nuce," 9.

27. For an overview of recent challenges to the coherence of modern historical criticism, see the helpful anthology of essays by Brevard Childs, David C. Steinmetz, Jon Levenson, Walter Wink, Phyllis Trible, Edgar V. McKnight, Elisabeth Schüssler Fiorenza, Dale Patrick, and Fernando Segovia in William Yarchin, ed., *History of Biblical Interpretation: A Reader* (Peabody, MA: Hendrickson, 2004), 307–429. See also Craig Bartholomew, Colin Greene, and Karl Möller, eds., *Renewing Biblical Interpretation* (Grand Rapids, MI: Zondervan, 2000) and Craig Bartholomew et al., *"Behind the Text": History and Biblical Interpretation* (Grand Rapids, MI: Zondervan, 2003).

28. John Barton, *The Nature of Biblical Criticism* (Louisville, KY: Westminster John Knox, 2007).

29. Barton, *Biblical Criticism*, 117–36.

30. Barton, *Biblical Criticism*, 5.

31. John J. Collins, *The Bible after Babel: Historical Criticism in a Postmodern Age* (Grand Rapids, MI: Eerdmans, 2005). For a more extensive discussion of this book, see Michael Legaspi, "What Ever Happened to Historical Criticism?" *Journal of Religion and Society* 9 (2007).

32. Collins, *Bible after Babel*, 10–11.

33. Legaspi, "Historical Criticism," paragraph 12.

34. Legaspi, "Historical Criticism," paragraph 17; see also John J. Collins, "The Zeal of Phinehas: The Bible and the Legitimation of Violence," *Journal of Biblical Literature* 122 (2003): 3–21.

35. Collins, *Bible after Babel*, 4–11.

Bibliography

Assmann, Jan. *Moses the Egyptian: The Memory of Egypt in Western Monotheism.* Cambridge, MA: Harvard University Press, 1997.
Astruc, Jean. *Conjectures sur la Genèse.* Edited by Pierre Gibert. Paris: Éditions Noêsis, 1999.
Auerbach, Erich. *Mimesis: The Representation of Reality in Western Literature.* Translated by Willard R. Trask. Princeton: Princeton University Press, 2003.
Augustijn, Cornelis. "The Ecclesiology of Erasmus." In *Scrinium Erasmianum,* edited by Joseph Coppens, 135–55. Leiden: Brill, 1969.
———. *Erasmus: His Life, Works, and Influence.* Translated by J. C. Grayson. Toronto: University of Toronto Press, 1991.
Bartholomew, Craig, C. Stephen Evans, Mary Healy, and Murray Rae, eds. *"Behind the Text": History and Biblical Interpretation.* Grand Rapids, MI: Zondervan, 2003.
Bartholomew, Craig, Colin Greene, and Karl Möller, eds. *Renewing Biblical Interpretation.* Grand Rapids, MI: Zondervan, 2000.
Barton, John. *The Nature of Biblical Criticism.* Louisville, KY: Westminster John Knox, 2007.
Bauermeister, Christopher C. W. "Hanover: *Milde Regierung* or *Ancien Régime?*" *German History* 20, no. 3 (2002): 288–308.
Baur, Jörg. "Die Anfänge der Theologie an der 'wohl angeordneten evangelischen Universität' Göttingen." In *Zur geistigen Situation der Zeit der Göttinger Universitätsgründung 1737. Eine Vortragsreihe aus Anlaß des 250jährigen Bestehens der Georgia Augusta,* edited by Jürgen von Stackelberg, 9–56. Göttingen: Vandenhoeck & Ruprecht, 1988.
Beaucour, Fernand, Yves Laissus, and Chantal Orgogozo. *The Discovery of Egypt.* Paris: Flammarion, 1990.

Becker, Carl L. *The Heavenly City of the Eighteenth-Century Philosophers*. New Haven: Yale University Press, 1932.

Berghahn, Klaus L. *Grenzen der Toleranz. Juden und Christen im Zeitalter der Aufklärung*. Köln: Böhlau, 2000.

Bernays, Jacob. *Phokion und Seine Neueren Beurtheiler. Ein Beitrag zur Geschichte der Griechischen Philosophie und Politik*. Berlin: Wilhelm Hertz, 1881.

Bernstein, J. M., ed. *Classical and Romantic German Aesthetics*. Cambridge: Cambridge University Press, 2003.

Berthold, Heinz. "Bewunderung und Kritik. Zur Bedeutung der Mittlerstellung Christian Gottlob Heynes." In *Winckelmanns Wirkung auf seine Zeit. Lessing, Herder, Heyne*, edited by Johannes Irmscher, 161–70. Stendal, 1988.

Bödeker, Hans Erich, Georg G. Iggers, Jonathan B. Knudsen, and Peter H. Reill, eds. *Aufklärung und Geschichte. Studien zur deutschen Geschichtswissenschaft im 18. Jahrhundert*. Göttingen: Vandenhoeck & Ruprecht, 1986.

Bourel, Dominique. "Die deutsche Orientalistik im 18. Jahrhundert. Von der Mission zur Wissenschaft." In *Historische Kritik und biblischer Kanon in der deutschen Aufklärung*, edited by Henning Graf Reventlow, Walter Sparn, and John Woodbridge, 113–26. Wiesbaden: Otto Harrassowitz, 1988.

Bultmann, Christoph. "After Horace: Sacred Poetry at the Centre of the Hebrew Bible." In *Sacred Conjectures: The Context and Legacy of Robert Lowth and Jean Astruc*, edited by John Jarick, 62–82. New York: T & T Clark, 2007.

———. *Die biblische Urgeschichte in der Aufklärung: Johann Gottfried Herders Interpretation der Genesis als Antwort auf die Religionskritik David Humes*. Tübingen: Mohr Siebeck, 1999.

Burckhardt, Jacob. *The Civilization of the Renaissance in Italy*. Translated by S. G. C. Middlemore. New York: Macmillan, 1904.

Burnett, Stephen. *From Christian Hebraism to Jewish Studies. Johannes Buxtorf (1564–1629) and Hebrew Learning in the Seventeenth Century*. Leiden: Brill, 1996.

Butler, Eliza Marian. *The Tyranny of Greece over Germany*. Cambridge: Cambridge University Press, 1935.

Bühler, Axel, and Luigi Cataldi Madonna. "Von Thomasius bis Semler. Entwicklungslinien der Hermeneutik in Halle." In *Hermeneutik der Aufklärung*, edited by Axel Bühler and Luigi Cataldi Madonna, 49–70. Hamburg: Felix Meiner, 1994.

Cameron, Euan. *The European Reformation*. Oxford: Clarendon, 1991.

Carhart, Michael C. *The Science of Culture in Enlightenment Germany*. Harvard Historical Series. Cambridge, MA: Harvard University Press, 2007.

Childs, Brevard. "Foreword." In *Renewing Biblical Interpretation*, edited by Craig Bartholomew, Collin Greene, and Karl Möller, xv–xvii. Grand Rapids, MI: Zondervan, 2000.

Christ, Karl. *Römische Geschichte und deutsche Geschichtswissenschaft*. Munich: C. H. Beck, 1982.

Clark, William. *Academic Charisma and the Origins of the Research University*. Chicago: University of Chicago Press, 2006.

Collins, John J. *The Bible after Babel: Historical Criticism in a Postmodern Age*. Grand Rapids, MI: Eerdmans, 2005.

———. "The Zeal of Phinehas: The Bible and the Legitimization of Violence." *Journal of Biblical Literature* 122 (2003): 3–21.

Coudert, Allison P., and Jeffrey S. Shoulson, eds. *Hebraica Veritas? Christian Hebraists and the Study of Judaism in Early Modern Europe*. Philadelphia: University of Pennsylvania Press, 2004.

Cramer, Konrad. "Die Stunde der Philosophie. Über Göttingens ersten Philosophen und die philosophische Theorielage der Gründungszeit." In *Zur geistigen Situation der Zeit der Göttinger Universitätsgründung 1737. Eine Vortragsreihe aus Anlaß des 250jährigen Bestehens der Georgia Augusta*, edited by Jürgen von Stackelberg, 101–43. Göttingen: Vandenhoeck & Ruprecht, 1988.

Cullhed, Anna. "Original Poetry: Robert Lowth and Eighteenth-Century Poetics." In *Sacred Conjectures: The Context and Legacy of Robert Lowth and Jean Astruc*, edited by John Jarick, 25–47. New York: T & T Clark, 2007.

Deetjen, Werner. "Johann Matthias Gesner und die Weimarer Bibliothek." In *Festschrift Armin Tille zum 60. Geburtstag*. Weimar: Hermann Böhlaus Nachfolger, 1930.

Diehl, Carl. *Americans and German Scholarship 1770–1870*. New Haven: Yale University Press, 1978.

Dohm, Christian Wilhelm. *Ueber die bürgerliche Verbesserung der Juden*. Reprinted from 1781 (Teil 1) and 1783 (Teil 2) editions. New York and Hildesheim: Georg Olms, 1973.

Ebel, Wilhelm, ed. *Catalogus Professorum Gottingensium 1734–1962*. Göttingen: Vandenhoeck & Ruprecht, 1962.

———. *Göttinger Universitätsreden aus zwei Jahrhunderten (1737–1934)*. Göttingen: Vandenhoeck & Ruprecht, 1978.

———. *Memorabilia Gottingensia. Elf Studien zur Sozialgeschichte der Universität*. Göttingen: Vandenhoeck & Ruprecht, 1969.

———. *Die Privilegien and ältesten Statuten der Georg-August-Universität zu Göttingen*. Göttingen: Vandenhoeck & Ruprecht, 1961.

Ebeling, Gerhard. "The Significance of the Critical Historical Method for Church and Theology in Protestantism." In *Word and Faith*, 17–61. London: SCM Press, 1963.

Eichhorn, Johann Gottfried. "Bemerkungen über J. D. Michaelis litterarischen Character." In *Lebensbeschreibung von ihm selbst abgefasst*, by Johann David Michaelis, 145–226. Leipzig, 1793.

Enderle, Wilfried. "Britische und Europäische Wissenschaft in Göttingen—Die Göttingischen Anzeigen von gelehrten Sachen als Wissensportal im 18. Jahrhundert." In *"Eine Welt allein ist nicht genug": Großbritannien, Hannover und Göttingen 1714–1837*, edited by Elmar Mittler, 161–78. Göttingen: Niedersächsische Staats- und Universitätsbibliothek Göttingen, 2005.

Farrar, Frederic W. *History of Interpretation*. London: Macmillan, 1886.

Flavell, M. Kay. "Winckelmann and the German Enlightenment: On the Recovery and Uses of the Past." *Modern Language Review* 74, no. 1 (1979): 79–96.

Fornaro, Sotera. "Deutschland. III. Bis 1806." In *Der Neue Pauly. Enzyklopädie der Antike*, edited by Manfred Landfester, 792–805. Stuttgart: J. B. Metzler, 1999.

Freimarck, Vincent. "Introduction." In *Lectures on the Sacred Poetry of the Hebrews*, by Robert Lowth. Hildesheim: Georg Olms, 1969.

Friedrich, Reinhold. *Johann Matthias Gesner: Sein Leben und sein Werk*. Roth: Genniges, 1991.

Friedrich, Wolf Hartmut. "Heyne als Philologe." In *Der Vormann der Georgia Augusta. Christian Gottlob Heyne zum 250. Geburtstag. Sechs akademische Reden*, 15–31. Göttingen: Vandenhoeck & Ruprecht, 1980.

Frye, Northrop. *The Great Code: The Bible and Literature*. New York: Harvest/HBJ, 1982.

Funke, Hermann. "F. A. Wolf." In *Classical Scholarship: A Biographical Encyclopedia*, edited by Ward W. Briggs and William M. Calder, 523–28. New York: Garland, 1990.

Gabler, Johann Philip. "*De justo discrimine theologiae biblicae et dogmaticae regundisque recte utriusque finibus*." In *The Flowering of Old Testament Theology: A Reader in Twentieth-Century Old Testament Theology, 1930–1990*, edited by Ben C. Ollenburger, Elmer A. Martens, and Gerhard F. Hasel, 492–502. Winona Lake: Eisenbrauns, 1992.

Gawthrop, Richard L. *Pietism and the Making of Eighteenth-Century Prussia*. Cambridge: Cambridge University Press, 1993.

Geerken, John H. "Machiavelli's Moses and Renaissance Politics." *Journal of the History of Ideas* 60, no. 4 (1999): 579–95.

Gericke, Theodor. *Joh. Matth. Gesners und Joh. Gottfr. Herders Stellung in der Geschichte der Gymnasialpädogogik*. Borna-Leipzig: PhD diss., University of Erlangen, 1911.

Gesenius, Wilhelm. *Geschichte der hebräischen Sprache und Schrift. Eine philologisch-historische Einleitung in die Sprachlehren und Wörterbücher der hebräischen Sprache*. Leipzig, 1815.

Gesner, Johann Matthias. *Enchiridion sive prudentia privata ac civilis*. Göttingen, 1745.

———. *Kleine deutsche Schriften*. Göttingen, 1756.

———. *Schulordnung vor die Churfürstlich Braunschweigisch-Lüneburgischen Lande*. Göttingen: Vandenhoeck, 1738.

Gibert, Pierre. "De l'intuition a l'évidence: La multiplicité documentaire dans la Genèse chez H. B. Witter et Jean Astruc." In *Sacred Conjectures: The Context and Legacy of Robert Lowth and Jean Astruc*, edited by John Jarick, 174–89. New York: T & T Clark, 2007.

Goethe, Johann Wolfgang. *Maxims and Reflections*. Edited by Peter Hutchinson. Translated by Elisabeth Stopp. New York: Penguin, 1998.

———. "Winckelmann und sein Jahrhundert (1805)." In *Goethe Werke. Band XII*, edited by Herbert von Einem and Hans Joachim Schrimpf, 96–129. Hamburg: Christian Wegner, 1967.

Graffmann, Heinrich. *Die Stellung der Religion im Neuhumanismus*. Göttingen, 1929.

Grafton, Anthony. *Defenders of the Text: The Traditions of Scholarship in an Age of Science, 1450–1800*. Cambridge, MA: Harvard University Press, 1991.

———. "'Man muß aus der Gegenwart heraufsteigen': History, Tradition, and Traditions of Historical Thought in F. A. Wolf." In *Aufklärung und Geschichte. Studien zur deutschen Geschichtswissenschaft im 18. Jahrhundert*, edited by Hans Erich Bödeker, Georg G. Iggers, Jonathan B. Knudsen, and Peter H. Reill, 416–362. Göttingen: Vandenhoeck & Ruprecht, 1986.

———. "Polyhistor into *Philolog*: Notes on the Transformation of German Classical Scholarship, 1780–1850." *History of Universities* 3 (1983): 159–92.

———. "Prolegomena to Friedrich August Wolf." In *Defenders of the Text: The Traditions of Scholarship in an Age of Science, 1450–1800*, 214–43. Cambridge, MA: Harvard University Press, 1991.

Graham, Loren, Wolf Lepenies, and Peter Weingart, eds. *Functions and Uses of Disciplinary Histories*. Dordrecht: D. Reidel, 1983.

Graham, William A. *Beyond the Written Word: Oral Aspects of Scripture in the History of Religion*. Cambridge: Cambridge University Press, 1987.

Grair, Charles A. "Antiquity and Weimar Classicism." In *The Literature of Weimar Classicism*, edited by Simon Richter, 63–88. Rochester, NY: Camden House, 2005.

Grandazzi, Alexandre. *The Foundation of Rome: Myth and History*. Translated by Jane Marie Todd. Ithaca: Cornell University Press, 1997.

Griffiths, Paul J. *Religious Reading: The Place of Reading in the Practice of Religion*. New York: Oxford University Press, 1999.

Gründer, Karlfried. "Johann David Michaelis und Moses Mendelssohn." In *Begegnung von Deutschen und Juden in der Geistesgeschichte des 18. Jahrhunderts*, edited by Jakob Katz and Karl Heinrich Rengstorf, 25–20. Tübingen: Max Niemeyer, 1994.

Hakemeyer, Ida. *Kleines Universitätsmosaik*. Göttingen, 1960.

Hamann, Johann Georg. "Aesthetica in nuce: A Rhapsody in Cabbalistic Prose." In *Classical and Romantic German Aesthetics*, J. M. Bernstein, 1–23. Cambridge: Cambridge University Press, 2003.

———. *Sämtliche Werke*. Edited by Josef Nadler. Wien: Thomas-Morus-Presse, 1949.

Hammerstein, Notker. "Die Universitätsgründungen im Zeichen der Aufklärung." In *Beiträge zu Problemen deutscher Universitätsgründungen der frühen Neuzeit*, edited by Peter Baumgart and Notker Hammerstein, 263–91. Nendeln: KTO Press, 1978.

Haye, Thomas. "Göttingens Ruhm in der Dichtung des Johann Matthias Gesner (1691–1761)." In *1050 Jahre Göttingen. Streiflichter auf die Göttinger Stadtgeschichte*, edited by Klaus Grubmüller, 48–77. Wallstein, 2004.

Hazard, Paul. *The European Mind: 1680–1715*. Cleveland and New York: Meridian, 1964.

Hecht, Hans. *T. Percy, R. Wood und J. D. Michaelis. Ein Beitrag zur Literaturgeschichte der Genieperiode*. Stuttgart, 1933.

Heeren, A. H. L. *Christian Gottlob Heyne. Biographisch dargestellt*. Göttingen: Johann Friedrich Röwer, 1813.

Heidenreich, Marianne. *Christian Gottlob Heyne und die Alte Geschichte*. München: K. G. Saur, 2006.

Hepworth, Brian. *Robert Lowth*. Boston: Twayne, 1978.

Herder, Johann Gottfried. *Philosophical Writings*. Edited and translated by Michael N. Forster. Cambridge: Cambridge University Press, 2002.

———. *Sämtliche Werke*. Edited by Bernhard Suphan. Hildesheim: Olms, 1967–68.

———. *The Spirit of Hebrew Poetry*. 2 vols. Translated by James Marsh. Burlington, VT: Edward Smith, 1833.

Hess, Jonathan M. *Germans, Jews, and the Claims of Modernity*. New Haven: Yale University Press, 2002.

Heyne, Christian Gottlob. *Einleitung in das Studium der Antike, oder Grundriß einer Anführung zur Kenntniß der alten Kunstwerke*. Göttingen and Gotha: Johann Christian Dieterich, 1772.

———. "Prüfung einiger Nachrichten und Behauptungen vom Laocoon im Belvedere." In *Sammlung antiquarischer Aufsätze. Zweites Stück*, 1–52. Leipzig: Weidmanns, Erben, und Reich, 1779.

Hinrichs, Carl. *Preußentum und Pietismus. Der Pietismus in Brandenburg-Preußen als religiös-soziale Reformbewegung*. Göttingen: Vandenhoeck & Ruprecht, 1971.

Hofstetter, Michael J. *The Romantic Idea of a University: England and Germany, 1770–1850*. New York: Palgrave, 2001.

Howard, Thomas Albert. *Protestant Theology and the Making of the Modern German University*. New York: Oxford University Press, 2006.

Humboldt, Wilhelm. *Briefe an Friedrich August Wolf*. Berlin: Walter de Gruyter, 1990.

———. "Ueber den Charakter der Griechen, die idealische und historische Ansicht desselben." In *Schriften zur Altertumskunde und Ästhetik. Die Vasken*, edited by Andreas Flitner and Klaus Giel, 65–72. Stuttgart: J.G. Cotta'sche Buchhandlung, 1961.

Hunger, Ulrich. "Die Georg-August-Universität als Landesherrliche Gründung. Ein Bericht über ihre Genese." In *"Eine Welt allein ist nicht genug": Großbritannien, Hannover und Göttingen 1714–1837*, edited by Elmar Mittler, 99–111. Göttingen: Niedersächsische Staats- und Universitätsbibliothek Göttingen, 2005.

Hunter, Ian. "Multiple Enlightenments: Rival *Aufklärer* at the University of Halle, 1690–1730." In *The Enlightenment World*, edited by Martin Fitzpatrick, Peter Jones, Christa Knellwolf, and Ian McCalman, 576–95. London: Routledge, 2007.

Israel, Jonathan. *Enlightenment Contested: Philosophy, Modernity, and the Emancipation of Man 1670–1752*. Oxford: Oxford University Press, 2006.

Jarausch, Konrad H. "The Institutionalization of History in 18th-Century Germany." In *Aufklärung und Geschichte. Studien zur deutschen Geschichtswissenschaft im 18. Jahrhundert*, edited by Hans Erich Bödeker, Georg G. Iggers, Jonathan B. Knudsen, and Peter H. Reill, 25–48. Göttingen: Vandenhoeck & Ruprecht, 1986.

Jaumann, Herbert. "Bibelkritik und Literaturkritik in der frühen Neuzeit." *Zeitschrift für Religions- und Geistesgeschichte* 49, no. 2 (1997): 123–34.

Jenkins, Allan K., and Patrick Preston. *Biblical Scholarship and the Church: A Sixteenth-Century Crisis of Authority*. Hampshire: Ashgate, 2007.

Jørgensen, Sven-Aage. "Hamanns hermeneutische Grundsätze." In *Aufklärung und Humanismus. Wolfenbütteler Studien zur Aufklärung. Bd. 6*, edited by Richard Toellner, 219–31. Heidelberg: Lambert Schneider, 1980.

Kling, David W. *The Bible in History: How the Texts Have Shaped the Times*. New York: Oxford University Press, 2004.

Klingner, Friedrich. *Christian Gottlob Heyne*. Leipzig: Poeschel & Trepte, 1937.

Köster, Beate. "'Mit Tiefem Respekt, mit Furcht und Zittern': Bibelübersetzungen im Pietismus." In *Beiträge zur Geschichte des Württembergischen Pietismus. Festschrift für Gerhard Schäfer zum 75. Geburtstag am 2. Juni 1998 und Martin Brecht zum 65. Geburtstag am 6. März 1997*, edited by Hermann Ehmer and Udo Sträter, 95–115. Göttingen: Vandenhoeck & Ruprecht, 1998.

Kraus, Hans-Joachim. *Geschichte der historisch-kritischen Erforschung des Alten Testaments*. Neukirchen-Vluyn: Neukirchener Verlag, 1982.

Kugel, James. *How to Read the Bible: A Guide to Scripture Then and Now*. New York: Free Press, 2007.

———. *The Idea of Biblical Poetry: Parallelism and Its History*. Baltimore: Johns Hopkins University Press, 1998.

La Vopa, Anthony J. *Grace, Talent, and Merit: Poor Students, Clerical Careers, and Professional Ideology in Eighteenth-Century Germany*. Cambridge: Cambridge University Press, 1988.

Lamb, Jonathan. *The Rhetoric of Suffering: Reading the Book of Job in the Eighteenth Century*. Oxford: Clarendon Press, 1995.

Lange, Horst. "Reconstructing a Nation's Birth: Monotheism, Nationalism, and Violence in Goethe's Reading of the Pentateuch." *Colloquia Germanica* 33, no. 2 (2000): 103–21.

Le Brun, Jacques. "Das Entstehen der historischen Kritik im Bereich der religiösen Wissenschaften im 17. Jahrhundert." *Trierer Theologische Zeitschrift* 89, no. 2 (1980): 100–17.

Legaspi, Michael. Review of *Academic Charisma and the Origins of the Modern University*, by William Clark. *Journal of Early Modern History* 11, no. 4/5 (2007): 389–91.

———. "What Ever Happened to Historical Criticism?" *Journal of Religion and Society* 9 (2007). Available at http://moses.creighton.edu/JRS/pdf/2007-22.pdf (accessed October 7, 2009).

Levenson, Jon D. *The Hebrew Bible, the Old Testament, and Historical Criticism*. Louisville, KY: Westminster John Knox, 1993.

Leventhal, Robert. *The Disciplines of Interpretation: Lessing, Herder, Schlegel, and Hermeneutics in Germany 1750–1800*. Berlin: Walter de Gruyter, 1994.

Levering, Miriam, ed. *Rethinking Scripture*. Albany: SUNY Press, 1989.

Levi, Anthony. *Renaissance and Reformation: The Intellectual Genesis*. New Haven: Yale University Press, 2002.

Lindbeck, George. *The Nature of Doctrine: Religion and Theology in a Post-Liberal Age*. Philadelphia: Westminster, 1984.

Love, Harold. *Attributing Authorship: An Introduction*. Cambridge: Cambridge University Press, 2002.

Löwenbruck, Anna-Ruth. "Johann David Michaelis' Verdienst um die philologisch-historische Bibelkritik." In *Historische Kritik und biblischer Kanon in der deutschen Aufklärung*, edited by Henning Graf Reventlow, Walter Sparn, and John Woodbridge. Wiesbaden: Otto Harrassowitz, 1988.

———. "Johann David Michaelis und Moses Mendelssohn. Judenfeindschaft im Zeitalter der Aufklärung." In *Moses Mendelssohn und die Kreise seiner Wirksamkeit. Wolfenbütteler Studien zur Aufklärung. Bd. 19*, edited by Michael Albrecht, Eva J. Engel, and Norbert Hinske, 315–32. Tübingen: Niemeyer, 1994.

———. *Judenfeindschaft im Zeitalter der Aufklärung. Eine Studie zur Vorgeschichte des modernen Antisemitismus am Beispiel des Göttinger Theologen und Orientalisten Johann David Michaelis (1717–1791)*. Frankfurt: Peter Lang, 1995.

Lowth, Robert. *De sacra poesi Hebraeorum praelectiones*. 2nd ed. Göttingen: Joan. Christ. Dieterich, 1770.

———. *Lectures on the Sacred Poetry of the Hebrews*. Translated by G. Gregory. 1787. Reprint, Hildesheim: Georg Olms, 1969.

Machiavelli, Niccolò. *Discourses on Livy*. Translated by Julia Conway Bondanella and Peter Bondanella. Oxford: Oxford University Press, 1997.

Mager, Inge. "Zu Johann Lorenz von Mosheims theologischer Biographie." In *Johann Lorenz Mosheim (1693–1755). Theologie im Spannungsfeld von Philosophie, Philologie und Geschichte*, edited by Martin Mulsow, Ralph Häfner, Florian Neumann, and Helmut Zedelmaier, 277–96. Wiesbaden: Harrassowitz, 1997.

Manuel, Frank. *The Broken Staff: Judaism through Christian Eyes*. Cambridge, MA: Harvard University Press, 1992.

Marchand, Suzanne L. *Down from Olympus: Archaeology and Philhellenism in Germany, 1750–1970*. Princeton: Princeton University Press, 1996.

———. "German Orientalism and the Decline of the West." *Proceedings of the American Philosophical Society* 145, no. 4 (2001): 465–73.

Marino, Luigi. "Der 'Geist der Auslegung.' Aspekte der Göttinger Hermeneutik (am Beispiel Eichhorns)." In *Hermeneutik der Aufklärung*, edited by Axel Bühler and Luigi Cataldi Madonna, 71–89. Hamburg: Felix Meiner, 1994.

———. *Praeceptores Germaniae: Göttingen 1770–1820*. Göttingen: Vandenhoeck & Ruprecht, 1995.

Marsch, Robert. "Neoclassical Poetics." In *Encyclopedia of Poetry and Poetics*, edited by Alex Preminger, 559–64. Princeton: Princeton University Press, 1965.

Marx, Steven. "Moses and Machiavellism." *Journal of the American Academy of Religion* 65, no. 3 (1997): 551–71.

McClelland, Charles E. *State, Society, and University in Germany 1700–1914*. Cambridge: Cambridge University Press, 1980.

McConica, James K. "Erasmus and the Grammar of Consent." In *Scrimium Erasmianum*, edited by Joseph Coppens, 77–99. Leiden: Brill, 1969.

McGrath, Alister. *The Intellectual Origins of the European Reformation*. Oxford: Basil Blackwell, 1987.

Meijering, E. P. "Mosheim und die Orthodoxie." In *Johann Lorenz Mosheim (1693–1755). Theologie im Spannungsfeld von Philosophie, Philologie und Geschichte*, edited by Martin Mulsow, Ralph Häfner, Florian Neumann, and Helmut Zedelmaier, 261–75. Wiesbaden: Harrassowitz, 1997.

Menze, Clemens. *Wilhelm von Humboldt und Christian Gottlob Heyne*. Ratingen: A. Henn, 1966.

Mettler, Werner. *Der junge Friedrich Schlegel und die griechische Literatur. Ein Beitrag zum Problem der Historie*. Zurich: Atlantis, 1955.

Michaelis, Johann David. *Abhandlung von der Syrischen Sprache, und ihrem Gebrauch: Nebst dem ersten Theil einer Syrischen Chrestomathie*. Göttingen, 1786.

———. *Arabische Grammatik, Nebst einer Arabischen Chrestomathie, und Abhandlungen vom Arabischen Geschmack, sonderlich in der poetischen und historischen Schreibart*. 2nd rev. ed. Göttingen: Victorinus Botziegel, 1781.

———. *Beurtheilung der Mittel, welche man anwendet, die ausgestorbene Hebräische Sprache zu verstehen*. Göttingen, 1757.

———. *The Burial and Resurrection of Jesus Christ: According to the Four Evangelists*. London: J. Hatchard, 1827.

———. *Commentaries on the Laws of Moses*. 4 vols. Translated by Alexander Smith. London, 1814.

———. *Dissertation qui a remporté le prix proposé par l'Académie Royale des Sciences et Belles Lettres de Prusse, sur l'influence réciproque de langage sur les opinions, et des opinions sur le langage*. Berlin, 1760.

———. *Einleitung in die Göttlichen Schriften des Alten Bundes*. Hamburg: Bohnsche Buchhandlung, 1787.

———. *Entwurf einer typischen Gottesgelahrtheit*. Göttingen: G. L. Förster, 1763.

———. *Erklärung der Begräbnis- und Auferstehungsgeschichte Christi nach den vier Evangelisten, mit Rücksicht auf die in den Fragmenten gemachte Einwürfe und deren Beantwortung*. Halle, 1783.

———. *Fragen an eine Gesellschaft gelehrter Männer, die auf Befehl Ihro Majestät des Königes von Dännemark nach Arabien reisen*. Frankfurt, 1762.

———. *Gedanken über die Lehre der Heiligen Schrift von Sünde und Genugthuung, als eine der Vernunft gemässe Lehre*. Göttingen and Bremen: Johann Heinrich Cramer, 1779.

———. *Hebräische Grammatik*. Halle, 1745.

———. *Lebensbeschreibung von ihm selbst abgefaßt, mit Anmerkungen von Hassencamp. Nebst Bemerkungen über dessen litterarischen Character von Eichhorn, Schulz—und dem Elogium von Heyne*. Rinteln and Leipzig, 1793.

———. *Poetischer Entwurf der Gedanken des Prediger-Buch Salomons*. Bremen and Leipzig: Georg Ludewig Förster, 1762.

———. *Raisonnement über die protestantischen Universitäten in Deutschland*. Frankfurt and Leipzig, 1768–76.

———. Review of Lowth's *Praelectiones*. *Göttingische Anzeigen von gelehrten Sachen* (1753), 947–50.

———. Review of Lowth's *Praelectiones*. *Relationes de libris novis* X (1754): 317–37.

———. *Uebersetzung des Alten Testaments, mit Anmerkungen für Ungelehrte*. Göttingen and Gotha: Johann Christian Dieterich, 1769–85.

———. "Von dem Geschmack der Morgenländischen Dichtkunst." In *Poetische Nebenstunden*, Johann Friedrich Löwens. Leipzig, 1752.

Michaelis, Johann Heinrich. *Biblia Hebraica, ex aliquot manuscriptis*. Halle, 1720.

———. *Gründlicher Unterricht von den Accentibus prosaicis u. metricis oder Hebräischen Distinctionibus der Heil. Schrift A.T.* Halle: Wäysen-Hause, 1720.

Miller, Peter N. "The 'Antiquarianization' of Biblical Scholarship and the London Polyglot Bible (1653–57)." *Journal of the History of Ideas* 62, no. 3 (July 2001): 463–82.

Moeller, Bernd. "Johann Lorenz von Mosheim und die Gründung der Göttinger Universität." In *Theologie in Göttingen. Eine Vorlesungsreihe*, edited by Bernd Moeller, 9–40. Göttingen: Vandenhoeck & Ruprecht, 1987.

Monk, Samuel H. *The Sublime: A Study of Critical Theories in XVIII-Century England*. New York: Modern Language Association, 1935.

Morgan, Robert, and John Barton. *Biblical Interpretation*. New York: Oxford University Press, 1988.

Morin, Jean. *Exercitationes biblicae*. Paris, 1633.

Muhlack, Ulrich. "Historie und Philologie." In *Aufklärung und Geschichte. Studien zur deutschen Geschichtswissenschaft im 18. Jahrhundert*, edited by Hans Erich Bödeker, Georg G. Iggers, Jonathan B. Knudsen, and Peter H. Reill, 49–81. Göttingen: Vandenhoeck & Ruprecht, 1986.

———. "Klassische Philologie zwischen Humanismus und Neuhumanismus." In *Wissenschaften im Zeitalter der Aufklärung*, edited by Rudolf Vierhaus, 93–119. Göttingen: Vandenhoeck & Ruprecht, 1985.

Müllenbrock, Heinz-Joachim. "Aufklärung im Zeichen der Freiheit—das Vorbild Englands." In *Zur geistigen Situation der Zeit der Göttinger Universitätsgründung 1737. Eine Vortragsreihe aus Anlaß des 250jährigen Bestehens der Georgia Augusta*, edited by Jürgen von Stackelberg, 101–43. Göttingen: Vandenhoeck & Ruprecht, 1988.

Mulsow, Martin. "Eclecticism or Skepticism? A Problem of the Early Enlightenment." *Journal of the History of Ideas* 58, no. 3 (1997): 465–77.

Nauert, Charles G. *Humanism and the Culture of Renaissance Europe*. 2nd ed. Cambridge: Cambridge University Press, 2006.

Neumann, Florian. "Mosheim und die westeuropäische Kirchengeschichtsschreibung." In *Johann Lorenz Mosheim (1693–1755). Theologie im Spannungsfeld von Philosophie, Philologie und Geschichte*, edited by Martin Mulsow, Ralph Häfner, Florian Neumann, and Helmut Zedelmaier, 111–46. Wiesbaden: Harrassowitz, 1997.

Newman, Amy. "The Death of Judaism in German Protestant Thought from Luther to Hegel." *Journal of the American Academy of Religion* LXI, no. 3 (1993): 455–84.

Niebuhr, B. G. *Vorträge über alte Länder- und Völkerkunde, an der Universität gehalten*. Berlin, 1851.

Norton, David. *A History of the Bible as Literature. Volume Two: From 1700 to the Present Day*. Cambridge: Cambridge University Press, 1993.

Oberman, Heiko A. "Discovery of Hebrew and Discrimination against the Jews: The *Veritas Hebraica* as Double-Edged Sword in the Renaissance and Reformation." In *Germania Illustrata: Essays on Early Modern Germany Presented to Gerald Strauss*, edited by Andrew C. Fix and Susan C. Karant-Nunn, 19–34. Kirksville, MO: Sixteenth Century Journal Publishers, 1992.

Oden, Robert. *The Bible without Theology*. San Francisco: Harper & Row, 1987.

Panke-Kochinke, Birgit. *Göttinger Professorenfamilien. Strukturmerkmale weiblichen Lebenszusammenhangs im 18. und 19. Jahrhunderts*. Pfaffenweiler: Centaurus-Verlagsgesellschaft, 1993.

Paulsen, Friedrich. *Geschichte des gelehrten Unterrichts auf den deutschen Schulen und Universitäten vom Ausgang des Mittelalters bis zur Gegenwart*. Vol. 2. 3rd ed. Berlin: Walter de Gruyter, 1921.

Polke, Irene. *Selbstreflexion im Spiegel des Anderen. Eine wirkungsgeschichtliche Studie zum Hellenismusbild Heynes und Herders*. Königshausen: Neumann, 1999.

Popkin, Richard. *The History of Skepticism: From Savonarola to Bayle*. Rev. ed. New York: Oxford University Press, 2003.

———. "Spinoza and Bible Scholarship." In *The Cambridge Companion to Spinoza*, edited by Don Garrett, 383–407. New York and Cambridge: Cambridge University Press, 1996.

Preiss, Bettina. *Die archäologische Beschäftigung mit der Laokoongruppe. Die Bedeutung Christian Gottlob Heynes für die Archäologie des 18. Jahrhunderts*. PhD diss., University of Bonn, 1992.

Prickett, Stephen. *Origins of Narrative: The Romantic Appropriation of the Bible.* Cambridge: Cambridge University Press, 1996.

———. *Words and the Word: Language, Poetics, and Biblical Interpretation.* Cambridge: Cambridge University Press, 1986.

Pütter, Johann Stephen, ed. *Denkwürdiges und Merkwürdiges aus Johann Stephen Pütters "Versuch einer academischen Gelehrten-Geschichte von der Georg-August-Universität zu Göttingen" (1765). Ausgewählt und mit Anmerkungen versehen von Friedrich Ellermeier.* Herzberg: Junger, 1966.

———. *Versuch einer academischen Gelehrten-Geschichte von der Georg-August-Universität zu Göttingen.* Göttingen: Vandenhoeck & Ruprecht, 1788.

Radner, Ephraim. *The End of the Church: A Pneumatology of Christian Division in the West.* Grand Rapids, MI: Eerdmans, 1998.

Rehm, Walter. *Griechentum und Goethezeit: Geschichte eines Glaubens.* 4th ed. Bern and Munich: Francke Verlag, 1969.

Reill, Peter Hanns. *The German Enlightenment and the Rise of Historicism.* Berkeley: University of California Press, 1975.

———. "Science and the Science of History in the Spätaufklärung." In *Aufklärung und Geschichte. Studien zur deutschen Geschichtswissenschaft im 18. Jahrhundert*, edited by Hans Erich Bödeker, Georg G. Iggers, Jonathan B. Knudsen, and Peter H. Reill, 430–51. Göttingen: Vandenhoeck & Ruprecht, 1986.

Rengstorf, Karl Heinrich. "Die deutschen Pietisten und ihr Bild von Judentums." In *Begugnungen von Deutschen und Juden in der Geistesgeschichte des 18. Jahrhunderts. Wolfenbütteler Studien zur Aufklärung. Bd. 6*, edited by Jacob Katz and Karl Heinrich Rengstorf, 1–16. Heidelberg: Lambert Schneider, 1994.

———. "Johann Heinrich Michaelis und seine *Biblia Hebraica* von 1720." In *Halle. Aufklärung und Pietismus. Wolfenbütteler Studien zur Aufklärung. Bd. 15*, edited by Norbert Hinske, 15–64. Heidelberg: Lambert Schneider, 1989.

Reno, R. R. "Theology in the Ruins of the Church." *Pro Ecclesia* XII, no. 1 (2003): 15–36.

Reventlow, Henning Graf. *Epochen der Bibelauslegung. Band III. Renaissance, Reformation, Humanismus.* München: C. H. Beck, 1997.

———. *Epochen der Bibelauslegung. Band IV. Von der Aufklärung bis zum 20. Jahrhundert.* München: C. H. Beck, 2001.

———. "Johen Lorenz Mosheims Auseinandersetzung mit John Toland." In *Johann Lorenz Mosheim (1693–1755). Theologie im Spannungsfeld von Philosophie, Philologie und Geschichte*, edited by Martin Mulsow, Ralph Häfner, Florian Neumann, and Helmut Zedelmaier, 93–110. Wiesbaden: Harrassowitz, 1997.

———. "Wurzeln der Modernen Bibelkritik." In *Historische Kritik und Biblischer Kanon in der Deutschen Aufklärung*, edited by Henning Graf Reventlow, Walter Sparn, and John Woodbridge, 47–63. Wiesbaden: Otto Harrassowitz, 1988.

Richter-Uhlig, Uta. "London—Hannover—Göttingen: Die Reisen Georgs II. nach Hannover und sein Verhältnis zu Göttingen." In *"Eine Welt allein ist nicht genug": Großbritannien, Hannover und Göttingen 1714–1837*, edited by Elmar Mittler, 141–57. Göttingen: Niedersächsische Staats- und Universitätsbibliothek Göttingen, 2005.

Ringleben, Joachim. "Göttinger Aufklärungstheologie—von Königsberg her gesehen." In *Theologie in Göttingen. Eine Vorlesungsreihe*, edited by Bernd Moeller, 82–110. Göttingen: Vandenhoeck & Ruprecht, 1987.

Robertson, Ritchie. "Religion and the Enlightenment: A Review Essay." *German History* 25, no. 3 (2007): 422–32.

Rogerson, John. "Michaelis, Johann David." In *Dictionary of Major Biblical Interpreters*, edited by Donald K. McKim, 736–39. Downers Grove, IL: Intervarsity Press, 2007.

———. *Old Testament Criticism in the Nineteenth Century: England and Germany*. London: SPCK, 1984.

Rössler, Emil. *Die Gründung der Universität Göttingen: Entwürfe, Berichte und Briefe der Zeitgenossen*. Göttingen: Vandenhoeck & Ruprecht, 1855.

Roston, Murray. *Prophet and Poet: The Bible and the Growth of Romanticism*. London: Faber and Faber, 1965.

Rummel, Erika. *Erasmus*. London: Continuum, 2004.

———. *Erasmus and His Catholic Critics*. Nieuwkoop: De Graaf, 1989.

———. *The Humanist-Scholastic Debate in the Renaissance & Reformation*. Cambridge, MA: Harvard University Press, 1995.

Sauppe, Hermann. "Johann Matthias Gesner und Christian Gottlob Heyne." In *Göttinger Professoren. Ein Beitrag zur deutschen Cultur- und Literaturgeschichte in acht Vorträgen*, 59–98. Gotha: Friedrich Andreas Porthes, 1872.

———. ed. *Weimarische Schulreden*. Weimar: Böhlau, 1856.

Schaff, Philip. *Germany; Its Universities, Theology, and Religion*. Philadelphia: Lindsay & Blakiston, 1857.

Schiller, Friedrich. *On the Aesthetic Education of Man, in a Series of Letters*. Translated and edited by Elizabeth M. Wilkinson and L. A. Willoughby. Oxford: Clarendon, 1967.

Schindel, Ulrich. "Die Anfänge der Klassischen Philologie in Göttingen." In *Philologie in Göttingen: Sprach- und Literaturwissenschaft an der Georgia Augusta im 18. und beginnenden 19. Jahrhundert*, edited by Reinhard Lauer, 9–24. Göttingen: Vandenhoeck & Ruprecht, 2001.

———. "Heyne und die Historiographie." In *Memoria Rerum Veterum. Neue Beiträge zur antiken Historiographie und alten Geschichte. Festschrift für Carl Joachim Classen Zum 60. Geburtstag*, edited by Wolfram Ax, 191–210. Stuttgart: Franz Steiner, 1990.

———. "Historische Analyse und Prognose im 18. Jh. Christian Gottlob Heyne und die spätantike römische Historiographie." *Antike und Abendland* 50 (2004): 1–13.

———. "In Memoriam C. G. Heyne." *Göttingische Gelehrte Anzeigen* 232, no. 1/2 (1980): 1–6.

———. "Johann Matthias Gesner, Professor der Poesie und Beredsamkeit 1734–1761." In *Die Klassische Altertumswissenschaft an der Georg-August-Universität Göttingen. Eine Ringvorlesung zu ihrer Geschichte*, edited by Carl Joachim Classen, 9–26. Göttingen: Vandenhoeck & Ruprecht, 1989.

Schlegel, Friedrich. "Athenaeum Fragments." In *Classical and Romantic German Aesthetics*, edited by J. M. Bernstein, 246–60. Cambridge: Cambridge University Press, 2003.

Schneider, Werner. "Thomasius, Christian." In *Deutsche Biographische Enzyklopädie*, edited by Walther Killy and Rudolf Vierhaus, 10:20. München: K.G. Saur, 1999.

Schrader, Wilhelm. *Geschichte der Friedrichs-Universität zu Halle*. Berlin: Ferd. Dümmler, 1894.

Schultens, Albert. *Animadversiones philologicae et criticae ad varia loca Veteris Testamenti*. Amsterdam: Wetstenios & Smith, 1732.

———. *Institutiones ad fundamenta Linguae Hebraeae. Quibus via panditur ad ejusdem analogiam restituendam, et vindicandam*. Lugduni Batavorum: Johannem Luzac, 1737.

———. *Origines Hebraeae sive Hebraeae linguae antiquissima natura et indoles ex Arabiae penetralibus*. Lugduni Batavorum: Samuelem et Joannem Lucthtmans et Joannem Le Mair, 1761.

———. *Vetus et regia via hebraizandi, asserta contra novam et metaphysicam hodiernam*. Lugduni Batavorum: Joannem Luzac, 1738.

Sheehan, Jonathan. *The Enlightenment Bible: Translation, Scholarship, Culture*. Princeton: Princeton University Press, 2005.

———. "Enlightenment, Religion, and the Enigma of Secularization: A Review Essay." *American Historical Review* 108, no. 4 (2003): 1061–80.

Simonsuuri, Kirsti. *Homer's Original Genius: Eighteenth-Century Notions of the Early Greek Epic (1688–1798)*. Cambridge: Cambridge University Press, 1979.

Smend, Rudolf (1851–1913). "Johann David Michaelis." In *Festrede im Namen der Georg-August-Universität zur akademischen Preisvertheilung am VIII. Juni MDCCCXCVIII*. Göttingen, 1898.

Smend, Rudolf (1932–). "Aufgeklärte Bemühung um das Gesetz: Johann David Michaelis." In *Epochen der Bibelkritik*, by Rudolf Smend, 63–73. Munich: Chr. Kaiser, 1991.

———. *From Astruc to Zimmerli*. Tübingen: Mohr Siebeck, 2007.

———. "Jean Astruc: A Physician as a Biblical Scholar." In *Sacred Conjectures: The Context and Legacy of Robert Lowth and Jean Astruc*, edited by John Jarick, 157–73. New York: T & T Clark, 2007.

———. "Johann David Michaelis und Johann Gottfried Eichhorn—Zwei Orientalisten am Rande der Theologie." In *Theologie in Göttingen. Eine Vorlesungsreihe*, edited by Bernd Moeller, 59–71. Göttingen: Vandenhoeck & Ruprecht, 1987.

———. "Lowth in Deutschland." In *Epochen der Bibelkritik*, by Rudolf Smend, 43–62. Munich: Chr. Kaiser, 1991.

Smith, Steven G. "What is Scripture? Pursuing Smith's Question." *Anglican Theological Review* 90, no. 4 (2008): 753–75.

Smith, Wilfred Cantwell. *What Is Scripture? A Comparative Approach*. Minneapolis: Fortress, 1993.

Sparn, Walter. "Auf dem Wege zur theologischen Aufklärung in Halle: Von Johann Franz Budde zu Siegmund Jakob Baumgarten." In *Halle, Aufklärung und Pietismus*, edited by Norbert Hinske, 71–89. Heidelberg: Lambert Schneider, 1989.

Spinoza, Baruch. *Theological-Political Treatise*. 2nd ed. Translated by Samuel Shirley. Indianapolis: Hackett, 2001.

Stroup, John. "Protestant Church Historians in the German Enlightenment." In *Aufklärung und Geschichte. Studien zur deutschen Geschichtswissenschaft im 18. Jahrhundert*, Hans Erich Bödeker, Georg G. Iggers, Jonathan B. Knudsen, and Peter H. Reill, 169–92. Göttingen: Vandenhoeck & Ruprecht, 1986.

Tracy, James D. *Europe's Reformations, 1450–1650: Doctrine, Politics, and Community*. 2nd ed. Lanham: Rowan & Littlefield, 2006.

Turner, R. Steven. "Historicism, *Kritik*, and the Prussian Professoriate, 1790 to 1840." In *Philologie und Hermeneutik im 19. Jahrhundert*, edited by Martin Bollack, Heinz Wismann, and Theodor Lindken, 450–77. Göttingen: Vandenhoeck & Ruprecht, 1983.

Tzoref-Ashkenazi, Chen. "The Status of Hebrew in Friedrich Schlegel's *Über die Sprache und Weisheit der Indier*." *German Life and Letters* 60, no. 2 (2007): 165–79.

Veltri, Guiseppe, and Gerold Necker, eds. *Gottes Sprache in der Philologischen Werkstatt. Hebräistik vom 15. bis zum 19. Jahrhundert*. Leiden: Brill, 2004.

Vierhaus, Rudolf. "Christian Wilhelm Dohm. Ein politischer Schriftsteller der deutschen Aufklärung." In *Begegnungen von Deutschen und Juden in der Geistesgeschichte des 18. Jahrhunderts. Wolfenbütteler Studien zur Aufklärung. Bd. 6*, edited by Jacob Katz and Karl Heinrich Rengstorf, 107–23. Heidelberg: Lambert Schneider, 1994.

Vöhler, Martin. "Christian Gottlob Heyne und das Studium des Altertums in Deutschland." In *Disciplining Classics / Institutionalisierung der Antike*, edited by G. W. Most, 39–54. Göttingen: Vandenhoeck & Ruprecht, 2002.

von Hardenberg, Friedrich Leopold. *Novalis Werke*. Edited by Gerhard Schulz. Munich: Beck, 1969.

von Selle, Götz. *Die Georg-August-Universität zu Göttingen 1737–1937*. Göttingen: Vandenhoeck & Ruprecht, 1937.

von Stackelberg, Jürgen. "Klassizismus und Aufklärung—der Blick nach Frankreich." In *Zur Geistigen Situation der Zeit der Göttinger Universitätsgründung 1737. Eine Vortragsreihe aus Anlaß des 250jährigen Bestehens der Georgia Augusta*. Edited by Jürgen von Stackelberg, 167–85. Göttingen: Vandenhoeck & Ruprecht, 1988.

von Wilamowitz-Moellendorff, Ulrich. *History of Classical Scholarship*. 1927. Edited by Hugh Lloyd-Jones. Translated by Alan Harris. London: Duckworth, 1982.

Walker, Mack. "Johann Jacob Moser." In *Aufklärung und Geschichte. Studien zur deutschen Geschichtswissenschaft im 18. Jahrhundert*, edited by Hans Erich Bödeker, Georg G. Iggers, Jonathan B. Knudsen, and Peter H. Reill, 105–18. Göttingen: Vandenhoeck & Ruprecht, 1986.

Weber, Max. "Wissenschaft als Beruf." In *Gesammelte Aufsätze zur Wissenschaftslehre*, 524–55. Tübingen: J. C. B. Mohr, 1922.

Webster, John. "Biblical Reasoning." *Anglican Theological Review* 90, no. 4 (2008): 733–51.

———. *Holy Scripture: A Dogmatic Sketch*. Cambridge: Cambridge University Press, 2003.

Wellenreuther, Hermann. "Von der Manufakturstadt zum 'Leine-Athen.' Göttingen, 1714–1837." In *"Eine Welt allein ist nicht genug": Großbritannien, Hannover und Göttingen 1714–1837*, edited by Elmar Mittler, 11–28. Göttingen: Niedersächsische Staats- und Universitätsbibliothek Göttingen, 2005.

Winckelmann, Johann Joachim. *Reflections on the Imitation of Greek Works in Painting and Sculpture*. Translated by Elfriede Heyer and Roger C. Norton. La Salle, IL: Open Court, 1987.

Wolf, Friedrich August. *Darstellung der Alterthumswissenschaft nebst einer Auswahl seiner kleinen Schriften und literarischen Zugaben zu dessen Vorlesungen über die Alterthumswissenschaft*. Edited by S. F. W. Hoffmann. Leipzig, 1833.

———. *Prolegomena to Homer 1795*. Edited by Anthony Grafton, Glenn W. Most, and James E. G. Zetzel. Princeton: Princeton University Press, 1985.

Wood, Robert. *An Essay on the Original Genius and Writings of Homer: With a Comparative View of the Ancient and Present State of the Troade*. London: H. Hughs for T. Payne and P. Elmsly, 1775.

Yarchin, William, ed. *History of Biblical Interpretation: A Reader*. Peabody, MA: Hendrickson, 2004.

Index

Abulfeda, 95
Adelung, Johann Christoph, 50
Alexandria, 76
Alterthumswissenschaft, 30, 57, 59, 67
Ammonn, Christoph Friedrich, 48
Ansbach, 61–62
Apollodorus, 70
Arabia, 81, 95, 99, 120, 148, 162
Arabic, 84, 101, 158
   and Albert Schultens, 83, 86, 91
   and Hebrew, 89, 91–95, 122, 185 n.46
Aramaic, 91, 93
Aristotle, Aristotelianism, 14, 41, 49, 111–112, 114
Arndt, Johann, 53
Assmann, Jan, 134–135
Astruc, Jean, 135–140, 156
Auerbach, Erich, 106
avenger of blood, 143

Bach, Johann August, 69
Bach, Johann Sebastian, 63
Bacon, Francis, 162–163
Barth, Karl, 29
Barton, John, 3, 167–168
Bauermeister, Christopher C. W., 176 n.66, 178 n.103
Becker, Carl, 10
Benson, George, 119

Bentley, Richard, 32, 72
Berleburger Bible, 32
Bernays, Jacob, 75
Bible
   academic Bible, 9, 32–33, 164–169
   cultural Bible, 5, 9, 31–32, 159–160
   death of scripture, 4–5, 9–18
   Enlightenment Bible, 31–33, 159
   Erasmus on, 12–16
   as sacred or divine, 100, 109–111, 115, 160
   scriptural Bible, 3–4, 164, 168–169
   Spinoza on, 23–25
   textualization of, 10, 18–26, 167–168
biblical studies
   contemporary, 7, 25, 165–169
   eighteenth-century, 4–6, 25–26, 30–33, 164–165
   and Michaelis, 51, 101–103
   nineteenth-century, 29–31, 165–166
   at the university, 29–33
Bildung, 43–44, 58, 60–61, 64, 73, 75
Bohl, Samuel, 88
Böhmer, G. L., 41
Bredenbach, Mathias, 18
Buddeus, Johann Franz, 49, 60, 62, 66
Bultmann, Christoph, n.189 n.34, 192 n.102
Burckhardt, Jacob, 10–11
Burnet, Stephen, 83–84

Buxtorf, Johannes (elder), 19, 83–84
Buxtorf, Johannes (younger), 19

Calixtus, George, 45
Cameron, Euan, 12, 18
Canaanite, Canaanites, 91, 161–162
canon, 128, 167–168
Cappel, Louis, 19–21, 26
Carhart, Michael, 50–51, 166, 186 n.61
Champollion, Jean-François, 142
Childs, Brevard, 7, 167–168, 197 n.27
Christ, Johann Friedrich, 69
Cicero, 60, 63, 65–66, 112, 123, 149
Clark, William, 37–38
Classics, 33, 51, 57, 64, 83–84, 101, 156
Coleridge, Samuel Taylor, 105
Collins, John J., 168–169, 198 n.34
Cousturier, Pierre (Petrus Sutor), 14–15
Cullhed, Anna, 189
culture, study of, 50–51
Cyprian, 21–22

David, 88, 102, 104, 109, 113, 118, 128, 161
DeMille, Cecil B., 130
De Wette, Wilhelm M. L., 30
Dohm, Christian Wilhelm, 97–98
Dresden, 69

Ebeling, Gerhard, 30
eclecticism, 42, 49, 62
Egypt, 142, 145, 149, 157, 195 nn.52–53
    and Moses 129–130, 134–135, 141, 149
Eichhorn, Johann Gottfried, 50–51, 128, 156, 165, 177 n.81
Enlightenment, 5–6
    and universities (*see* Universities, Enlightenment)
    and the Bible (*see* Bible, Enlightenment; biblical studies, eighteenth-century)
Epictetus, 69
Erasmus, 10, 12–16
Ernesti, Johann August, 63, 66, 69, 83, 101
Ethiopic, 85, 91, 93, 165
Ethnography, 95–96, 120, 156
eudaimonism, 144–145

Faulkner, William, 105
Fichte, Johann Gottlob, 54, 158
Francke, August Hermann, 39, 49, 53, 84
Frei, Hans, 6

Freimarck, Vincent, 189 n.28
Friedrich III of Prussia, 39
Frye, Northrop, 3, 160

Gawthrop, Richard L., 175 n.45, 178 n.3
Gedike, Friedrich, 38
George II of Britain, 40, 106
Gesner, Johann Matthias
    background, 61–64
    and Heyne, 55, 60, 69–70, 72–73, 78, 100–101, 123, 158
    and Michaelis, 51, 81, 82–83, 102, 177 n.81, 187 n.81
    pedagogy, 64–68, 187 n.85
    and Philological Seminar, 66–68, 181 n.49
Gibert, Pierre, 194 n.30
Goethe, Johann Wolfgang, 81, 115, 135, 160, 179 n.7
    and philhellenism, 53, 54, 57–59, 105
Göttingen, university of (Georgia Augusta), 5, 9, 33, 44–45
    Academy of Sciences, 63, 68, 70, 77, 80, 82
    classical philology at, 54–55, 61, 73–74, 78
    founding, 37–45
    "Göttingen School," 50–51
    Göttingische Gelehrte Anzeigen (or *Göttingische Anzeigen von gelehrten Sachen*), 70, 75, 77, 80
    Philological Seminar, 66–68, 73–74, 77
    scholarship at, 45–51
    and theology, 27, 42
Gousset, Jacques, 88
grace, 117–119
Grafton, Anthony, 21–22, 159
Graham, William A., 171 n.2
Greece (ancient), 70–71, 112, 120–121, 139, 156–157, 161
    as model, 6, 75, 100, 130, 159 (*see also* philhellenism)
Griffiths, Paul, 171 n.2, 172 n.7
Gruber, J. D., 34, 40

Hakemeyer, Ida, 184 n.11, 190 n.62
Halle, university of, 38–40, 44, 81, 158
    and study of Hebrew, 84–85, 96
    and Pietism, 34, 53–54, 117
Haller, Albrecht, 177 n.81

Hamann, Johann Georg, 81, 155, 160–164
Hammerstein, Notker, 36
Hanover, 40, 43
Hardt, Hermann von der, 90–91
Hare, Francis, 113
Harnack, Adolf, 29
Hazard, Paul, 8
Hebrew, 19–21, 160
  and Arabic, 89, 91–95, 122, 185 n.46
  cognate languages, 91, 93, 165
  grammar, 92–94, 101–102, 184 n.24
  and Michaelis, 86–95
  philology, 84–86, 96, 161–164
  study of, 79–81, 88–90, 95–96, 101–102
Hecht, Hans, 190 n.62
Heeren, A. H. L., 61
Heidenreich, Marianne, 181 n.66
Hepworth, Brian, 189 n.28
Herder, Johann Gottfried, 58–59, 79,
    147–148, 152, 160
  and Lowth, 115, 128
  and Michaelis 51, 81, 107, 156–157
Hess, Jonathan, 96–97, 142
Heston, Charlton, 130
Hetzron, Robert, 185 n.45
Heumann, Christoph August, 48, 173 n.3
Heyne, Christian Gottlob, 50, 59–61, 121, 179
    n.22
  background, 68–70
  and Gesner, 55, 60, 69–70, 72–73, 78,
    100–101, 123, 158
  and Michaelis, 81, 82–84, 104, 164, 184 n.11
  and Philological Seminar, 73–74
  study of the ancient world, 70–76, 182
    n.69
Hiller, Matthaeus, 86
Hinrichs, Carl, 178 n.2
historical criticism (or historical-critical
  method), 8–9, 165–169
historicism, 8–9, 49–50, 166
Hofstetter, Michael J., 174 n.24
Hohenzollerns, 39
Hollmann, Samuel Christian, 42
Holy Spirit, 15, 16, 32, 109, 118,
    122, 129
Homer, 70, 71–72, 109, 140
  as poetic genius, 120, 127, 152
Horace, 108–109, 111–112, 186 n.48
Horkheimer, Max, 129
Howard, Thomas Albert, 28–29

humanism, 10–12, 60
Humboldt, Wilhelm, 54, 57–60, 71, 77, 158,
    179 n.22
Hunt, Thomas, 117
Hunter, Ian, 38–39

Ibsen, Henrik, 160
irenicism
  academic, 7, 41–42, 168–169
  political, 9, 164–165
  theological, 6, 47–48, 51, 152
Israel, Jonathan, 24
Israel, Israelites, 160, 161–162, 191 n.90
  as classical civilization, 100–104, 106–107,
    155–164
  and Moses, 132–134, 142–146, 151–153
Italian journeys, 57–58

Jenkins, Allan, and Patrick Preston, 13–14
Jesus, 49, 109–110, 123, 161
Job, book of, 102, 103, 114
  and Moses 131, 138, 140, 146–152
Josephus, 193 n.20
Judaism, Jews, 96–100, 107, 158–159
  and the study of Hebrew, 87–88, 90–91,
    94
jus consuetudinarium, 142–143

Kant, Immanuel, 29, 30, 48, 61, 111, 160
Kennicott, Benjamin, 165
Koch, Friedrich Christian, 89
Köhler, Georg Nikolaus, 62
Kraus, Hans-Joachim, 178 n.98, 183 n.7
Kugel, James, 25, 114, 127, 172 n.6, 190
    n.41

Lamb, Jonathan, 147, 193 n.22
Laocoön, 74–75
Le Brun, Jacques, 173 n.29
Leipzig, 62–63
Lessing, Gotthold Ephraim, 8, 74, 80,
    135
Levenson, Jon D., 7, 197 n.15, 197 n.27
Leventhal, Robert, 8
Levita, Elias, 19
Levites, 133
Lindbeck, George, 171 n.2
Longinus, 111, 127
Love, Harold, 139–140
Löwenbrück, Anna-Ruth, 98

Lowth, Robert, 81, 120, 147, 149, 167
  and Herder, 115, 128
  Lectures on the Sacred Poetry of the Hebrews, 107–118
  and Michaelis, 115–117, 121–128, 165
Ludolph, Hiob, 85
Luther, Martin, 12, 15–16, 100, 151
Lutheranism, Lutherans, 32, 39, 42, 48–49, 96, 98, 117

Machiavelli, Niccolò, 131–132, 135, 137
Macpherson, James, 112
Mager, Inge, 177 n.79, 177 n.85
Manetho, 193 n.20
Manuel, Frank, 96, 186 n.63
Marchand, Suzanne, 59, 196 n.7
Marino, Luigi, 177 n.77
Marsh, Herbert, 141
McClelland, Charles, 43, 175 n.42
McGrath, Alister, 12, 172 n.19
Meiners, Christoph, 50
Mendelssohn, Moses, 80, 115, 128
Menze, Clemens, 59, 77
Mettler, Werner, 71, 72
Michaelis, Caroline, 184 n.11
Michaelis, Christian Benedict, 84–85, 149, 187 n.85
Michaelis, Christian Friedrich, 121
Michaelis, Johann David, 5–6, 33, 50–51, 78, 84–85
  anti-Semitism of, 97–100 (*see also* Judaism)
  background, 27–28, 80–81, 84–85, 117–118
  and Bible translation, 100, 151, 187 n.78
  and the book of Job, 146–153
  in English context, 115–121
  ethnography, 95–97, 156
  Hebrew study, 86–95, 184 n.24, 185 n.46
  and Herder 51, 81, 107, 156–157
  legacy, 155–165
  and Lowth, 115–117, 121–128
  Mosaisches Recht, 95, 130, 140–146
  relation to Gesner and Heyne, 82–84, 184 n.11
  on the university, 33–37
Michaelis, Johann Heinrich, 49, 184 n.19
Michelangelo, 131
Midian, 140, 149
Miller, Peter, 22–23

Monk, Samuel, 111
monotheism, 24, 100, 130, 135, 142, 145–146, 152
Montesquieu, Charles Louis de Secondat, 131, 141, 144
Morin, Jean, 19–21
Moses, 156
  as author of the Pentateuch, 135–140, 193 n.14
  and the book of Job, 131, 138, 140, 146–152
  as classical paragon, 151–153, 157
  in early modern thought, 131–137
  Egyptian background, 129–130, 134–135, 141–142, 149
  as moral philosopher, 149–151
  as poet, 102, 104, 127–128
  as political leader, 131–135, 141–146
Mosheim, Johann Lorenz, 40–41, 45–51, 177 n.81
Münchhausen, Gerlach Adolph, 38, 40–45, 48, 69, 78, 146

neoclassicism, 111–115, 121, 123
neohumanism, 8, 59–61, 106, 152, 158
Neumann, Caspar, 89, 185 n.40
Neumann, Florian, 177 n.80, 177 n.89
Newman, Amy, 183 n.2
Nicodemus, 163
Niebuhr, Barthold Georg, 77
Niebuhr, Carsten, 81, 162
Novalis (G. P. F. von Hardenberg), 56

Oden Robert, 172 n.6
Oporinus, Joachim, 48
Orientalism, 98–99, 156–159
Ossian, 112

parallelism, 111, 113–115, 125–126
Paul, Saint, 60, 106, 124
Paulsen, Friedrich, 66
Peirce, James, 119
Percy, Thomas, 112, 119–120
Peyrère, Isaac, 7
philhellenism, 54–60, 105–106, 158–159
philology, 11, 21–22, 49, 83, 135, 158, 165–166
  (*see also* classical philology; Göttingen, classical philology at; Hebrew philology)
Phocion, 75

Pietism, 8, 32, 39–40, 53–54, 84–85, 118
Pindar, 70, 72
Plato, 140
poetry, 108, 120, 124, 129
　biblical poetry, 108–115, 121–128, 165
　classical, 109, 114
　meter, 112–113, 122
Poliziano, 21–22
polyglot Bibles, 20, 22–23
polytheism, 145
Popkin, Richard, 15, 139
preromanticism, 55, 111–112, 119, 121, 152
Prickett, Stephen, 188 n.12, 189 n.28, 192 n.103
Prophets, 104, 118, 128, 132
Protestantism, Protestants, 4–5, 17–21, 30, 98, 106–107, 158, 168
Prussia, 36, 39–40, 53, 56–58, 97

Radner, Ephraim, 17
Reformation, 3–4, 10–11, 17–19, 32, 167
Reformed, 33, 39
Rehm, Walter, 179 n.5
Reill, Peter Hanns, 8, 166, 178 n.99
Reimarus, Hermann Samuel, 7, 49
Reinhold, Karl, 135
Reiske, Johann Jakob, 158
Renaissance, 10–11, 18, 36, 82–84
Reno, R. R., 17, 188 n.7
Reventlow, Henning Graf, 177 n.84
Ribov, Georg Heinrich, 48
Richardson, Samuel, 119
Ringleben, Joachim, 177 n.92
Rogerson, John W., 183 n.7
Roman Catholicism, Roman Catholics, 4–5, 17–21, 30, 136, 179 n.7
Rome (ancient), 6, 75, 105–106, 112, 124
Roston, Murray, 110, 112, 189 n.28
Rubin, Aaron, 185 n.45
Ruhnken, David, 69, 72
Rummel, Erika, 16, 172 n.19

Savonarola, Girolamo, 131
Scaliger, Joseph, 22
scholasticism
　late medieval, 11–14
　Protestant, 9, 42–43, 48–49, 61
Schelling, Friedrich, 54, 56, 158
Schiller, Friedrich, 54, 56, 58, 135, 152

Schindel, Ulrich, 180 n.37, 181 nn.42, 45, 51, 63, 65, 182 n.81, 187 n.81
Schlegel, August, 54
Schlegel, Friedrich, 54, 60, 158
Schleiermacher, Friedrich, 29, 158
Schlözer, August Ludwig, 51, 75, 165
Schmauß, Johann Jacob, 42–43
Schultens, Albert, 83, 86, 91, 95, 149, 165
Scythian, 90
secularization, 8–9, 10–11
Semler, Johann Salomo, 53
Sheehan, Jonathan, 9, 31–32, 96, 159, 166, 186 n.61
Simon, Richard, 4, 136, 137, 167
Simonis, Johann, 86
Simonsuuri, Kirsti, 152
Smend, Rudolf, 116–117, 193 n.27, 194 n.47
Smith, Alexander, 141
Smith, Wilfred Cantwell, 171 n.2
Spinoza, Baruch, 4, 7, 23–25, 132–134, 136
Stäudlin, Karl Friedrich, 48
Strauss, David Friedrich, 7
sublime, 100, 111, 115, 130–131
　in poetry, 102–103, 111, 126–128, 138–140, 189 n.28
Syriac, 84, 91, 93, 101, 122, 165

Taylor, Charles, 178 n.94
textual criticism, 20–22, 67, 72, 165
textualization (*see* Bible, textualization of)
theologians, 23, 122, 133
theology, 11, 110–111
　apologetics, 46–47
　at Göttingen, 27, 42, 45–51
　at the university, 28–29, 35–36
Thiersch, Friedrich, 37
Tholuck, August, 173 n.2
Thomasius, Christian, 38–39, 42, 176 n.62
Thomasschule, 63, 83
Thomson, James, 119
Tibullus, 69
Toland, John, 32, 49, 134–135
Turner, Steven, 59

Universities, 28–29, 42–43
　Berlin, 29, 60, 158
　biblical studies at, 29–33
　Enlightenment 26, 33–38, 168
　Göttingen (*see* Göttingen, university of)
　Halle (*see* Halle, university of)

Universities (*continued*)
  Helmstedt, 40, 45–46
  Jena, 54, 60, 62, 66, 158
  Kiel, 45
  Leiden, 69
  Leipzig, 39, 63, 68–69
  Oxford, 107–108, 116–117

Valla, Lorenzo, 12, 22
Vatke, Wilhelm, 30
Virgil, 70, 104
Voigt, Rainer M., 185 n.45
Vulgate, 4, 10, 13–14

Walton, Brian, 22–23
Warburton, William, 134–135, 146, 148–149
Weber, Max, 31

Webster, John, 171 n.2
Weimar, 54, 62–63
Wilamowitz-Moellendorf, Ulrich, 57
Winckelmann, Johann Joachim, 54–60, 74–75, 76, 80, 179 n.7, 182 n.69
Witter, H. B., 194 n.30
Wolf, Friedrich August, 53, 69, 71, 73, 76, 182 n.82
  and philhellenism, 54, 57–60, 158
Wolff, Christian, 39, 53, 118
Wood, Robert, 81, 82, 119–121, 127

Yahweh, 132, 134

Zäunemann, Sidonia Hedwig, 37

Index of Biblical References

Genesis
1:1   85, 184 n.19
2:7   148
3:20   138
12:6   193 n.14
14   138
17:5   138
41:2   148
41:18   148

Exodus
2:11–12   132
9:10–11   148
14:21   148
15:20–21   113
20:18   133
20:22–23:33   193 n.14
22:26–27   149
23:19   145
32   132–133
32:9–14   132
34:26   145

Leviticus
13:18–20   148
25:25–28   143

Numbers
8:17   133
11:12   93

13:3   193 n.14
21:27–30   138
35:9–35   143
35:21   143

Deuteronomy
1:1   193 n.14
2:10–11   138
2:19–21   138
14:21   145
19:1–10   143
21:2   118
24:10–13   149
28:27   148
30:11–13   125
30:13   148
32:1–43   193 n.14
32:2   118

Judges
4   162
5   161–162
5:30   162

1 Samuel
18:7   113
21:13–15   161

Job
2:7   148

3   125
3:14   148
8:11–12   148
11:17   196 n.84
14:13   196 n.84
15:7   148
19:25   196 n.83
19:25–27   150–151
20:11   148
22:6   149
22:24–25   148
24:3, 7–9   149
24:18   196 n.84
26:5   148
27:3   148
27:21   148
28:1–28   148
29:22–23   118
40:15–24   148
40:25–41:26   148

Psalms
2:7   93
25:13   125
42   124
90   138–139
90:2   148
90:8   149
90:10   125, 148
147:9   125

Isaiah
14.9–20   191 n.90
55:3–5   118
55:10–11   118, 190 n.58

Jeremiah
2:27   93
38:11–13   161

Ezekiel
21:2   118
31:14, 16–18   191 n.90
32   191 n.90

Micah
2:6   118

Matthew
3:12   161
16:18   18

John
3:8   163
9:6   161

Acts
7:22   141

1 Corinthians
1:26   106
1–2   123

2 Timothy
2:23–24   47

1 Peter
3:20–21   32